IMAGES
of America

BUCYRUS

On the cover: Please see page 30. (Courtesy of the Bucyrus Historical Society.)

IMAGES
of America

BUCYRUS

Marian Schiefer Vance

ARCADIA
PUBLISHING

ISBN 978-0-7385-4081-8

Published by Arcadia Publishing
Charleston, South Carolina

Printed in the United States of America

Library of Congress Catalog Card Number: 2006930907

For all general information contact Arcadia Publishing at:
Telephone 843-853-2070
Fax 843-853-0044
E-mail sales@arcadiapublishing.com
For customer service and orders:
Toll-Free 1-888-313-2665

Visit us on the Internet at www.arcadiapublishing.com

Contents

ACKNOWLEDGMENTS

Compiling a book such as this requires the help and support of many people. I would like to thank everyone at Arcadia Publishing, especially my editor Melissa Basilone for seeing me through this process. A special thank-you goes to my friends at the Bucyrus Historical Society for making their collection available for use in the book and their willingness to be available when we needed them to be there. Of special note, Don and Mary Ellen Lust also deserve special recognition for their willingness to share what they know, and when they did not, helping us to find the answers. Thank you to everyone who came to the Pelican House with images. Nancy Clague, Rob Pirnstill, and Lucille Fullerton also made significant contributions. I also want to thank the Bucyrus fire and police departments and the mayor's office for their help in checking for the availability of images. Wayne Rish and Greg Northrup from the Bratwurst Festival helped with unlocking images for this book. Thank you to the Ohio Historical Society, Dr. William Laidlaw, and Duryea Kemp of the Archives Library. A special note of thanks goes to Rob Neff and Helen Picking Neff for making the chapter on the Picking family possible. I would also like to thank Jim Croneis and Arvin Kindinger for meeting with us over and over to help review the text and share some great laughter and stories. Thank you to my sister and brothers, Karen Scott, Norman Schiefer, and Allan Schiefer who were my eyes and ears on the ground in Bucyrus while I was making trips back and forth from Springfield to work on "the book". Thank you to my neighbors in Springfield, Rick, Michael, and Christe, for never tiring of hearing me talk about the text of the book and its challenges. E. Haley also deserves recognition for his help in getting the book ready for the publisher. Thank you to my husband and family for encouragement and support. And finally, a giant thank-you to Stuart Koblentz because none of this would have happened without his enthusiasm, support, determination, sheer genius, and image scanner.

INTRODUCTION

Our past is here
Our history is now.
Learn what you thought you knew.

This quote from a poster at the Ohio Historical Society expresses what I have been pondering since beginning this pictorial history of my hometown, Bucyrus, several months ago. I thought I knew a lot about this history, but I was wrong.

I was not aware of so many things that shaped my own destiny. Reading and talking with so many people has stimulated my mind and has helped me to understand my heritage more. I purposely tried to keep from writing about my relatives, thinking that it was too easy to do, until I realized there were so many commonalities between the families of Bucyrus, that I actually could talk about my own when referencing the others. I hope I have gained some character from my ancestors. I certainly appreciate how hard they worked and the legacy that they left.

I have such fond memories of bratwurst cooking on the street—every town had brats, right? I certainly thought so, until I met my future husband from southern Ohio, and he did not know what a bratwurst was! I would love to shop at Baumoel's just one more time and to cruise the streets with—oh who cares, just cruise the streets!

Each generation before and each generation since has added to or drawn from the ingenuity, inventiveness, and productivity of Bucyrus and its citizens. This book is a celebration of just that.

—Marian Schiefer Vance
August 3, 2006

One

Around and About Bucyrus

The first settlers of what is now Bucyrus, Ohio, arrived in 1819. Samuel and Mary Norton left the comfort of their Pennsylvania home for the relative unknown of the wilderness that north-central Ohio offered. Originally Norton and his party stopped near what is now Galion, Ohio, but the guide encouraged the group further west to a geographical ridge that forms the dividing point from which water either flows northward toward Lake Erie or southward toward the Ohio River. It was Col. William Kilbourne who platted the village that would become Bucyrus, the name for which is a combination of the word beautiful and the biblical Persian general Cyrus. Throughout times of great upheaval and halcyon days of calm, Bucyrus has remained what it began as, a community filled with good people who are blessed with good friends.

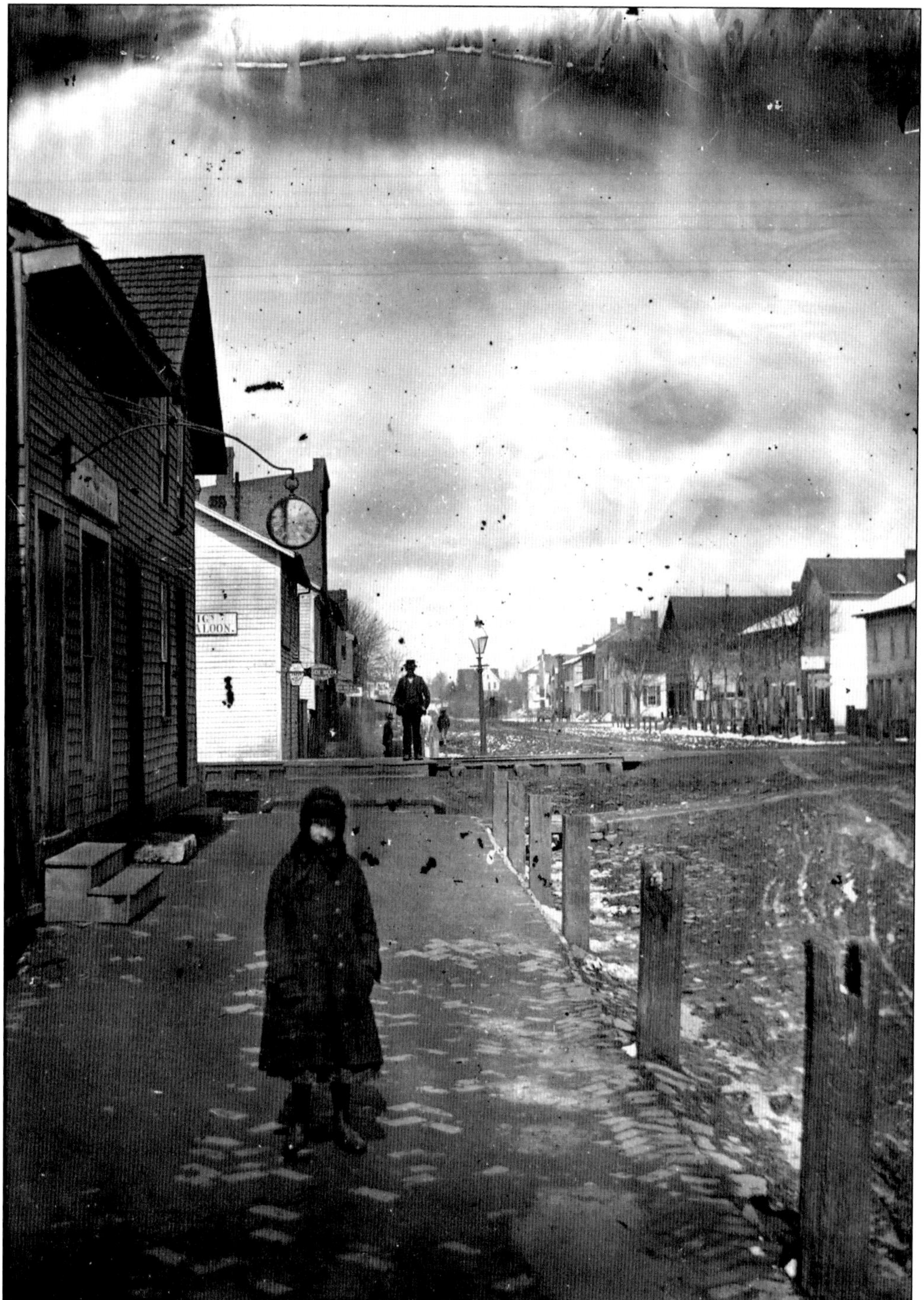

West Side of North Sandusky Street, c. 1870s. Long before the advent of concrete sidewalks and paved streets, roadbeds were usually made of dirt, which turned to mud when it rained. Sidewalks were either made of wooden planks, or if improved, were paved with bricks. (Courtesy of Don and Mary Ellen Lust.)

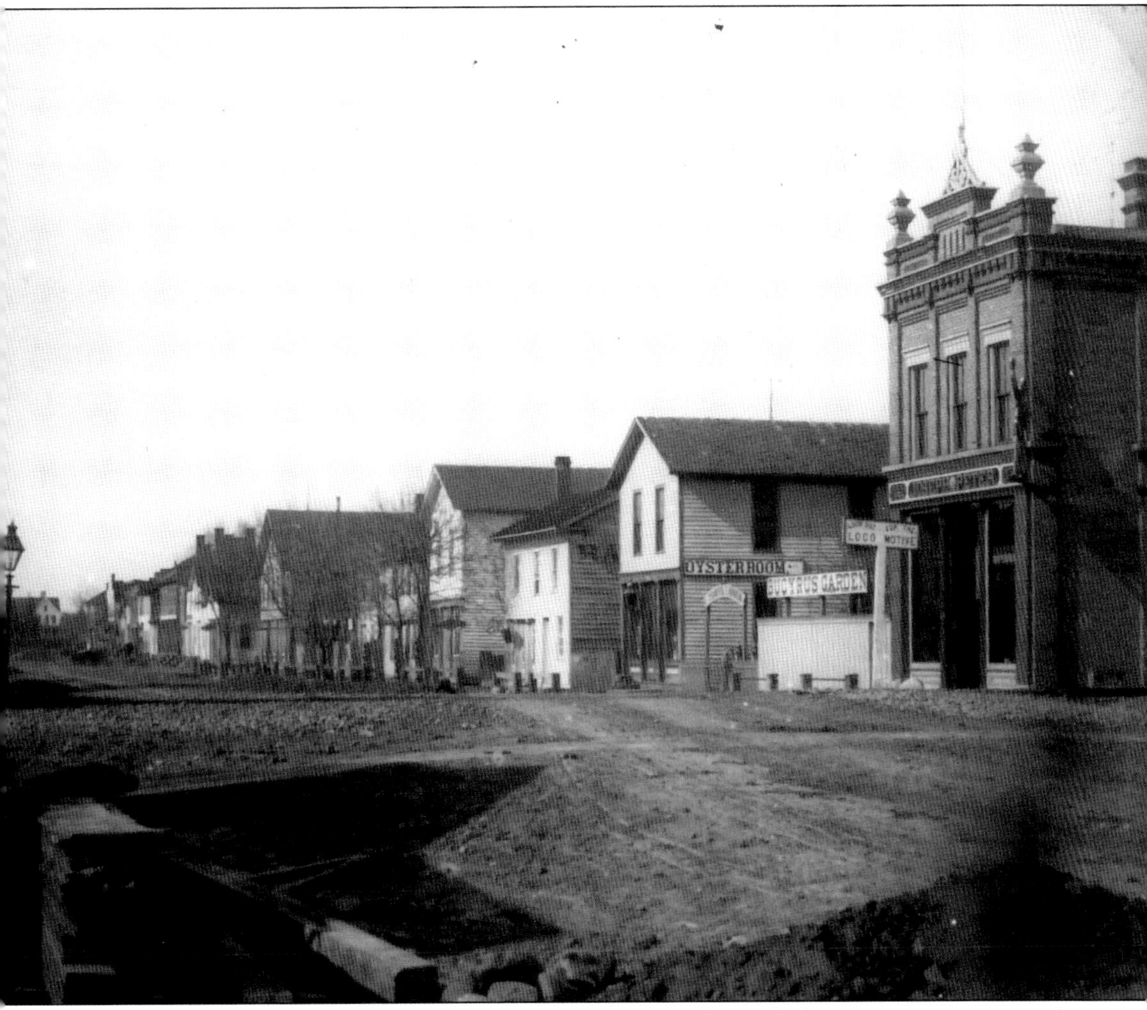

EAST SIDE OF NORTH SANDUSKY STREET, C. 1880S. North Sandusky Street was a street of businesses and fashionable homes. The building to the far right in this photograph has served numerous functions, including a saloon and a boardinghouse. Next to it is an "Oyster Room," so named because its dishes were made with canned oysters—a delicacy in an era when fresh saltwater seafood was only available along the U.S. coastal regions. In the distance, to the left of the gas streetlight is the Findlay residence that once stood at Sandusky and Plymouth Streets. (Courtesy of the Bucyrus Historical Society.)

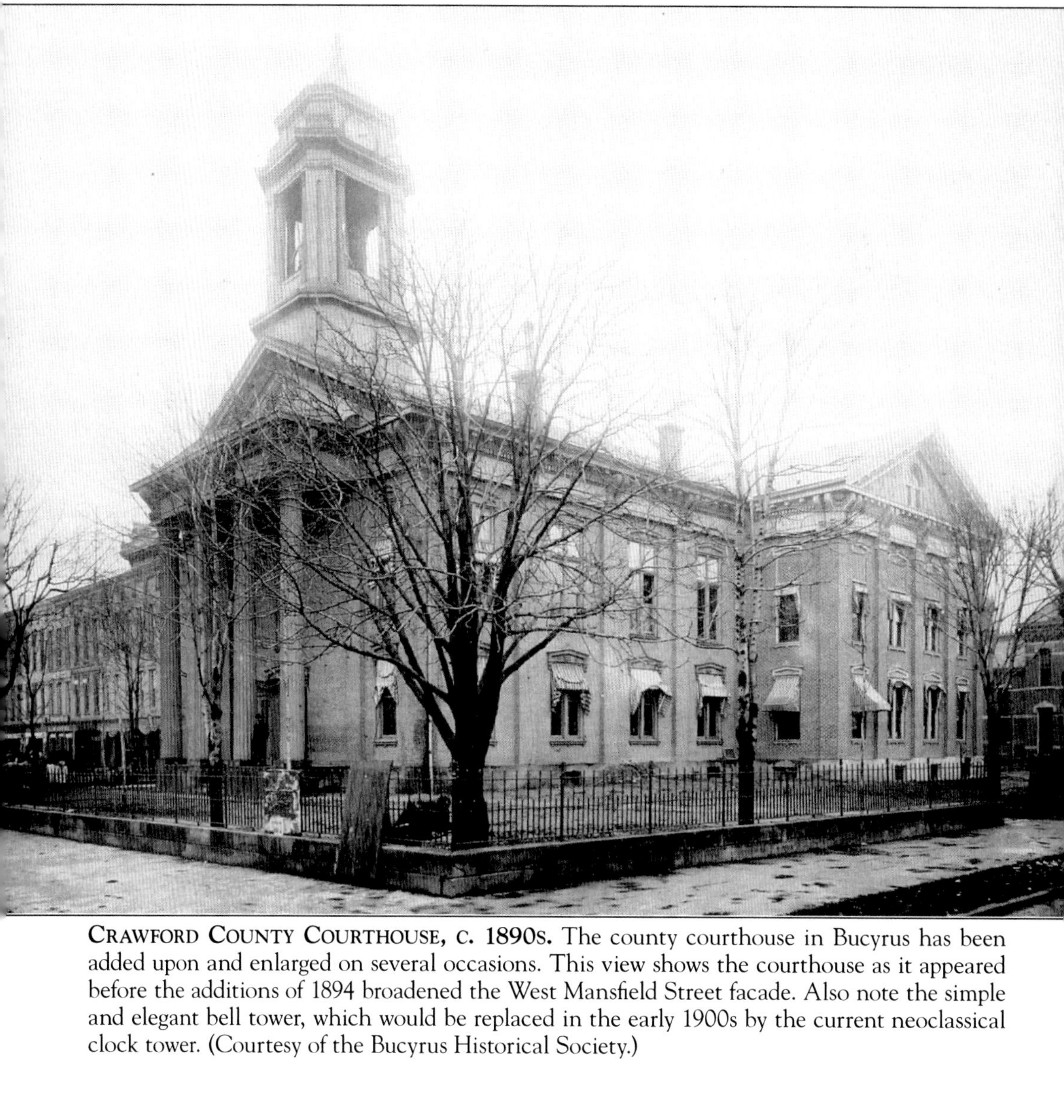

CRAWFORD COUNTY COURTHOUSE, C. 1890S. The county courthouse in Bucyrus has been added upon and enlarged on several occasions. This view shows the courthouse as it appeared before the additions of 1894 broadened the West Mansfield Street facade. Also note the simple and elegant bell tower, which would be replaced in the early 1900s by the current neoclassical clock tower. (Courtesy of the Bucyrus Historical Society.)

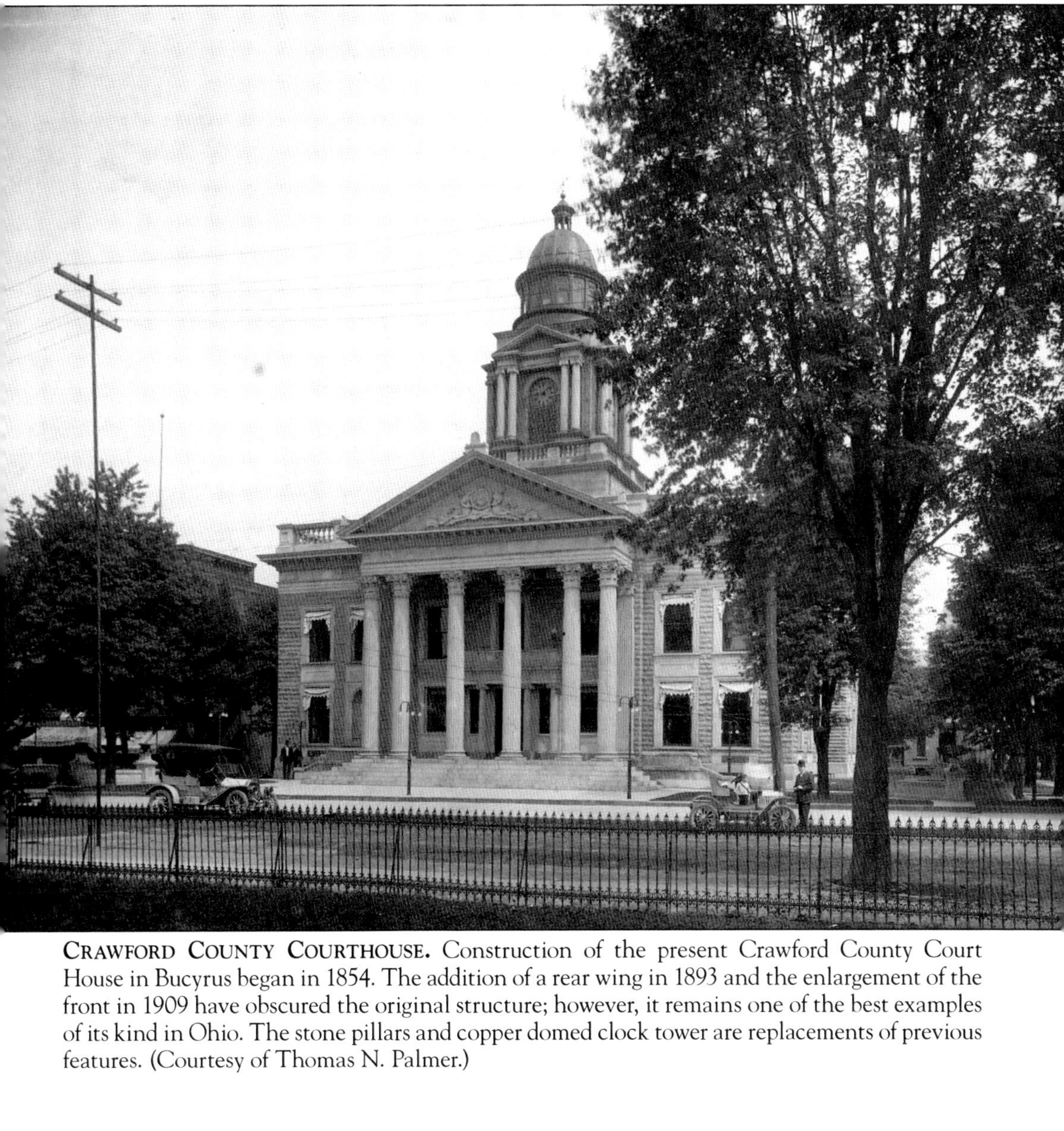

CRAWFORD COUNTY COURTHOUSE. Construction of the present Crawford County Court House in Bucyrus began in 1854. The addition of a rear wing in 1893 and the enlargement of the front in 1909 have obscured the original structure; however, it remains one of the best examples of its kind in Ohio. The stone pillars and copper domed clock tower are replacements of previous features. (Courtesy of Thomas N. Palmer.)

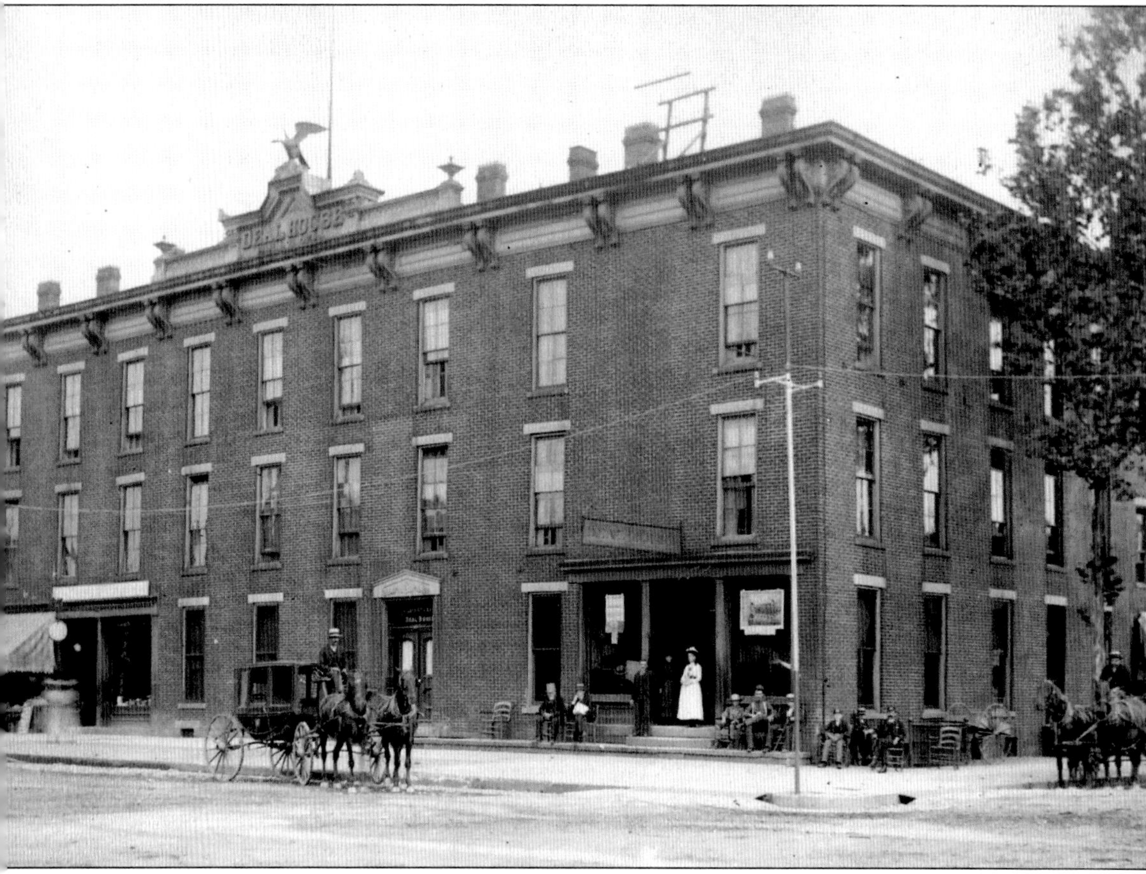

THE DEAL HOUSE, C. 1880S. Once occupying the southeast side of Washington Square was the Deal House, established by Horace Deal. Built of brick, the structure was crowned with an elaborate entablature bearing the Deal House name and an eagle. It is interesting to note that the middle set of doors was designated as the ladies entrance, where unescorted women could safely enter without being confronted by men or hearing whispers questioning their behavior. (Courtesy of the Bucyrus Historical Society.)

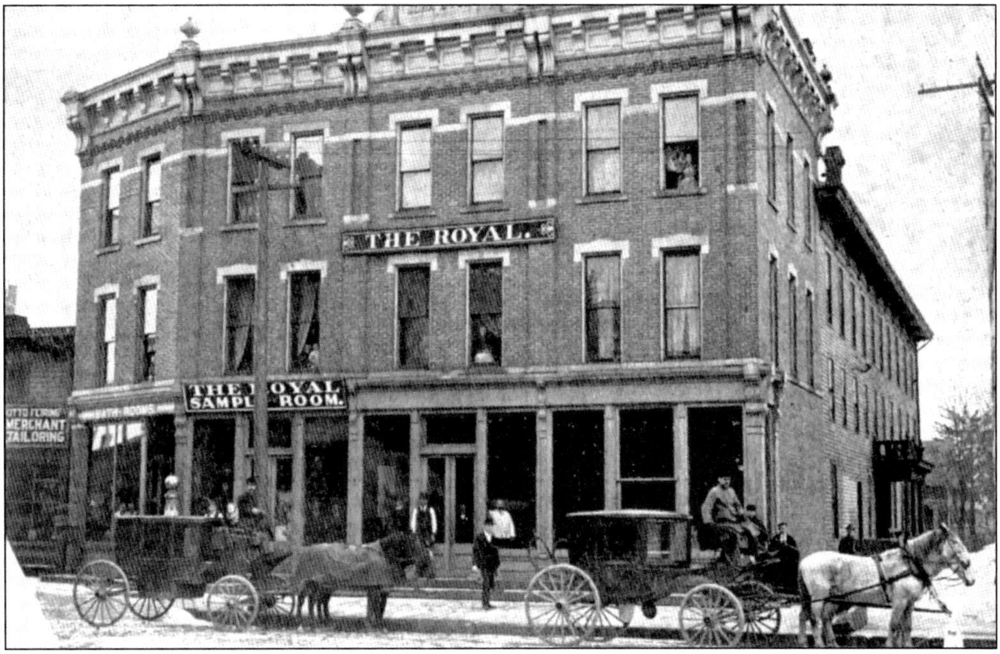

THE ROYAL. Located in the John Stoll building that once stood on Washington Square was the Hotel Royal. At street level was the Royal Sample Room, a place where manufacturers' representatives would exhibit their products to local merchants. (Courtesy of the Bucyrus Historical Society.)

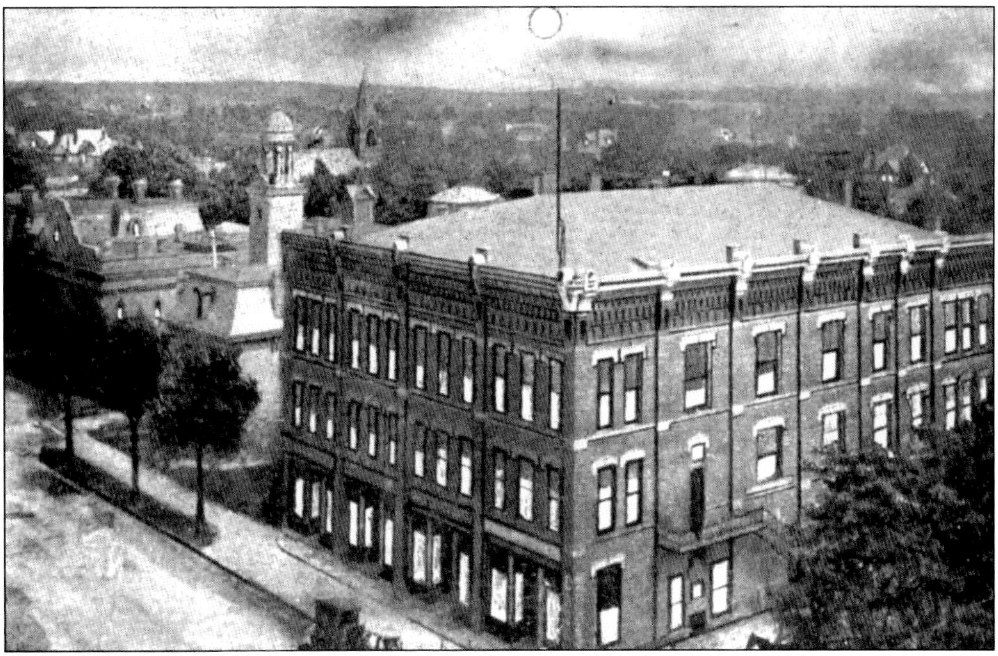

VOLLRATH BUILDING AND OPERA HOUSE. Standing on the south side of East Mansfield Street across from the courthouse was the Vollrath Building, which also was the home of the Bucyrus Opera House. Built in 1885 and 1886, the structure survived until 1936, when it was destroyed by fire. (Courtesy of Don and Mary Ellen Lust.)

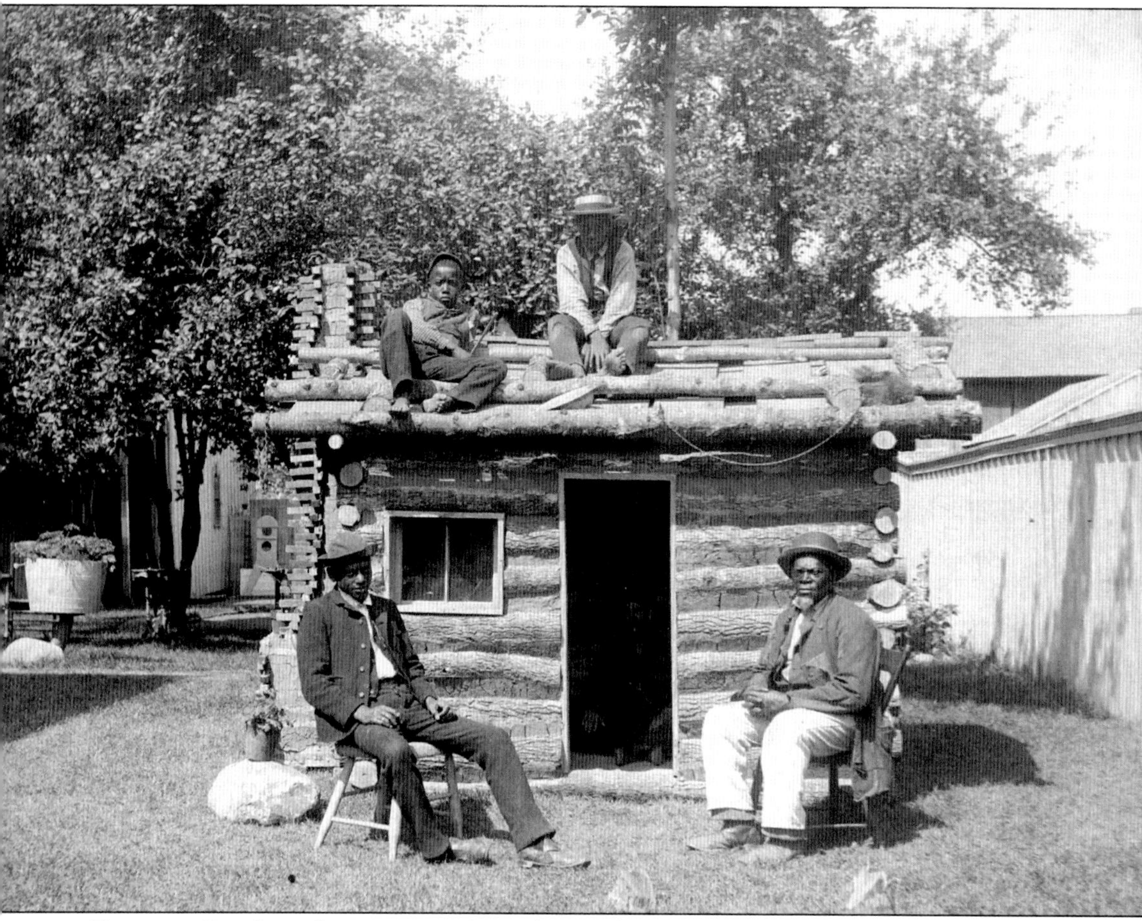

ELECTION-ERA LOG CABIN, 1888. According to the Hopley Collection at the Ohio Historical Society, this one-third-scale-size cabin was used during the presidential election campaign in 1888 in Bucyrus. However, little else is known about this fascinating photograph, the people in it, or how it factored into the race in which Ohio's Benjamin Harrison defeated Grover Cleveland. (Courtesy of the Ohio Historical Society, Hopley Collection.)

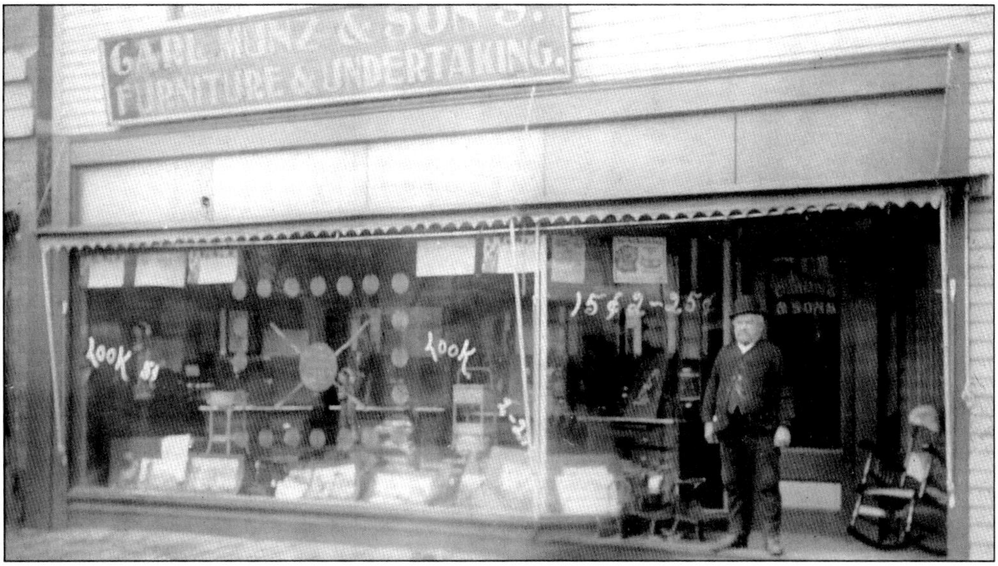

MUNZ FURNITURE AND UNDERTAKING. The combination of a furniture store and undertaker service was a common sight in the 19th century, as both dealt in fine furnishings built of wood that contained upholstery. The common and accepted custom of the day was for the family to prepare the deceased body and to hold the body in the family home until the funeral and burial. The early 20th century saw the division of business, with professionally operated funeral homes (some including overnight accommodations for out-of-town mourners) and morticians as the accepted practice of the day. (Courtesy of Dave Pirnstill, Munz and Pirnstil Funeral Home.)

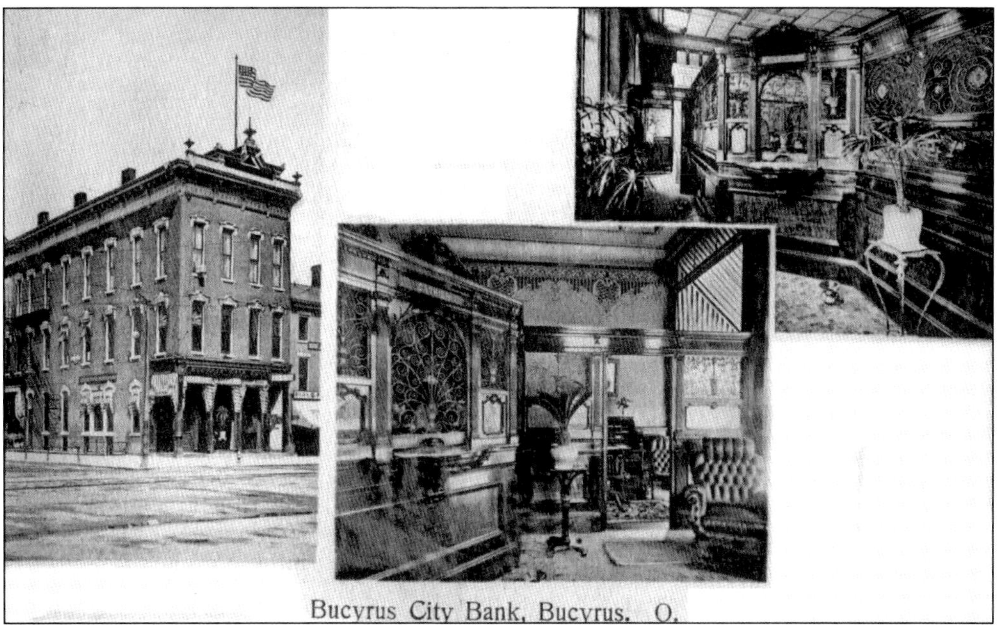

OLD BUCYRUS CITY BANK. This bank was originally established as the Monnett Bank in 1881 and was reincorporated as the Bucyrus City Bank in 1892 following the economic panic of 1890. Of note, the street facade on this building is crowned with an elaborate metal cornice that endures to this day. The Bucyrus City Bank used this structure until the late 1950s. (Courtesy of Don and Mary Ellen Lust.)

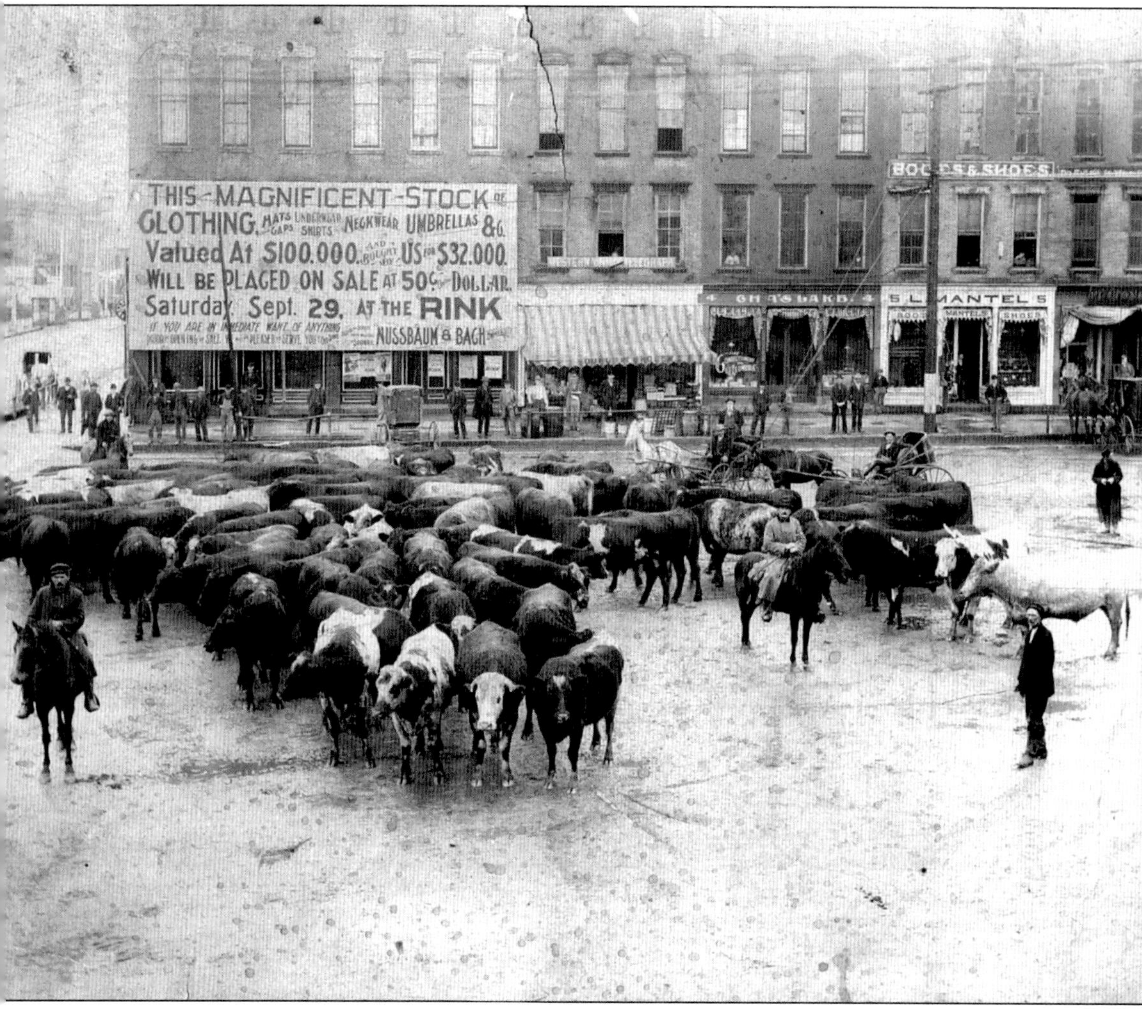

MALCOLM CATTLE, WASHINGTON SQUARE. In 1897, livestock breeder James Malcolm sold 207 of his "choicest and fattest stock" to a cattle broker, according to the Bucyrus newspaper. Because of the size of the sale, the cattle were driven to Bucyrus in smaller, manageable lots and then loaded onto boxcars and delivered to the new owner. (Courtesy of the Bucyrus Historical Society.)

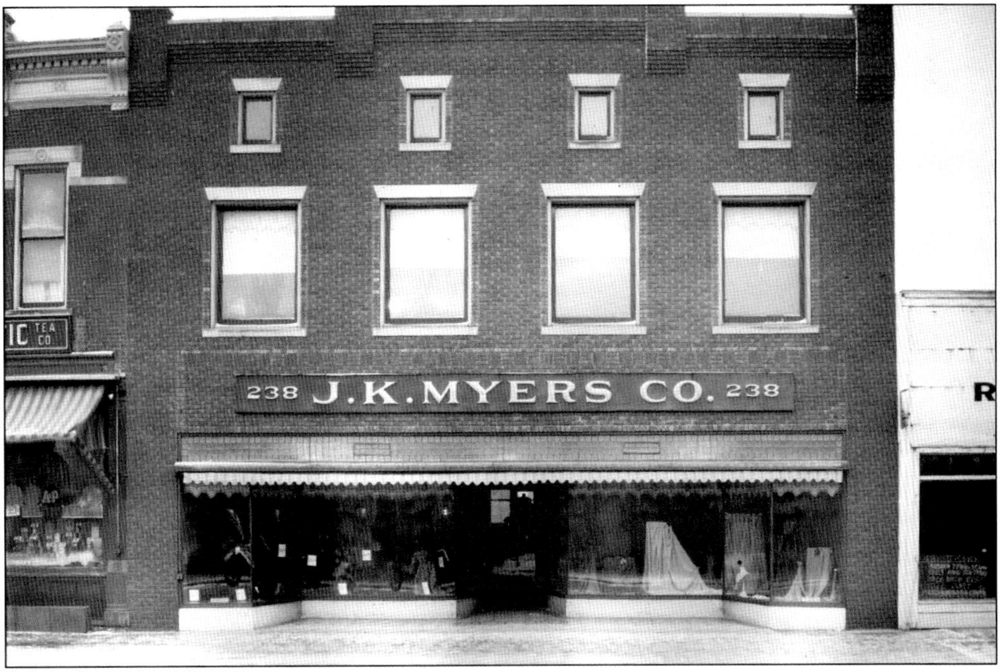

J. K. MYERS STORE. Once located on North Sandusky Street, the J. K. Myers Store sold dry goods. The building survives, although it is heavily remodeled. (Courtesy of the Bucyrus Historical Society.)

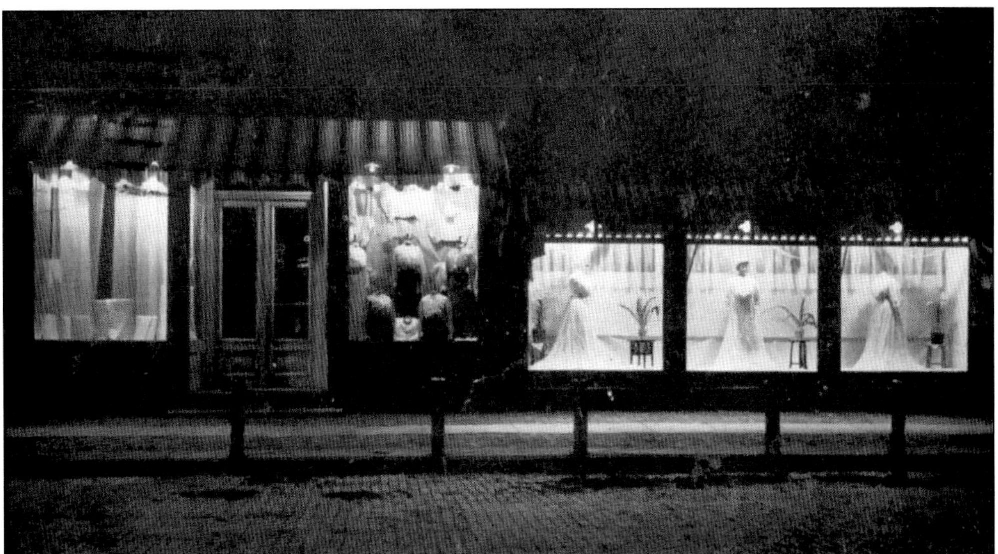

J. K. MYERS STORE, AT NIGHT. While electricity is taken for granted in the modern world, in 1900, it was still regarded somewhat as a novelty. This photograph of the windows of the J. K. Myers Store was taken specifically to show off the electrically lit storefront. (Courtesy of the Charles Spiegle collection.)

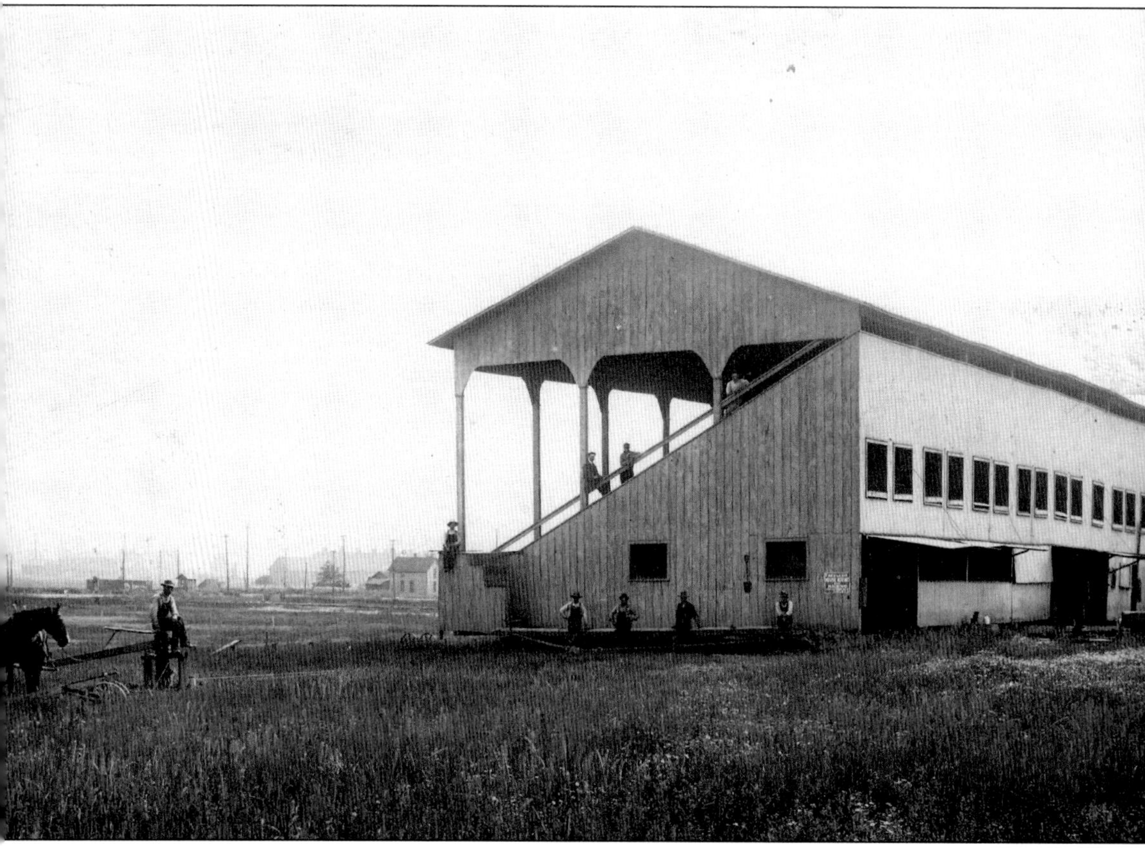

Grandstand Relocation, 1912. This photograph shows the relocation of the Crawford County Fairgrounds grandstand in 1912 by Fred Lewis. As impossible as it seems, the structure was relocated by temporarily reinforcing it, detaching it from its foundation, placing it on skids, and then pulling it slowly with workhorses to move it to its new location. (Courtesy of Don and Mary Ellen Lust.)

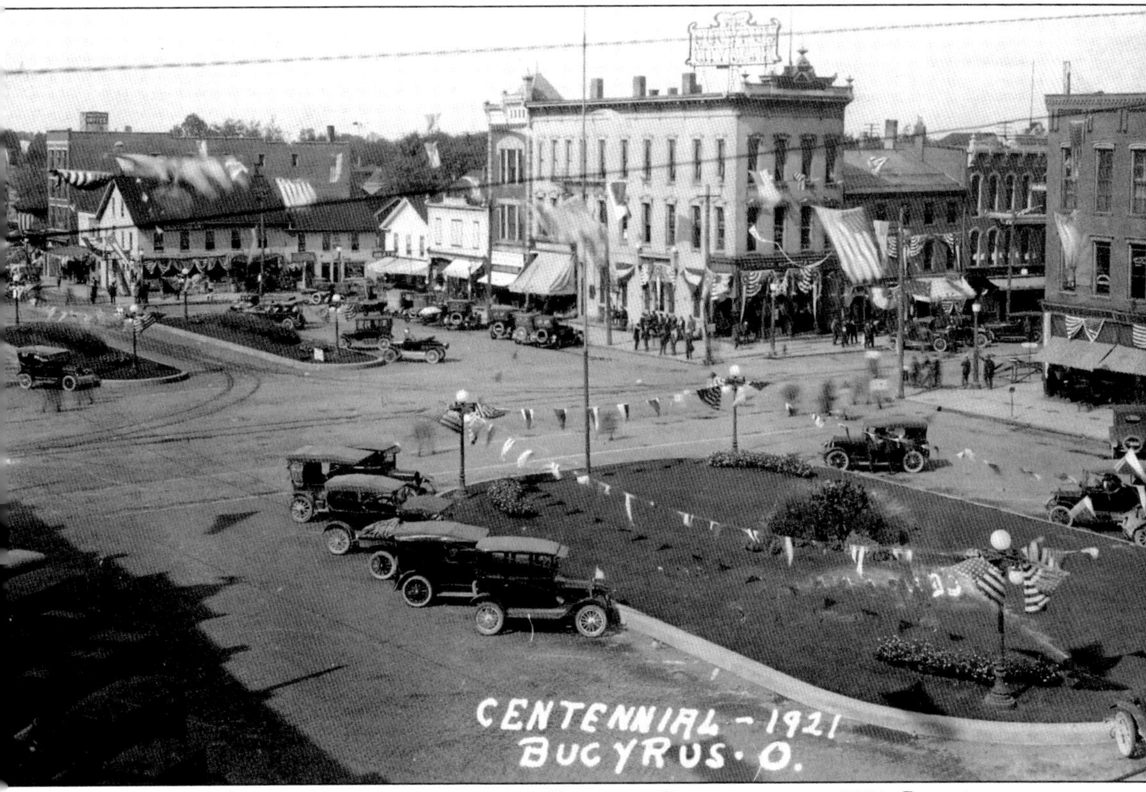

WASHINGTON SQUARE DECORATED FOR THE BUCYRUS CENTENNIAL OF 1921. Bucyrians went all out for the centennial of 1921 by hosting a number of events commemorating the celebration. This view shows the square looking northwest from the Vollrath Building, toward the former Bucyrus City Bank building. (Courtesy of the Bucyrus Historical Society.)

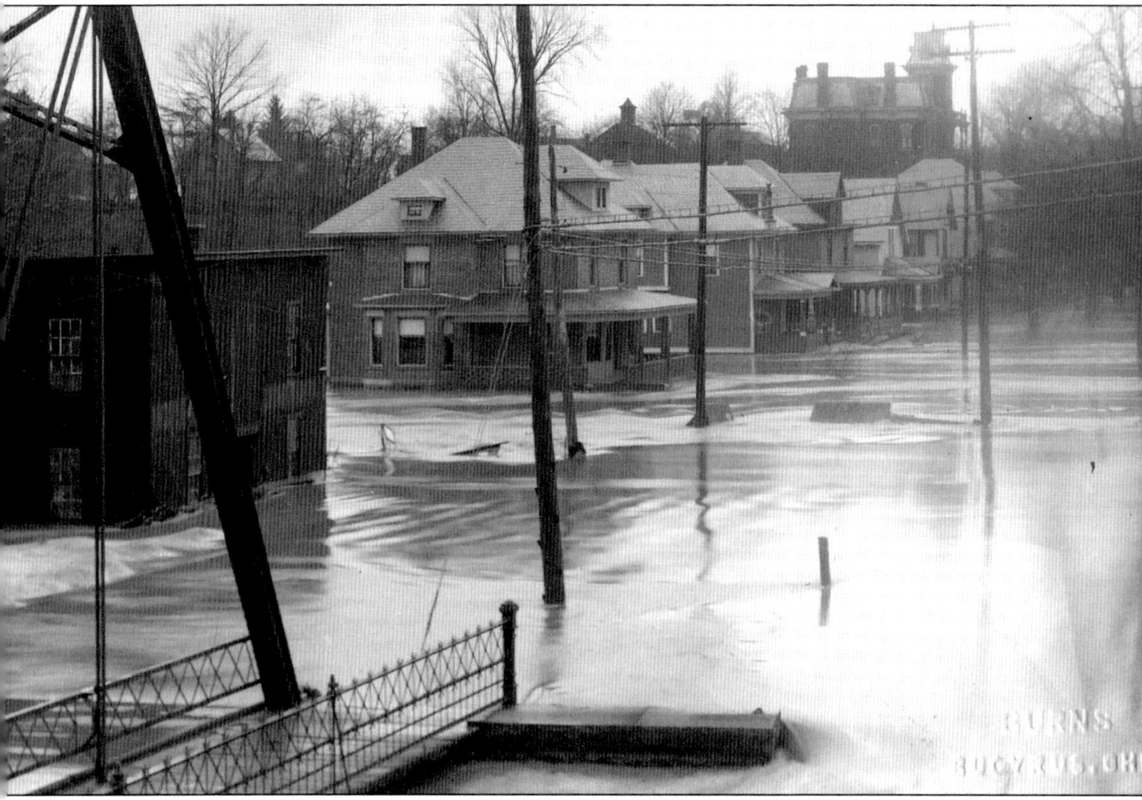

Great Flood of 1913, Looking North. Looking toward Monnett Memorial Hospital in the distance, this view provides an indication of the spread of the floodwaters in March 1913. (Courtesy of Stuart Koblentz.)

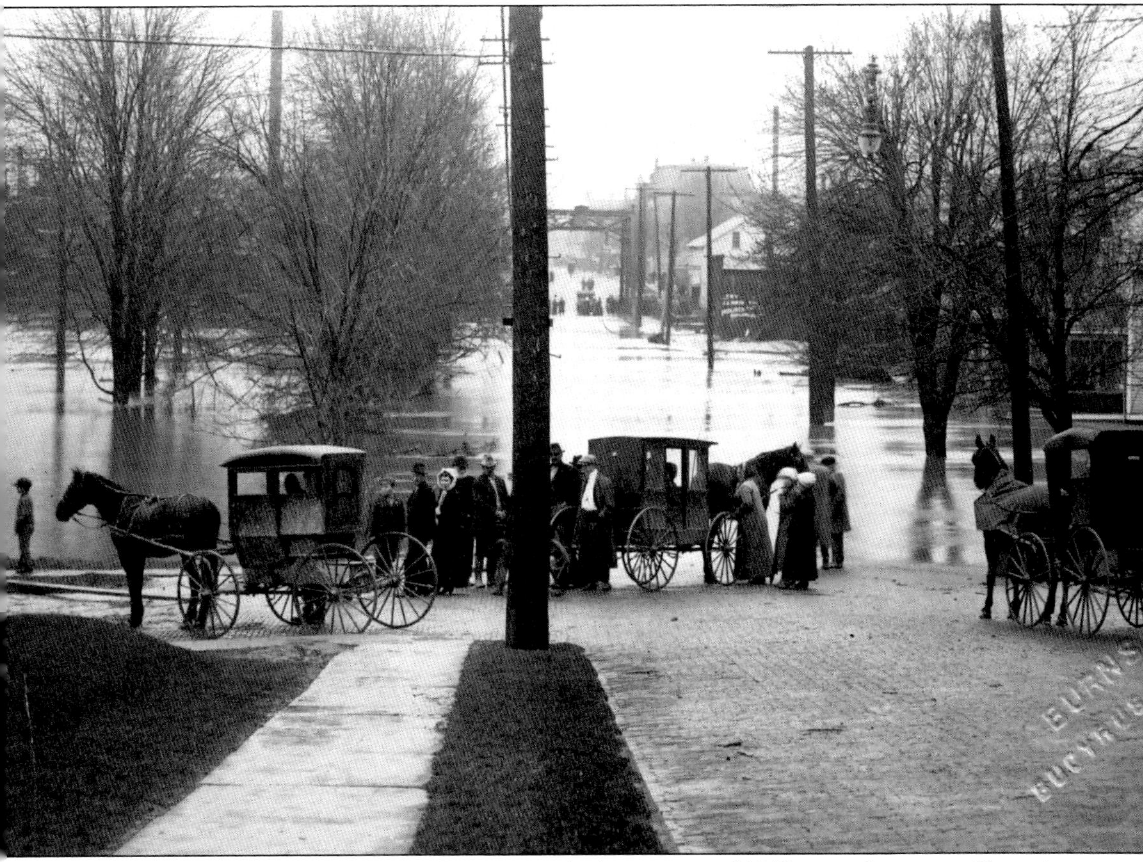

GREAT FLOOD OF 1913, LOOKING SOUTH. In the late winter of 1913, a combination of heavily packed snow and ice, persistent rains, and warming temperatures lead to the greatest flood catastrophe seen in western Ohio to that point. Throughout the region, rivers overran their banks, destroying lives, livelihoods, and property. This photograph shows the view from North Sandusky and Plymouth Streets looking south toward downtown. (Courtesy of Don and Mary Ellen Lust.)

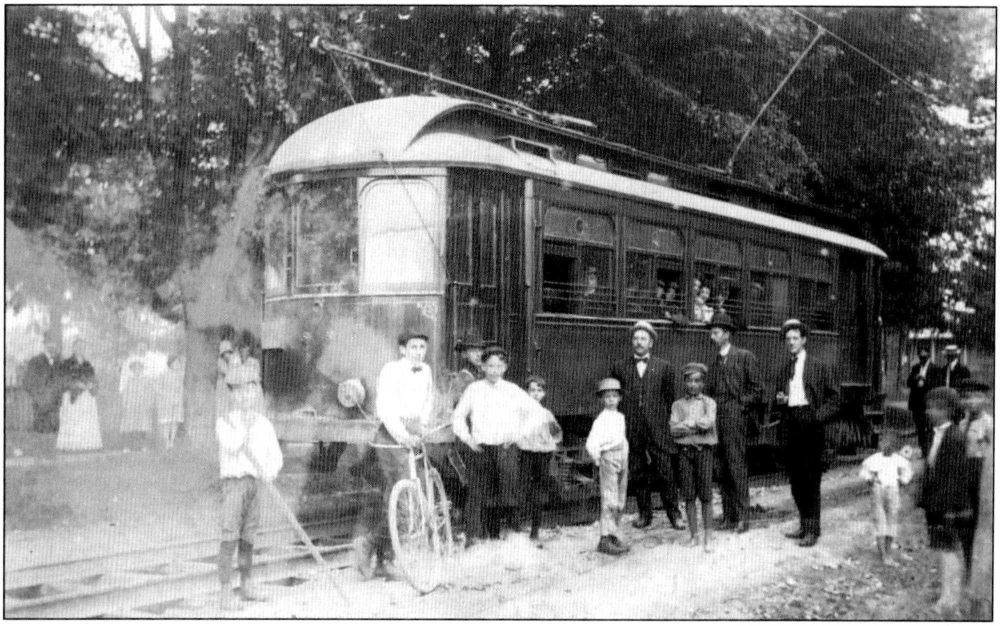

FIRST INTERURBAN CAR, 1908. An interurban was a form of high-speed intercity transportation found throughout America in the early 20th century. Powered by electricity, and oftentimes operated by the electric companies themselves, the cars could reach speeds of up to 70 miles per hour. This particular car traveled along Route 4 between Bucyrus and Marion. (Courtesy of the Bucyrus Historical Society.)

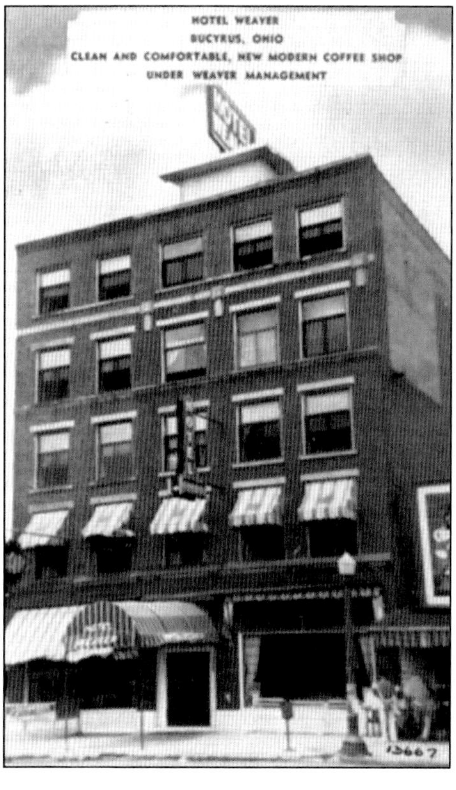

HOTEL WEAVER. Built on West Mansfield Street, just beyond Washington Square, stands the building once known as the Highway Hotel and later as the Hotel Weaver. According to local lore, Al Capone would spend the night at the Weaver while in Bucyrus; he was also known to spend the night in his private railcar. (Courtesy of Don and Mary Ellen Lust.)

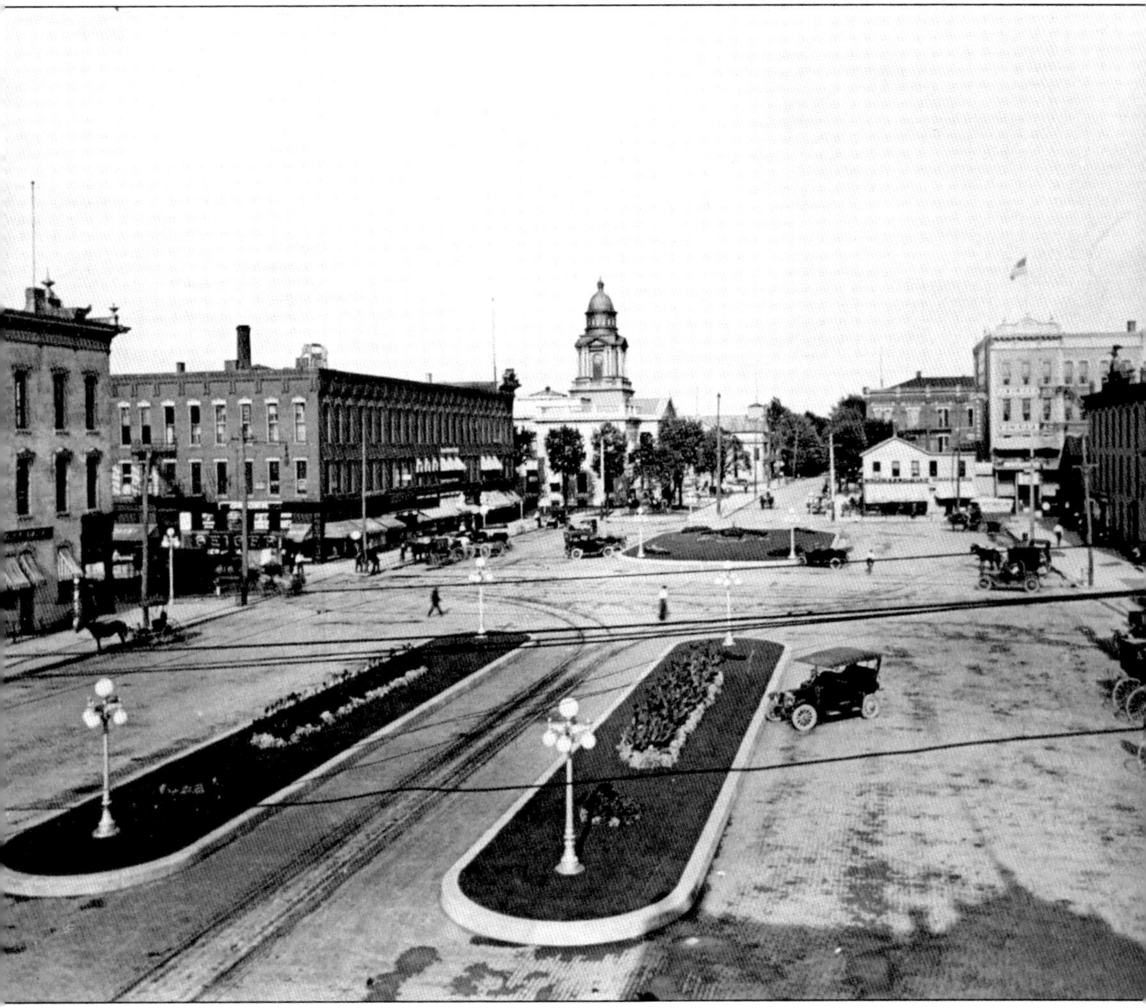

WASHINGTON SQUARE, LOOKING EAST. Bucyrus is unique in that it is one of the few Ohio cities to have a public square as large as Washington Square. The split green in the foreground provided a safe disembarking area for the interurban lines that connected Bucyrus to neighboring communities. (Courtesy of the Bucyrus Historical Society.)

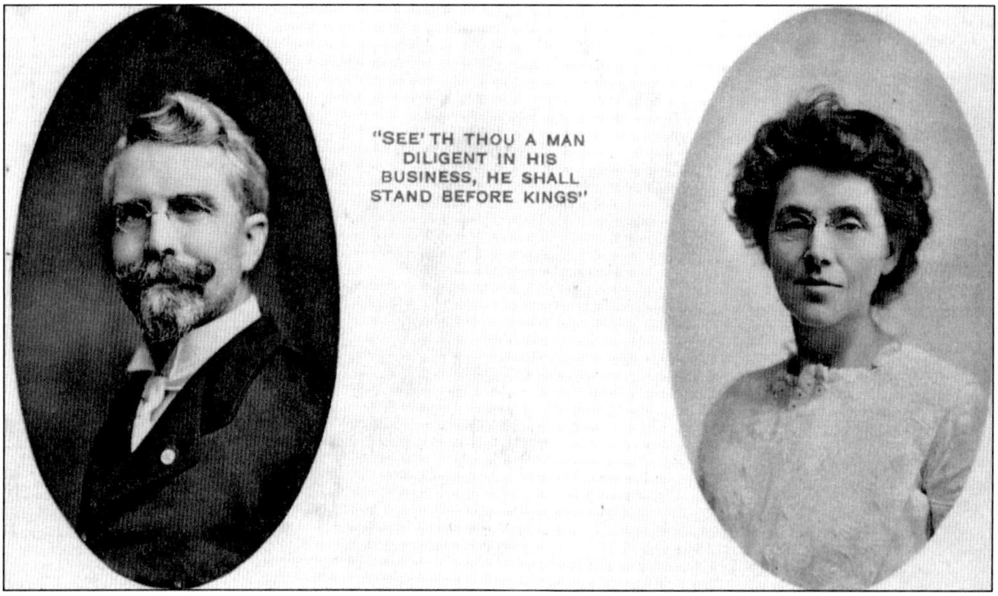

DR. W. C. AND DORA GATES. Dr. W. C. Gates and his wife, a trained nurse, established their first hospital in Bucyrus in 1906, and later the Bucyrus County Hospital at Popular and Warren Streets. Dr. Gates followed strict antiseptic procedures in his facility; he once admonished another Bucyrus physician for taking a cigarette break in the middle of performing a surgery and returning to the procedure without washing his hands. (Courtesy of Don and Mary Ellen Lust.)

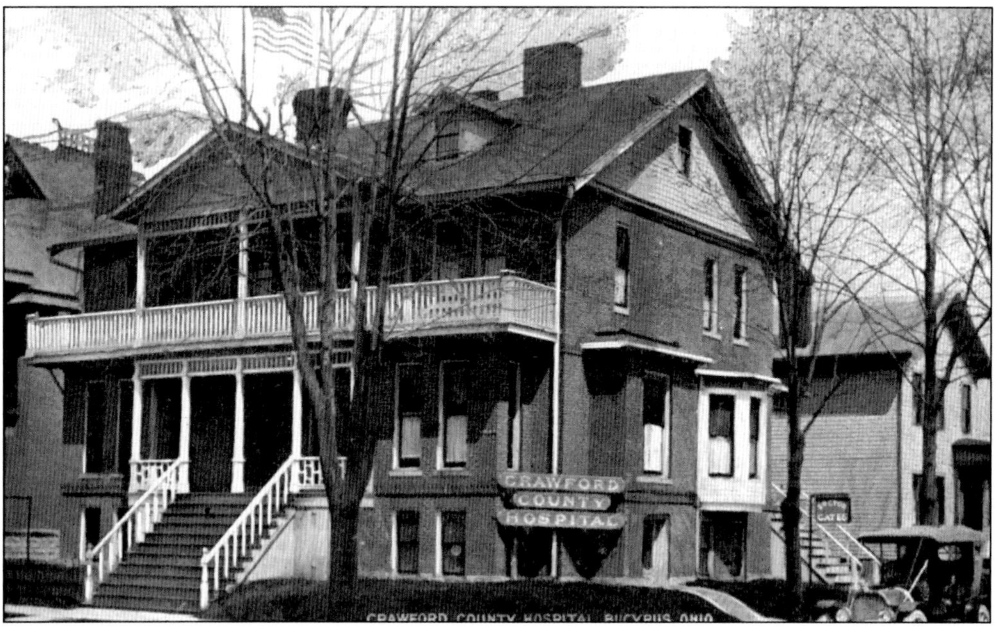

CRAWFORD COUNTY HOSPITAL. Like many small communities in the early 1900s, hospitals were housed in structures similar to houses and apartments, owed in part to the prevalence of in-home treatment of the sick. The Crawford County Hospital was established by Dr. W. C. Gates, who oversaw its operation until his death during World War I. (Courtesy of the Bucyrus Historical Society.)

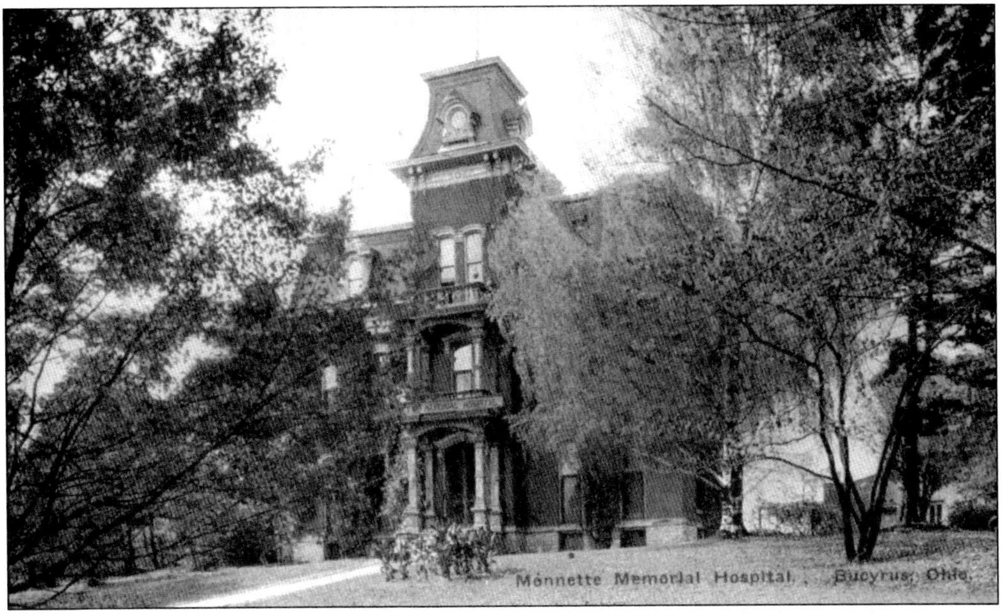

MONNETT MEMORIAL HOSPITAL, NORTH SANDUSKY STREET. In 1910, the former Tobias mansion on North Sandusky Street was converted to Monnett Memorial Hospital. The brother of Amina Tobias, Mervin J. Monnett made a $10,000 donation (equal to $204,000 in 2006) toward its conversion, and the facility was named in his honor. The structure held six wards and four private rooms, and the surgery area was placed in the third floor. An elevator was later installed, eliminating the need to carry surgical patients up several flights of stairs. (Courtesy of Stuart Koblentz.)

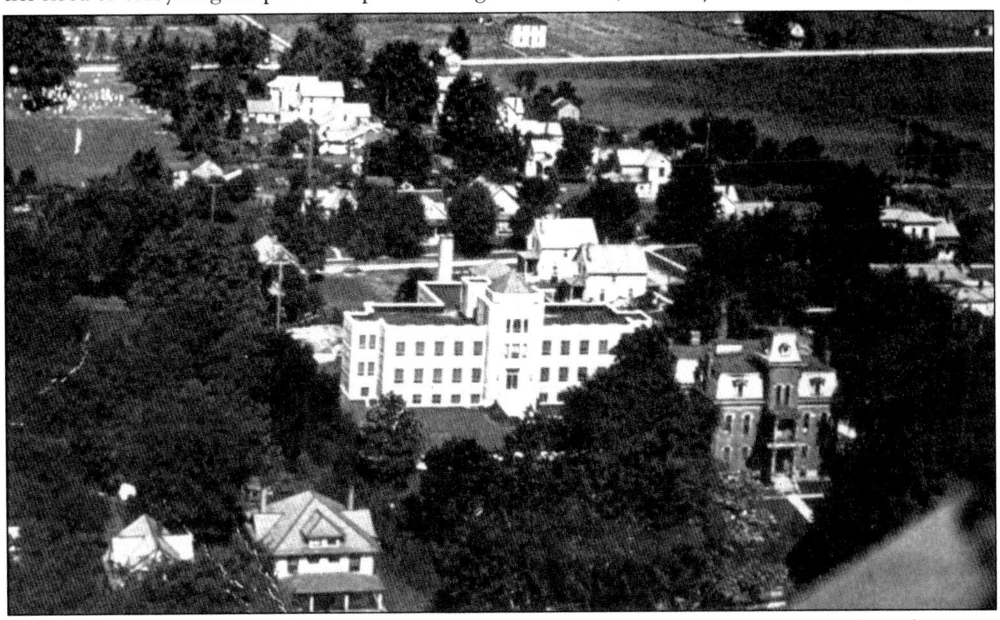

AERIAL VIEW, BUCYRUS COMMUNITY HOSPITAL, 1932. The advancement of facilities between the former Monnett Memorial Hospital and the new Bucyrus Community Hospital are evident in this postcard view from the era. Once decommissioned, the former hospital structure was razed. Since that time, the hospital has been enlarged and improved to serve the needs of the growing community. (Courtesy of Stuart Koblentz.)

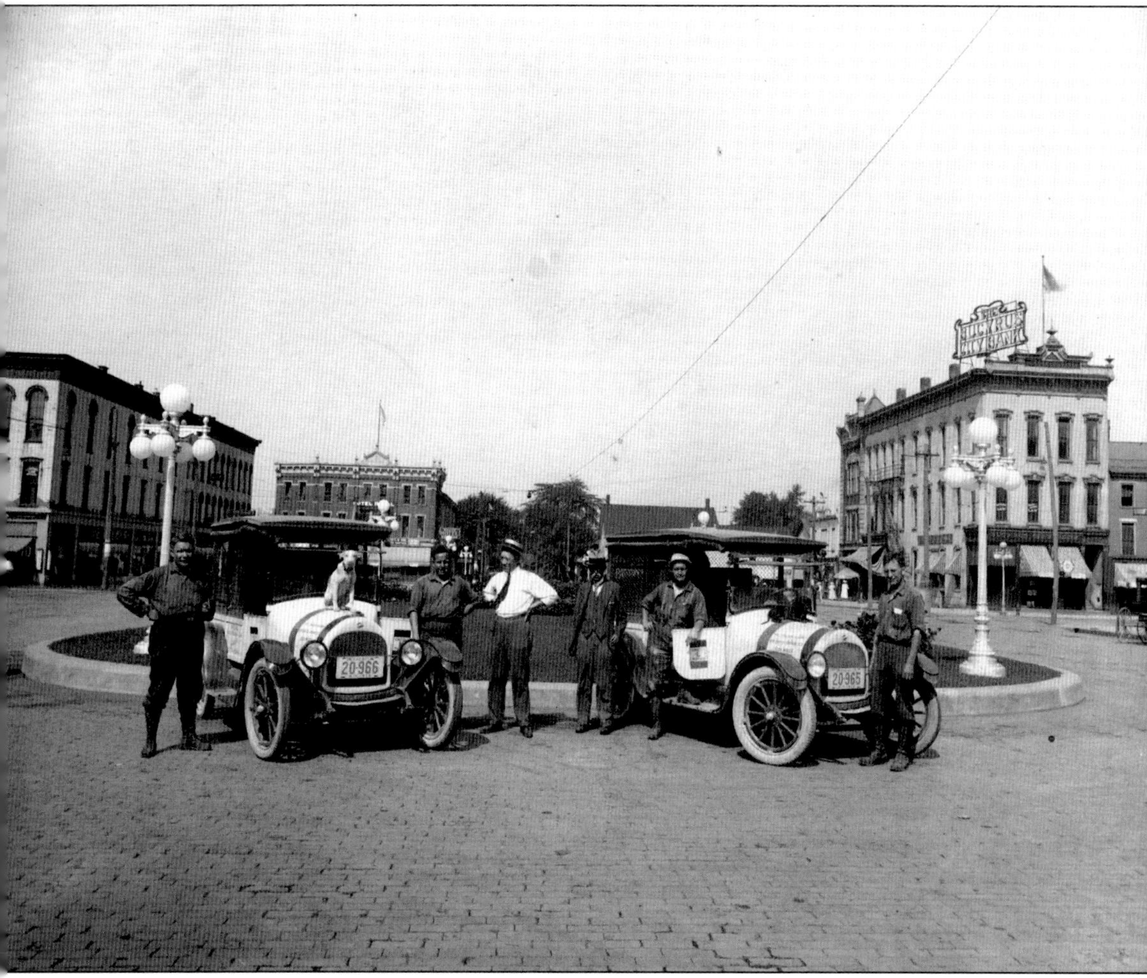

LINCOLN HIGHWAY SIGN PAINTERS. Stopping over in Bucyrus were sign painters employed by the Lincoln Highway Association, whose job it was to paint red, white, and blue bands on telephone poles along the route. Once completed, these same painters kept the painted bands in good shape. These bands were visual cues to motorists that they were traveling on the Lincoln Highway and had not been diverted off the route. (Courtesy of the Ohio Historical Society, Hopley Collection.)

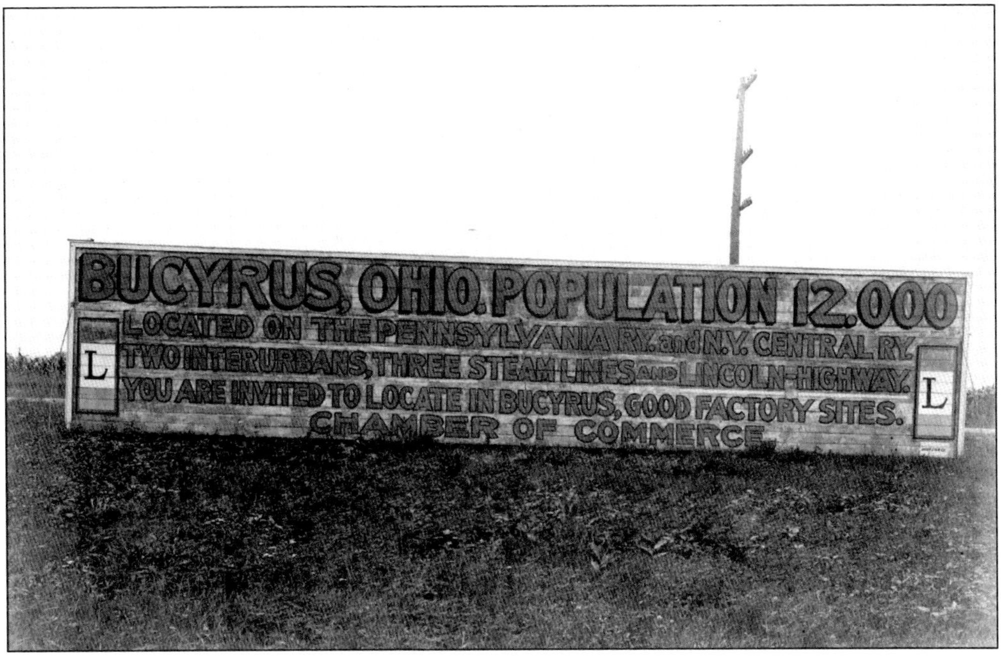

WELCOME TO BUCYRUS. In 1916, improved roads between communities were a rarity, so it was with great pride that Bucyrus erected this sign at the point where the Lincoln Highway, the nation's first improved coast-to-coast highway, entered the city's eastern incorporation limit. (Courtesy of the Ohio Historical Society, Hopley Collection.)

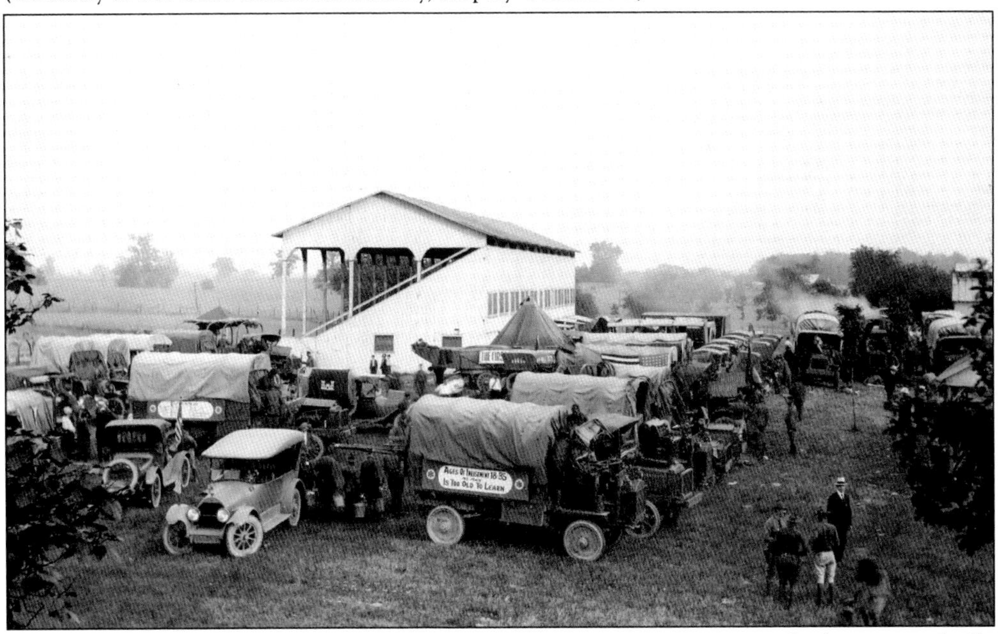

LINCOLN HIGHWAY CARAVAN. So novel was the idea of a coast-to-coast highway specifically designed for the automobile, that a caravan of cars and trucks set out from Times Square in New York City with the intention of celebrating the road's opening by crossing its entire length. Upon arriving in Bucyrus, they pitched their tents at the Crawford County Fairgrounds and spent the night. (Courtesy of the Ohio Historical Society, Hopley Collection.)

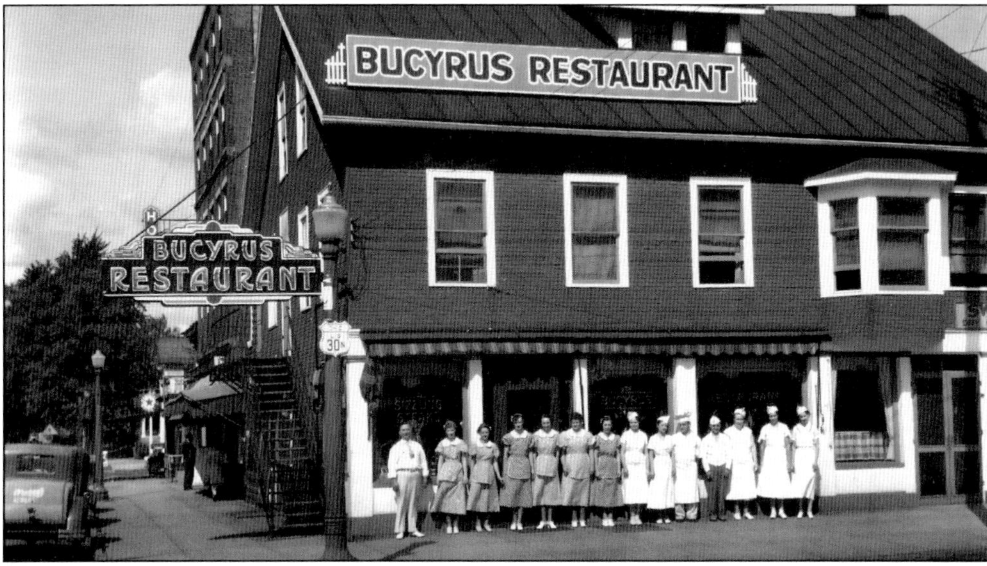

BUCYRUS RESTAURANT AND HIGHWAY HOTEL, 1934. The Bucyrus Restaurant was located on the northwest corner of Washington Square and Mansfield Street, and was a very busy and well-known restaurant. Standing are, from left to right, George Davis, the restaurant's owner; Lulu Luke-Wheeler (née Ulmer); Jenny Wertz (née Taylor); Hilly Parsel (née Lohr); Hazel Black (née Lutz); Phyllis Russell; Lena Heiby; Sally Light; Willy Myers; Ray Lahman; Bus Taylor; Kathryn Davis; Lena (née Merhling); and Rose Bentz (née Stader). (Courtesy of the Bucyrus Historical Society.)

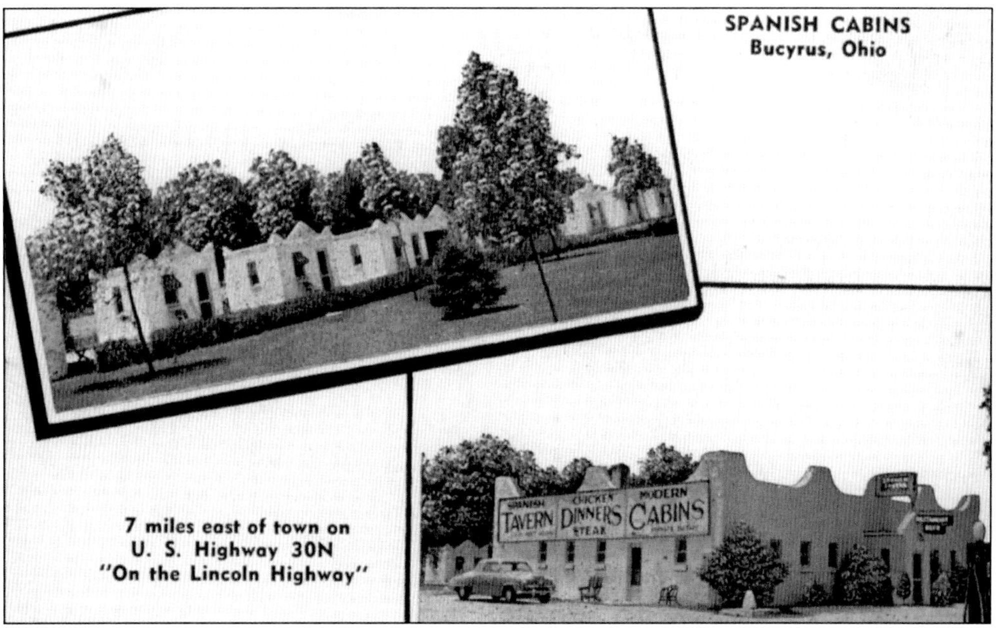

SPANISH CABINS, LINCOLN HIGHWAY, EAST OF BUCYRUS. As America took to modern and improved highways in their own automobiles, thousands of motor hotels (motels) and tourist cabins sprouted up to serve the public's hunger for inexpensive overnight accommodations. The Spanish Cabins, so named for the roadside style of architecture, was one such local landmark for many years. (Courtesy of Don and Mary Ellen Lust.)

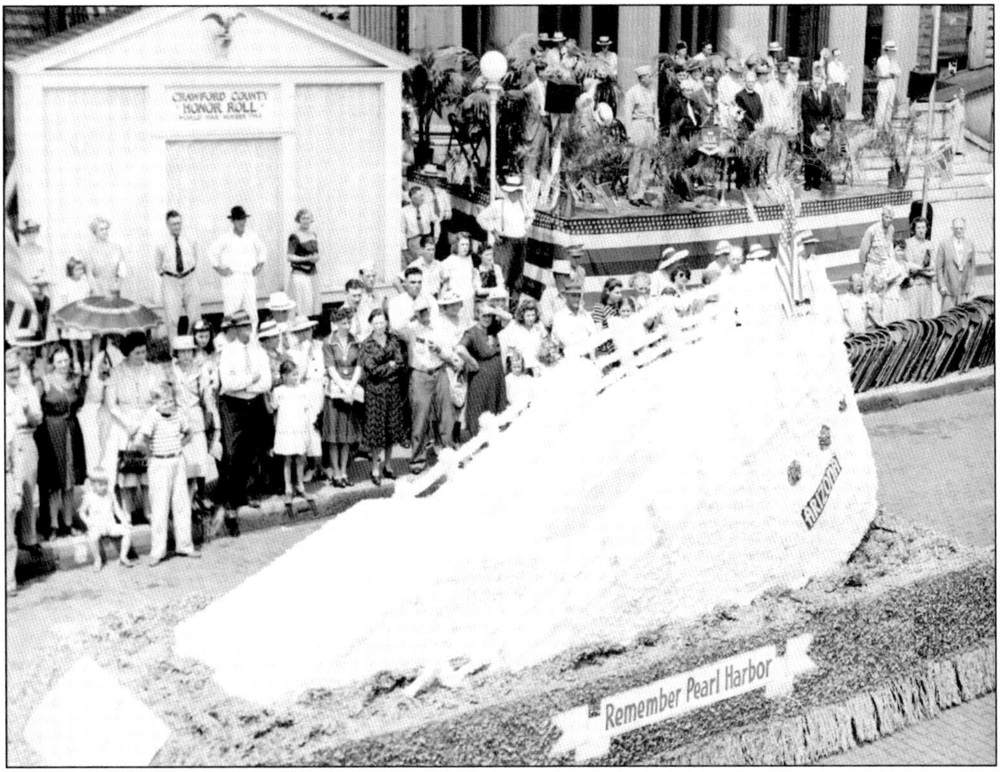

PEARL HARBOR FLOAT. Built for a parade in downtown Bucyrus, the float was designed to solemnly remind bystanders of what America was fighting for in World War II. (Courtesy of the Bucyrus Historical Society.)

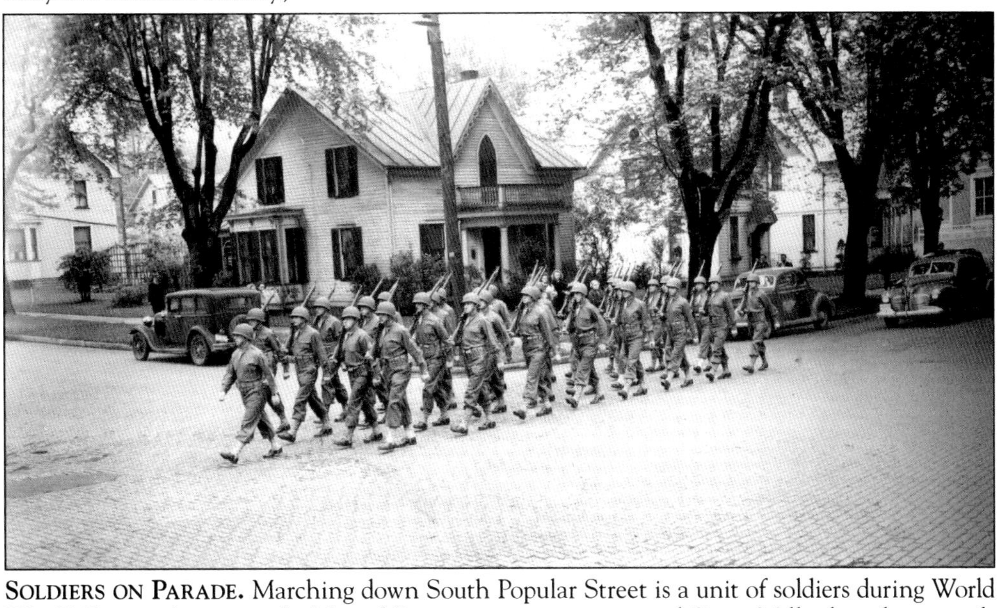

SOLDIERS ON PARADE. Marching down South Popular Street is a unit of soldiers during World War II. During that time, the United States government operated Camp Millard on the grounds of the Crawford County Fairgrounds as a training site for army engineers. (Courtesy of the Bucyrus Historical Society.)

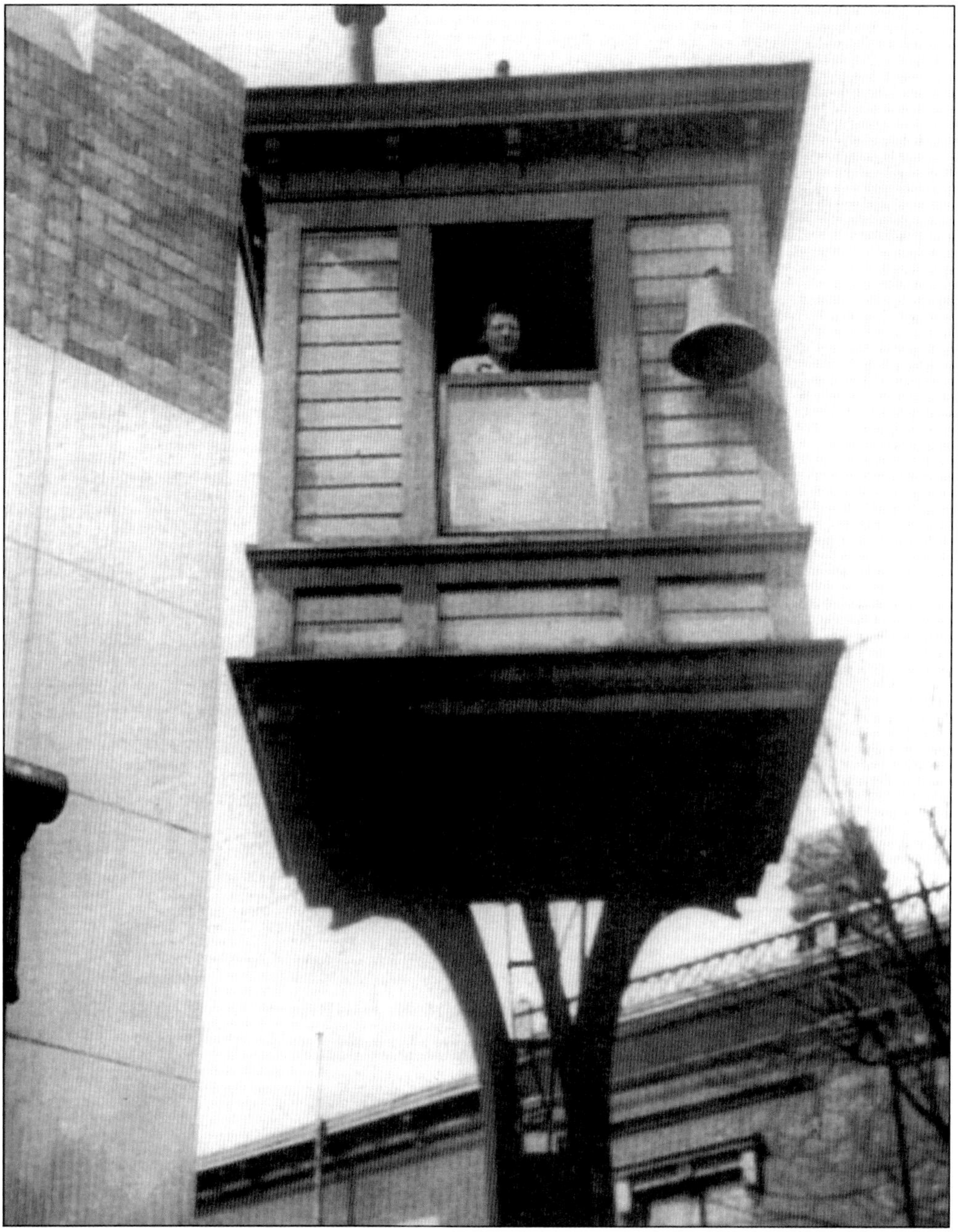

RAILROAD CROSSING TOWER. Before the advent of automatic gates, rail crossing gates were operated manually. In building-congested areas, like downtown Bucyrus, the crossing guard often had to be elevated to see far enough in either direction to allow for ample time to drop the gates. This tower, operated by a woman during World War II, was located on North Sandusky Street for many years. (Courtesy of the Bucyrus Historical Society.)

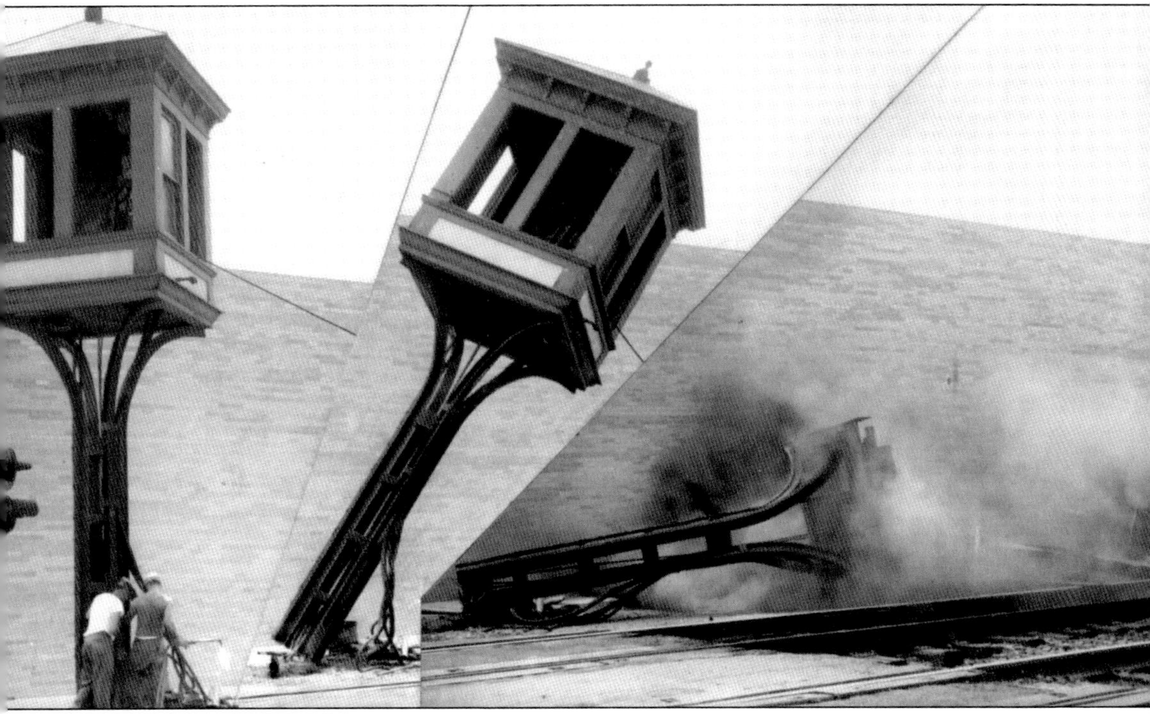

CROSSING TOWER DEMOLITION. With the advent of fully automated safety gates, the need for a manned crossing tower was eliminated. The demolition of the North Sandusky Street tower occurred in the early 1960s. (Courtesy of Jim Croneis.)

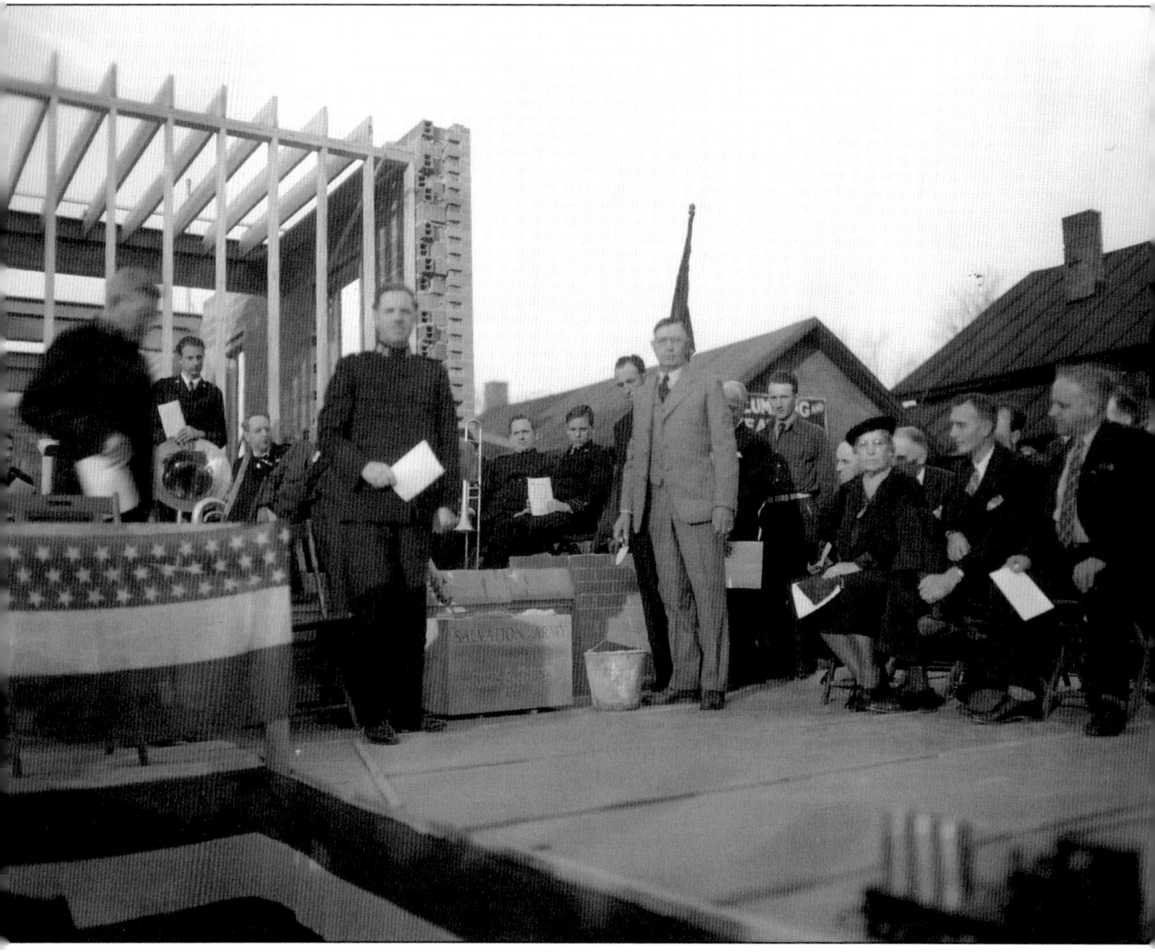

SALVATION ARMY CORNERSTONE. The Salvation Army found a permanent home in Bucyrus on Rensselaer Street in the 1930s through a generous gift by industrialist John Q. Shunk, who took part in the facility's cornerstone ceremony. (Courtesy of the Bucyrus Historical Society.)

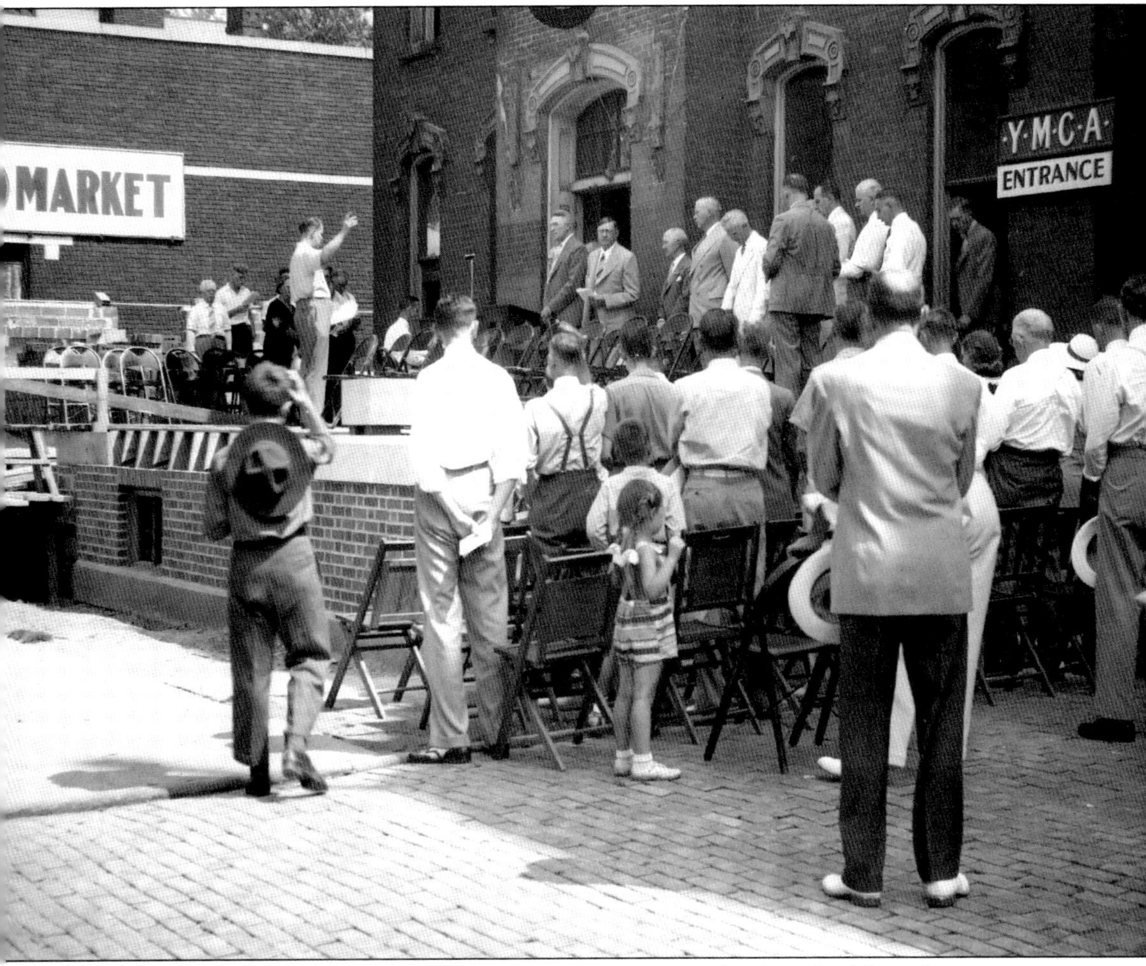

YMCA Modernization, 1941. Another Bucyrus institution that benefited from the generosity of John Q. Shunk was the YMCA, which used financial gifts to enlarge and construct a new facade. (Courtesy of the Bucyrus Historical Society.)

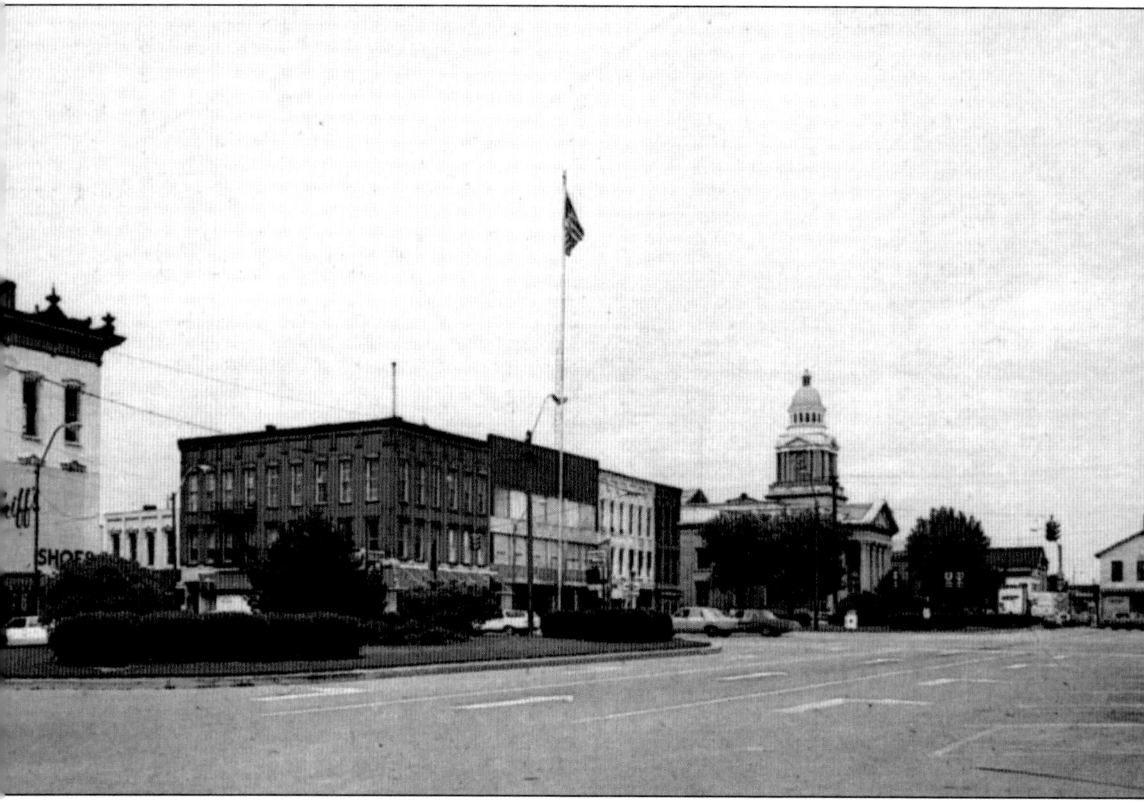

NORTH SIDE OF WASHINGTON SQUARE, C. 1960S. Washington Square has undergone numerous changes since its establishment, one of which was the demolition of the northeast quadrant for the new headquarters of the Farmers and Citizens Bank. The original block of buildings is seen in this view. (Courtesy of Stuart Koblentz.)

Two

To Serve and Protect

Since its earliest beginnings, Bucyrus has relied upon the service of a select group of men and women to ensure that the community was kept safe from harm's way. To do the jobs that the community's police and fire departments are expected to accomplish not only requires community support, but respect for the jobs that these brave and valiant public servants perform when they are needed most.

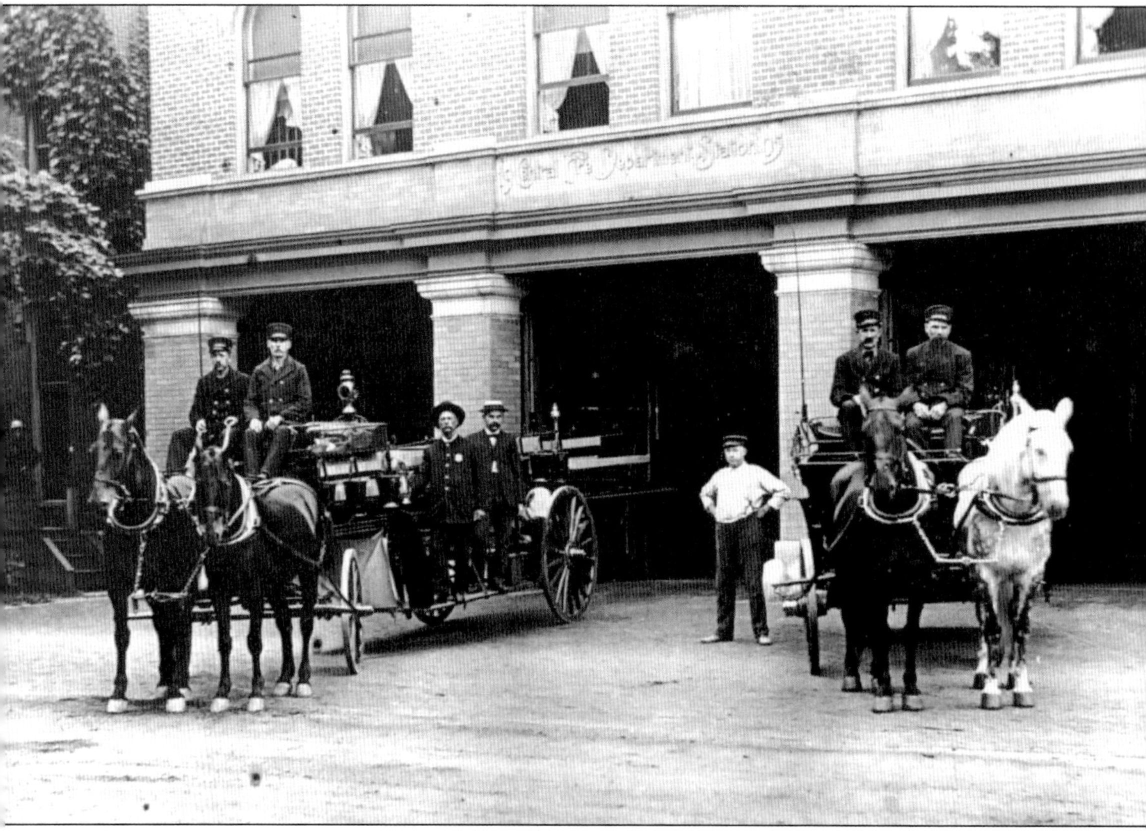

CENTRAL FIRE STATION. Opened in 1905, the Bucyrus Central Fire Station was among the largest and most modern of its kind for the era. The structure has remained in continuous use and celebrated its centennial of service in 2005. (Courtesy of the Bucyrus City Fire Department.)

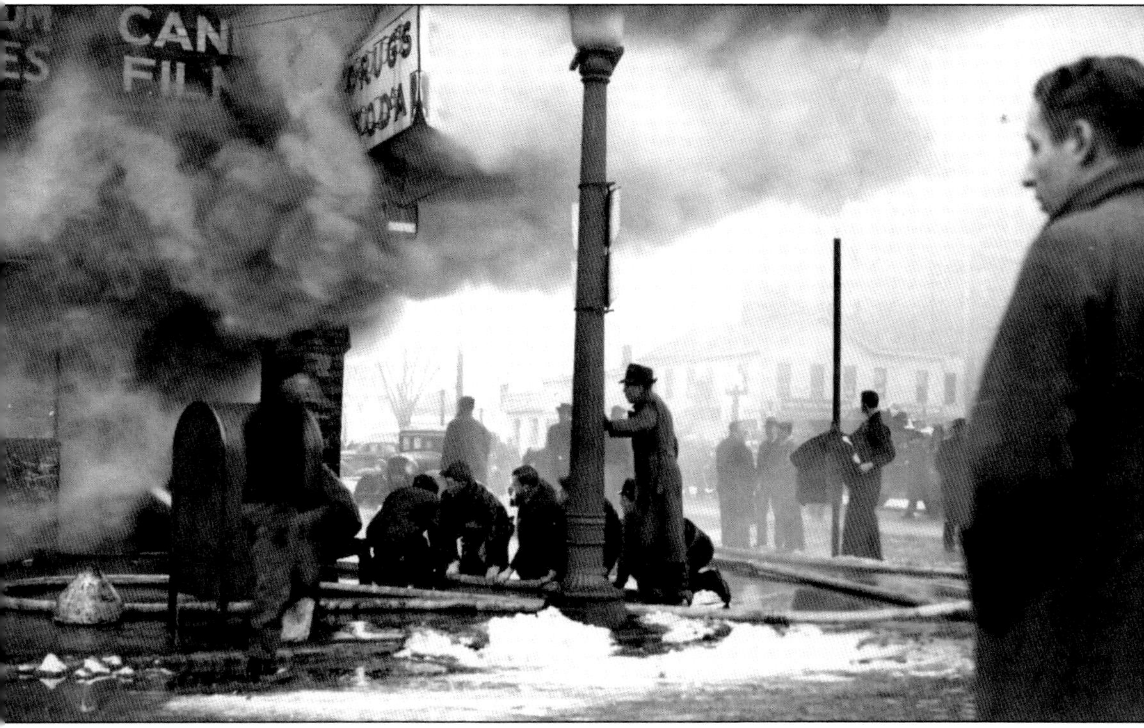

FOULK'S REXALL FIRE. A longtime landmark on Washington Square was Foulk's Rexall Drug Store. The building in which the shop was located caught fire in the mid-1930s. While damage to the building was sustained, Foulk's reopened, maintaining its presence in Bucyrus until its building was razed for the headquarters of the Farmers and Citizens Bank. (Courtesy of the Bucyrus City Fire Department.)

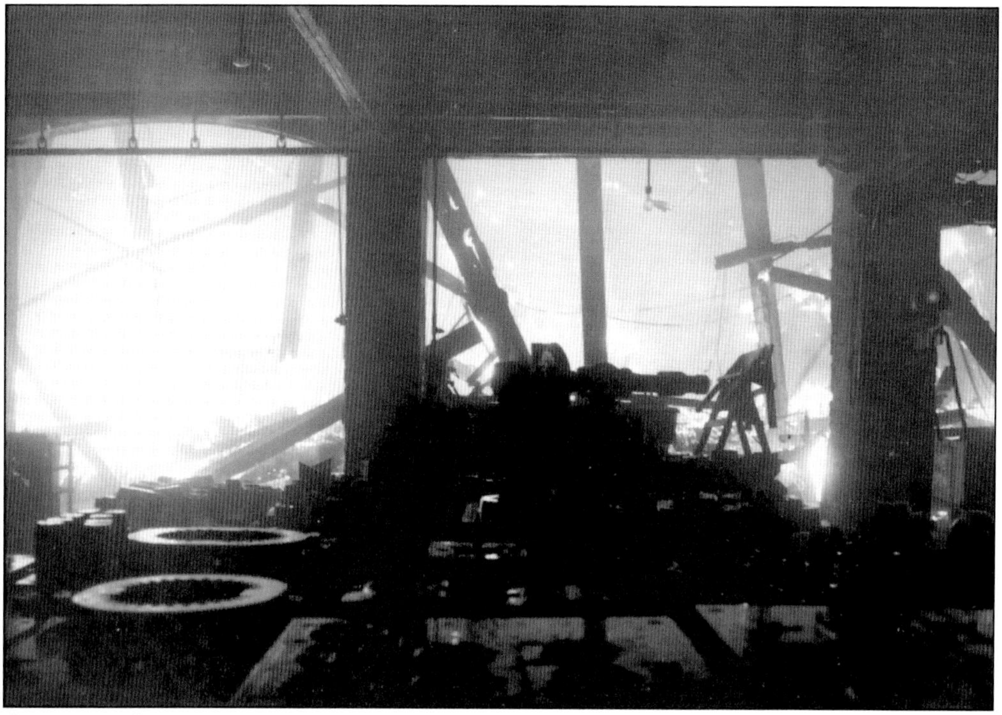

CRAWFORD STEEL FOUNDRY FIRE. This view looks toward the fire that destroyed the Crawford Steelworks on December 17, 1958. (Courtesy of the Bucyrus City Fire Department.)

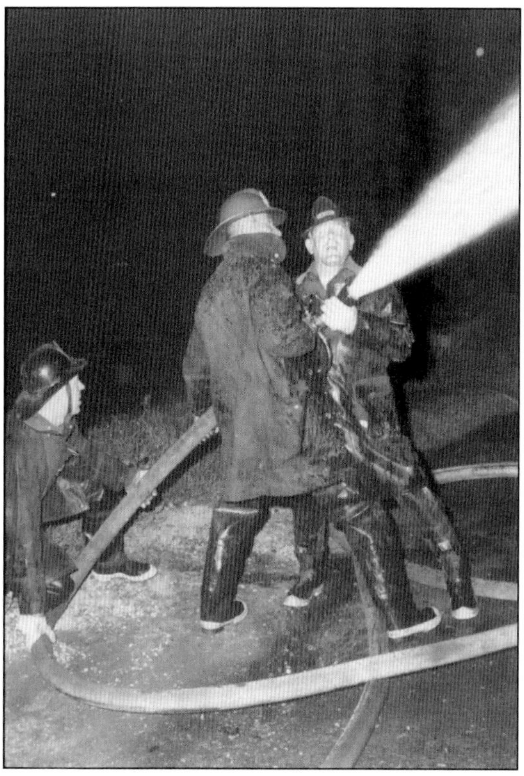

HEROES AT WORK. Jack Metzler, Red Rorick, and an unidentified firefighter (from left to right) control a water hose during a fire in downtown. (Courtesy of the Bucyrus City Fire Department.)

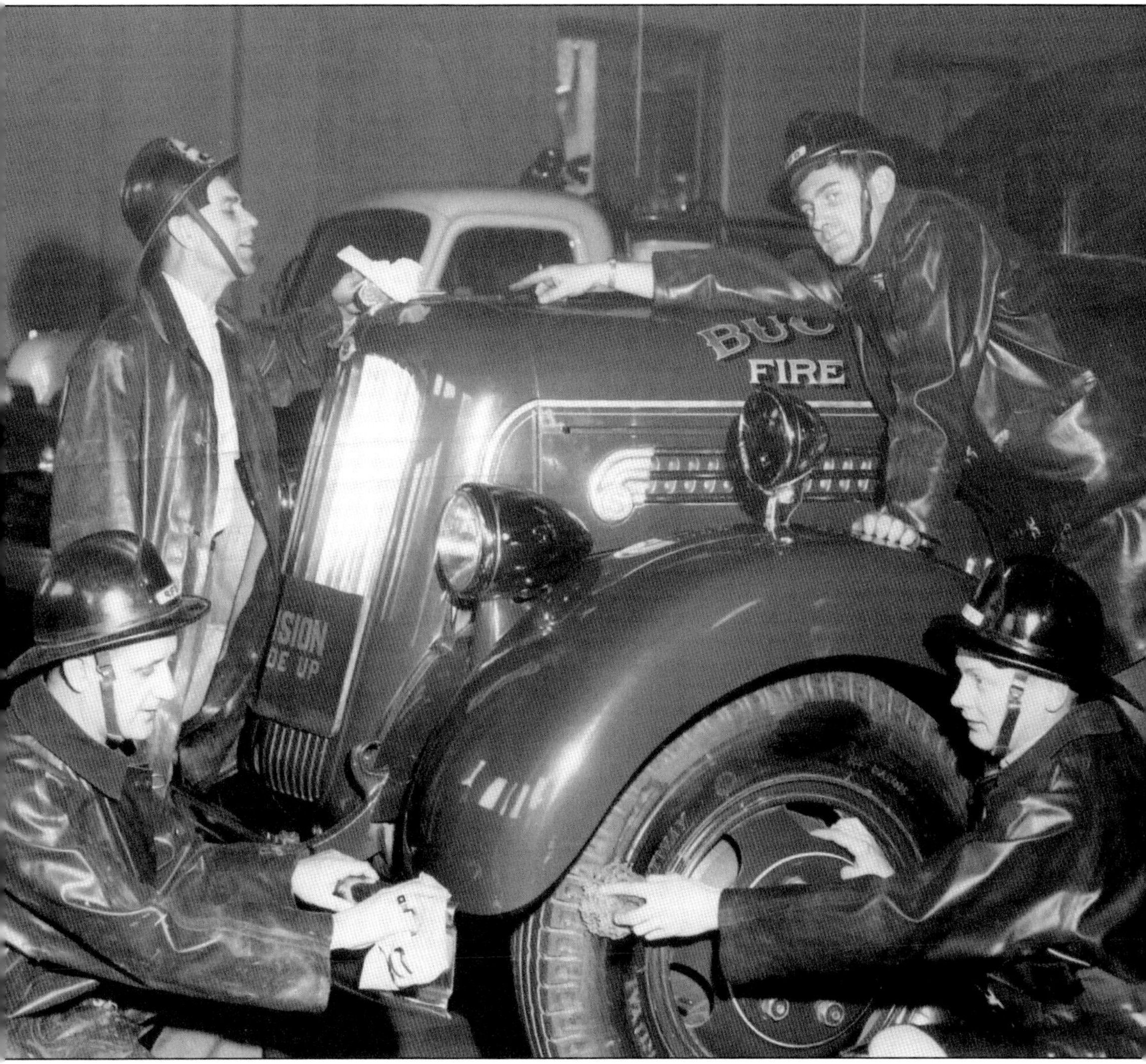

FIREFIGHTERS AND SEAGRAVE FIRE TRUCK, C. 1962–1963. From left to right, Rev. Pat Paetznick, Jack Metzger, Bob Gingery, and John Rorick, who are members of the Bucyrus Fire Department, pose with the department's Seagrave fire truck. (Courtesy of the Bucyrus City Fire Department.)

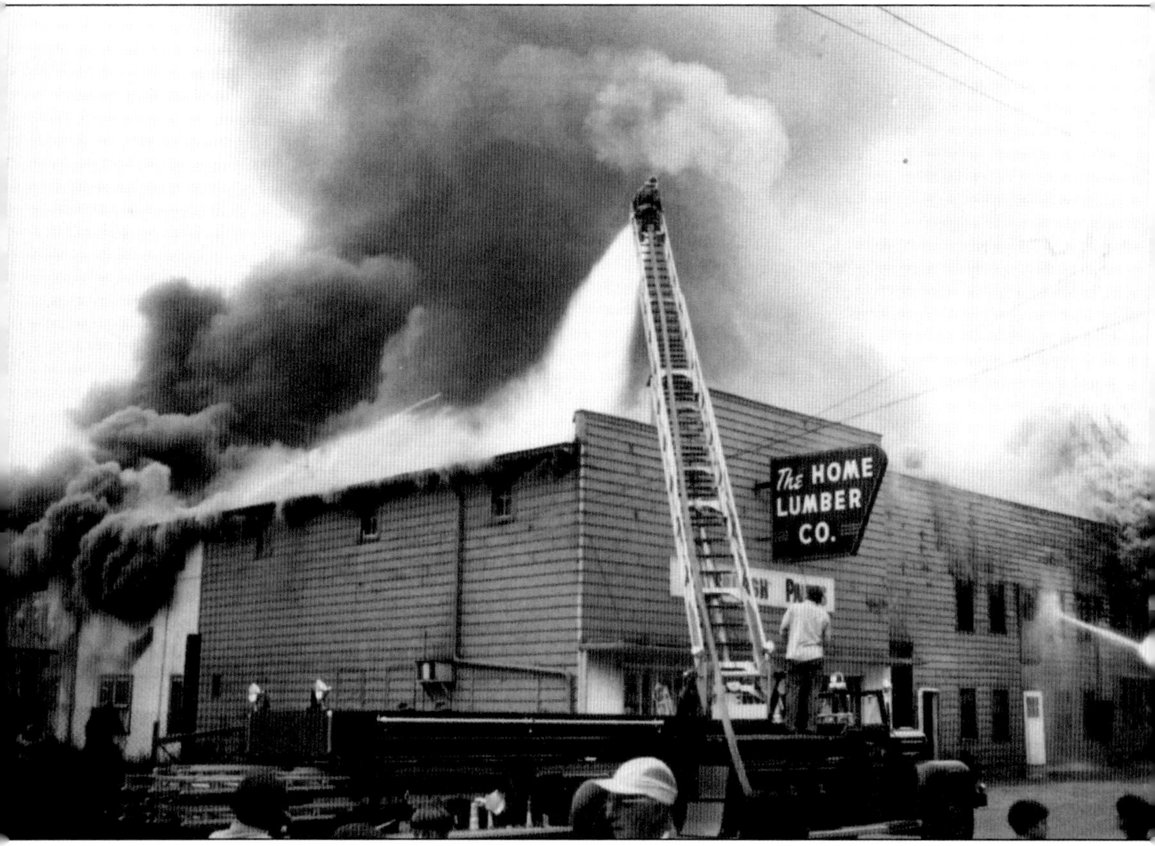

HOME LUMBER FIRE. When the Home Lumber Company in Bucyrus caught fire, despite attempts by firefighters to get the blaze under control, its contents—wood and painting solvents—fueled the flames. (Courtesy of the Bucyrus City Fire Department.)

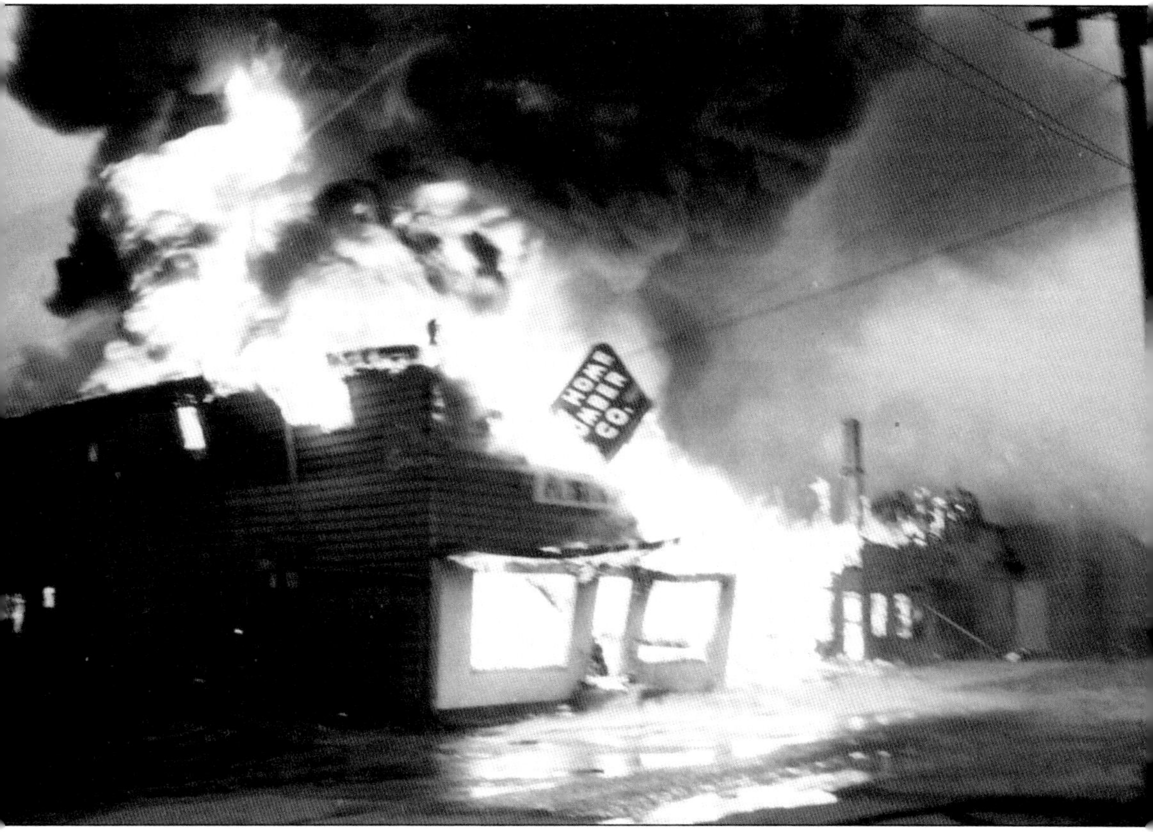

HOME LUMBER EXPLOSION. Ultimately the paint, solvents, and other materials pushed the fire at Home Lumber to the point of explosion. Fortunately no lives were lost as a result of the fire. (Courtesy of the Bucyrus City Fire Department.)

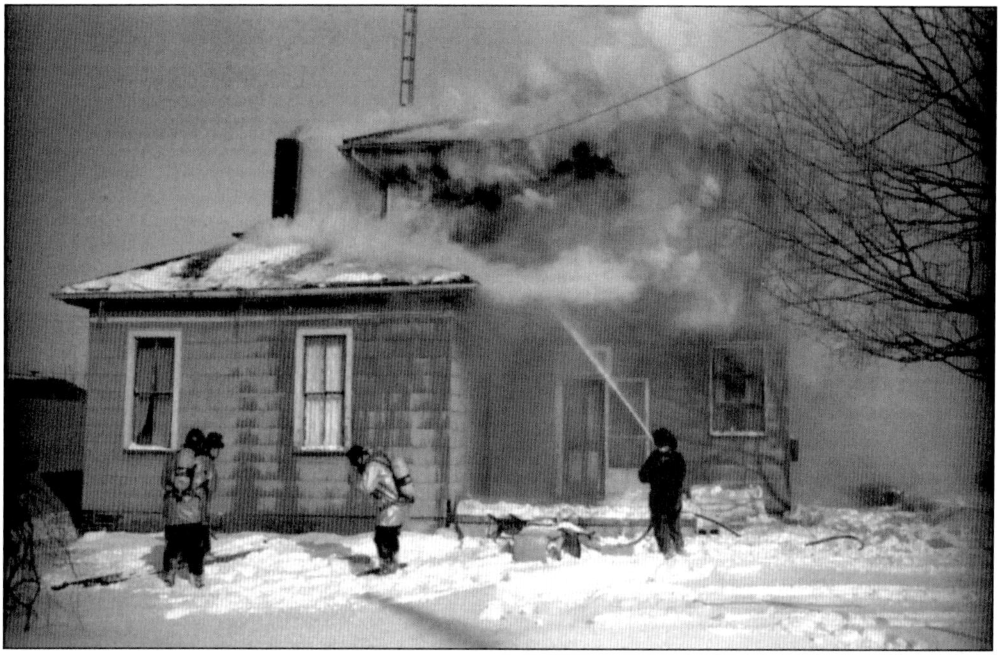

House Fire, Woodlawn Avenue. Firefighters are called to duty in all manner of weather, around the clock, on any day of the year. Despite the frigid temperatures, members of the Bucyrus Fire Department fight to control a fire on Woodlawn Avenue in February 1971. (Courtesy of the Bucyrus City Fire Department.)

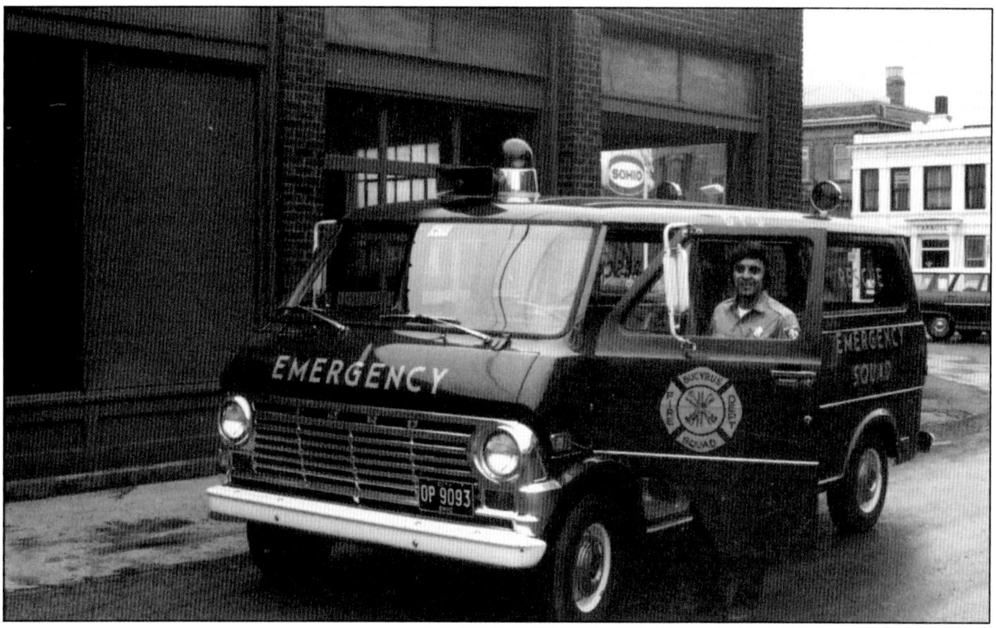

Emergency Squad Van, 1969. Bucyrus added this emergency squad vehicle in 1969. The transition from the point of purchase as a used standard Ford Econoline van to a finished EMT squad vehicle —including a trip to Columbus for a quick Earl Shibe paint job, lettering, and lights, and then to Lima for interior supplies—was accomplished in just 24 hours. (Courtesy of the Bucyrus City Fire Department.)

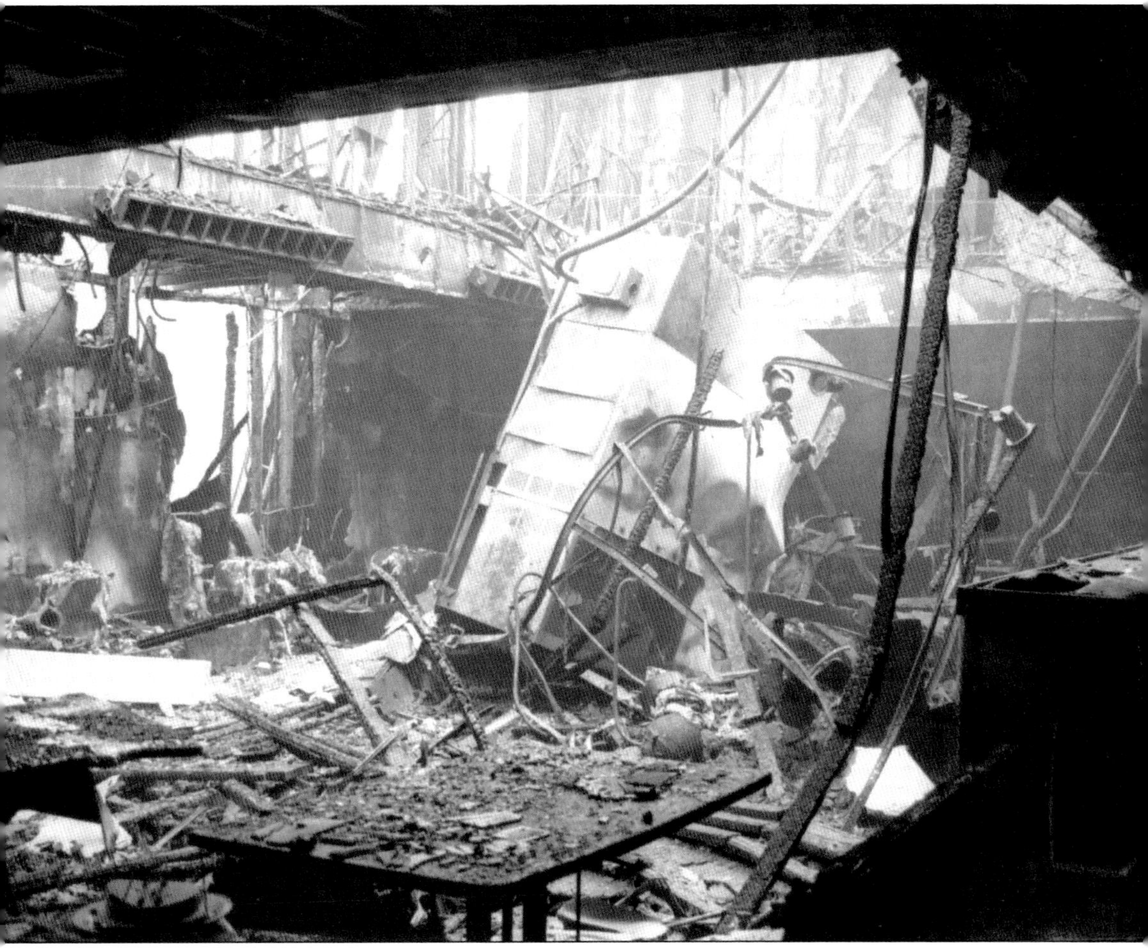

MAD BULL FIRE. Perhaps the action on the dance floor at Bucyrus's Mad Bull on Washington Square was a little too hot the night before this fire destroyed the regionally popular nightclub in April 1987. (Courtesy of the Bucyrus City Fire Department.)

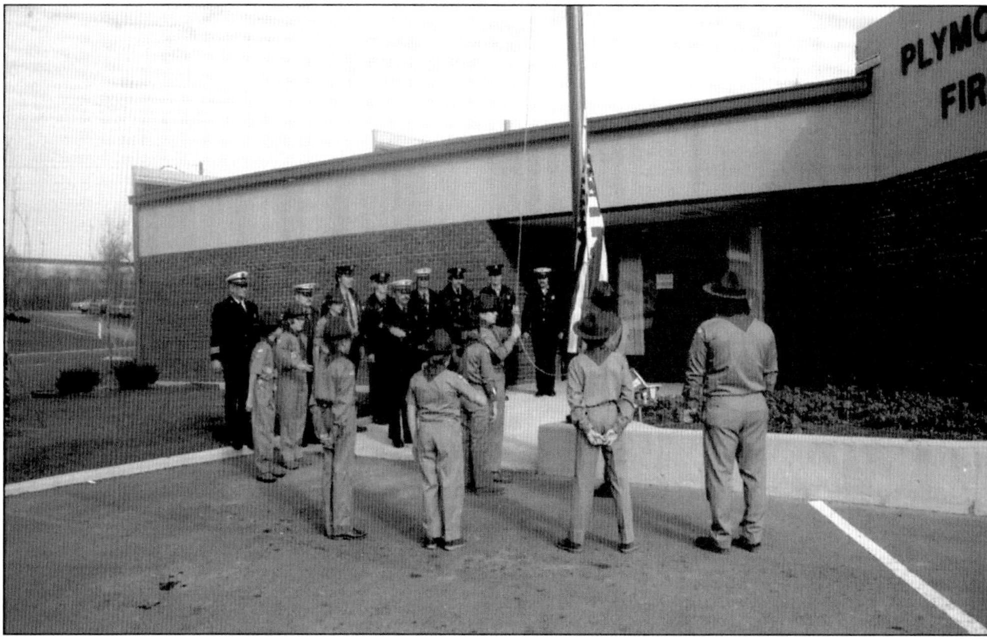

PLYMOUTH STREET STATION. Dedicated on November 13, 1977, the city's Plymouth Street Fire Department substation served the community until the mid-1980s. The structure has since been converted to private business use. (Courtesy of the Bucyrus City Fire Department.)

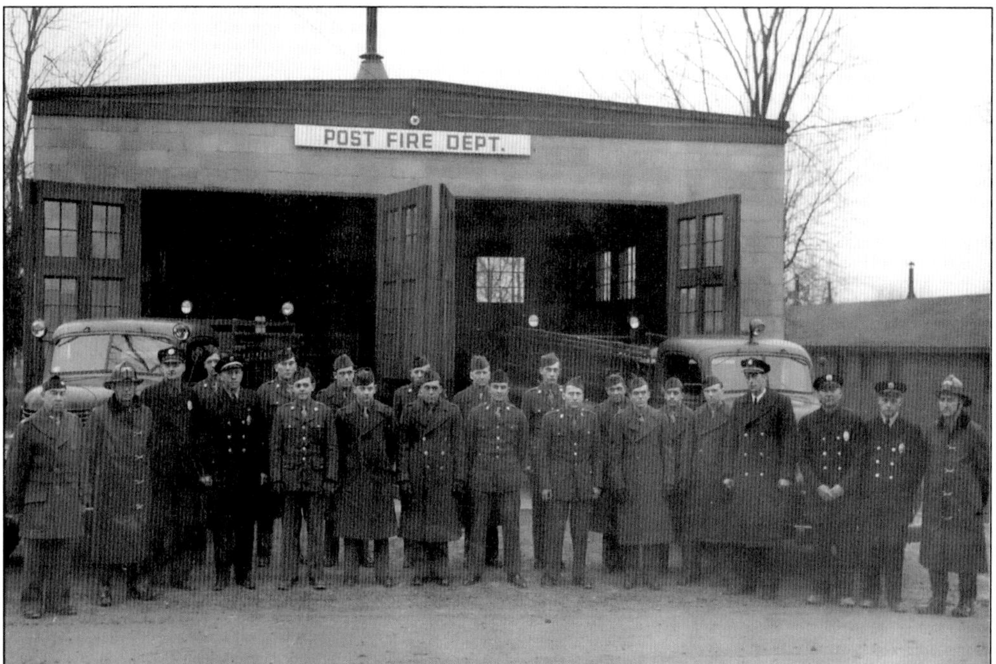

CAMP MILLARD FIRE DEPARTMENT. During World War II, the United States government converted the Crawford County Fairgrounds into Camp Millard, a training base for engineers. Members of the Camp Millard Fire Department pose for their picture. (Courtesy of the Holtshouse family.)

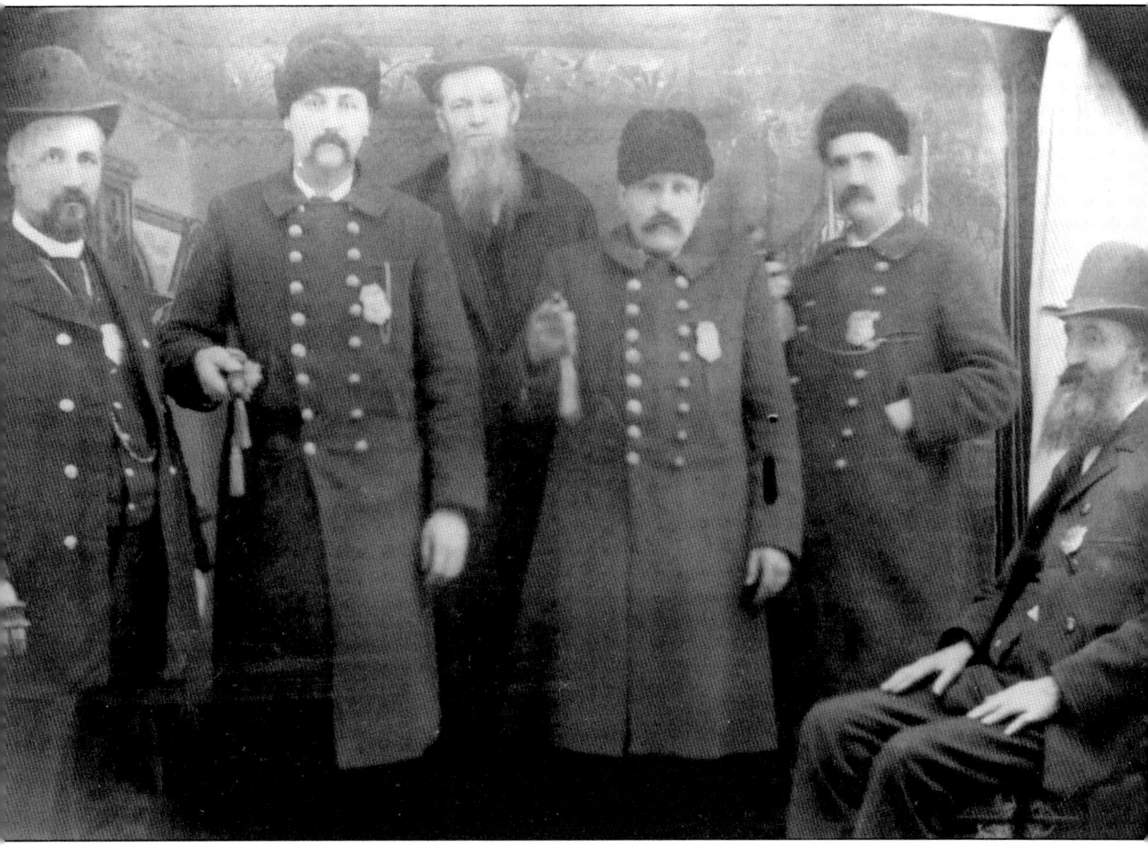

BUCYRUS CONSTABLES, 1890S. Members of the Bucyrus Police Department pose in this photograph from the 1890s. While each of the policemen (wearing double-breasted coats) has his billy club in hand, the lack of firearms is also notable. (Courtesy of the Bucyrus Police Department and Bucyrus Historical Society.)

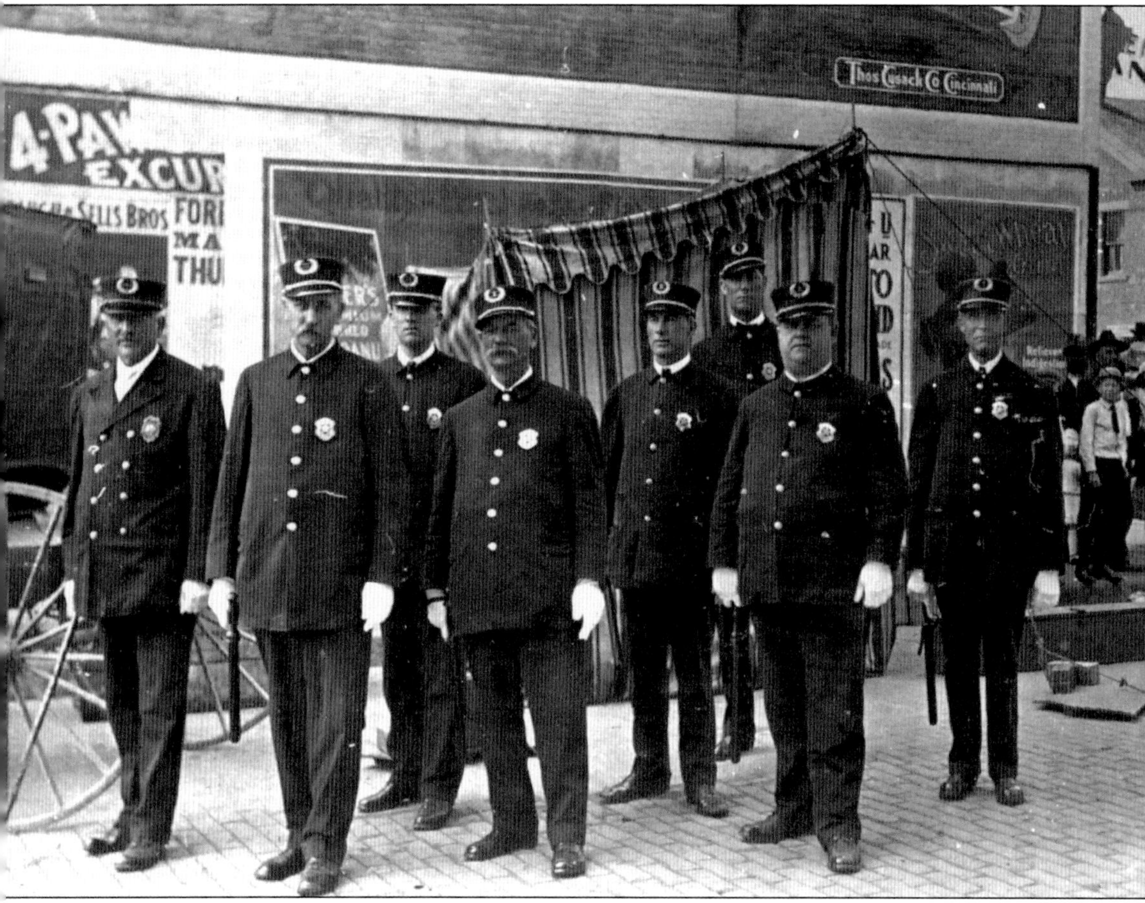

BUCYRUS POLICE FORCE, 1909. As Bucyrus grew in population, so did the police force. Longtime chief of police Phillip Trautman is standing at the far left in this group picture. (Courtesy of the Bucyrus Police Department and Bucyrus Historical Society.)

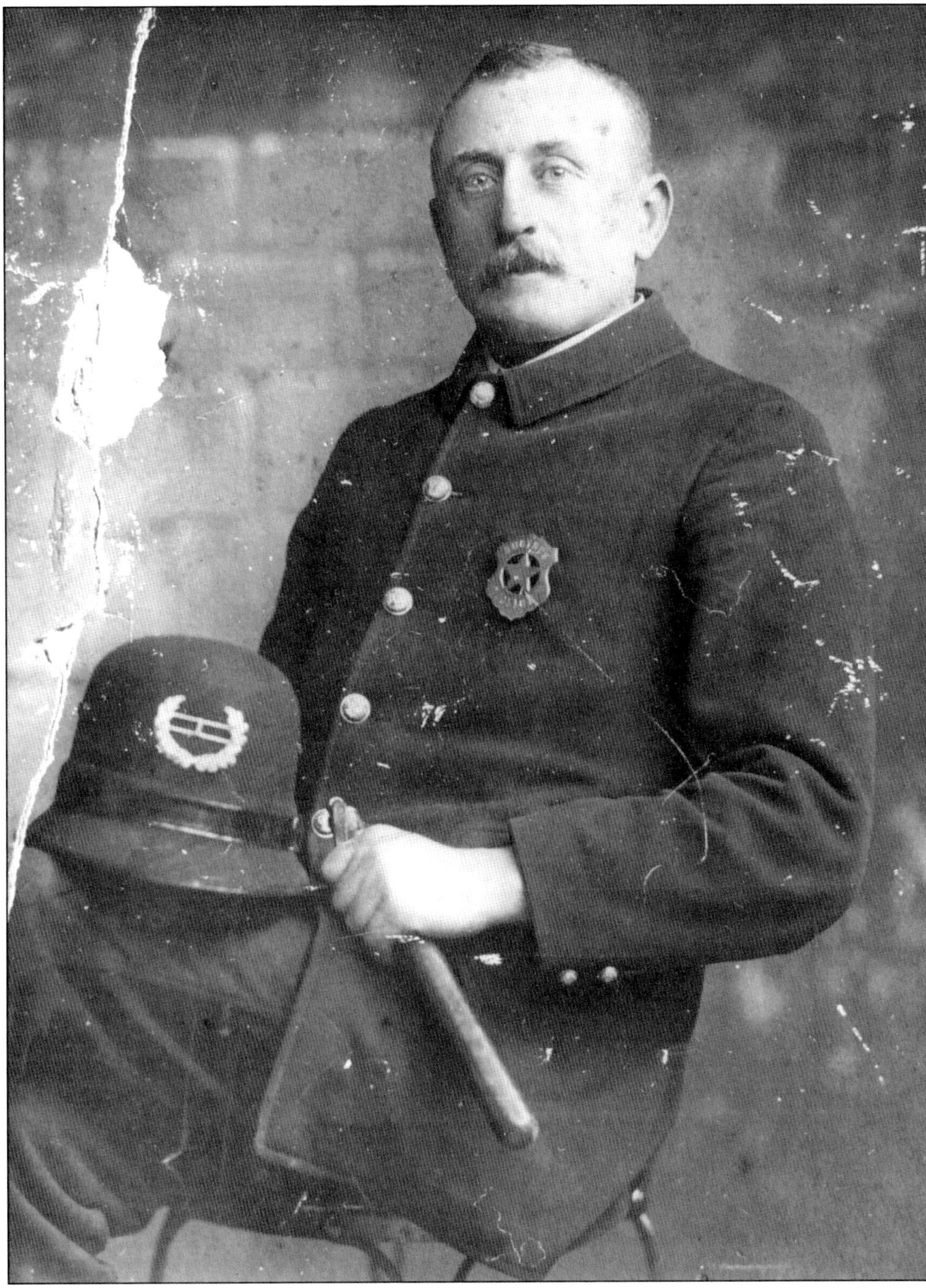

PHILLIP TRAUTMAN. Serving the citizens of Bucyrus for more than 50 years as chief of police, Phillip Trautman oversaw the transition of Bucyrus's police force into a modern, well-equipped law-enforcement agency. Trautman retired in 1938. (Courtesy of the Bucyrus Police Department and Bucyrus Historical Society.)

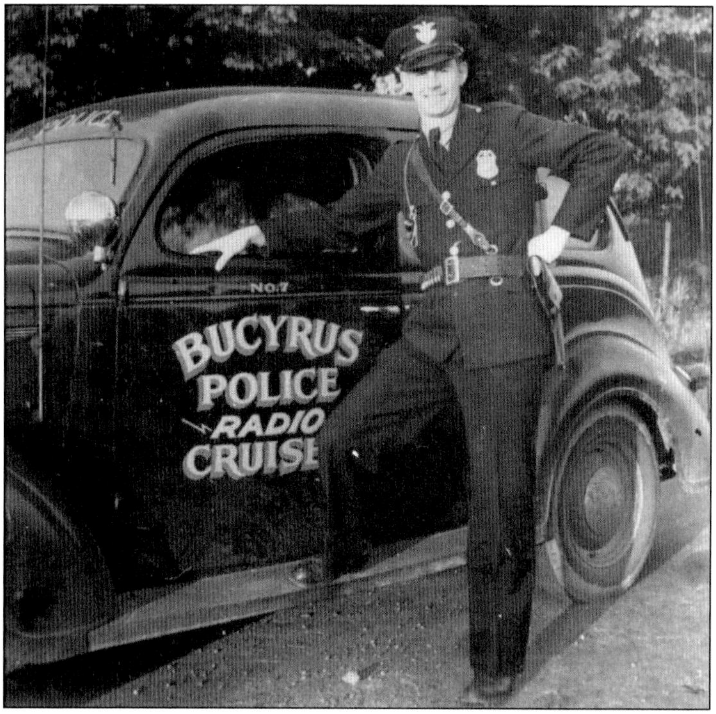

CHET WINKLEFOOS, C. 1940. A deep-sea diver by trade, Chet Winklefoos served as a policeman and a volunteer fireman. He founded the first community-based ambulance service in Bucyrus. As a side note, police cars from this era were equipped with a porthole in the windshield that allowed police to fire their weapons while traveling, if needed. (Courtesy of the Galion Historical Society.)

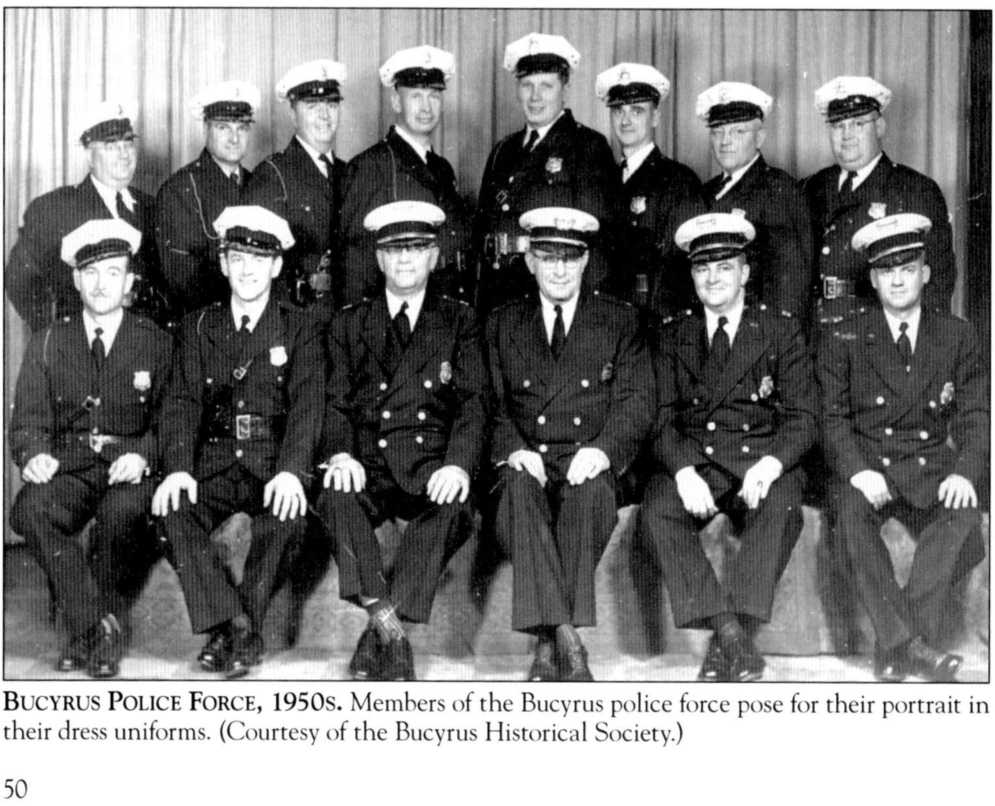

BUCYRUS POLICE FORCE, 1950S. Members of the Bucyrus police force pose for their portrait in their dress uniforms. (Courtesy of the Bucyrus Historical Society.)

Three

BUCYRIANS

Most Bucyrus natives know about the roles that the Norton family, Col. William Crawford, and Col. James Kilbourne played in the establishment of Bucyrus. Others, too, left their mark on the community just as those who are Bucyrians today will leave their mark for future generations. Each person in this chapter has touched the lives of numerous people around them, and causes one to reflect on how others in the future will regard each person who lives today.

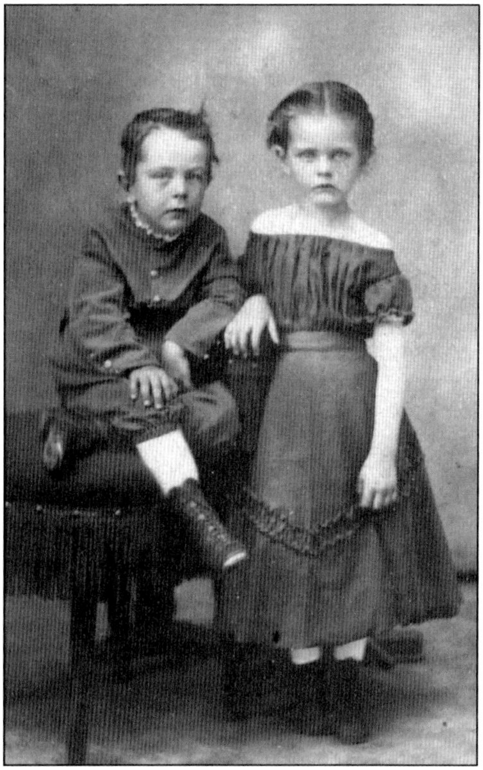

GILBERT FERRIS "TOM" AND KATHRYN MALCOLM, C. 1868. The children of Elsie Monnett and her husband James Malcolm, Gilber Ferris "Tom" and his older sister Kathryn pose for a portrait taken around 1868. Kathryn married Mitchell Aye. Tom married Elizabeth Hinamon and operated the family farm in southern Crawford County throughout his life. (Courtesy of James Campbell.)

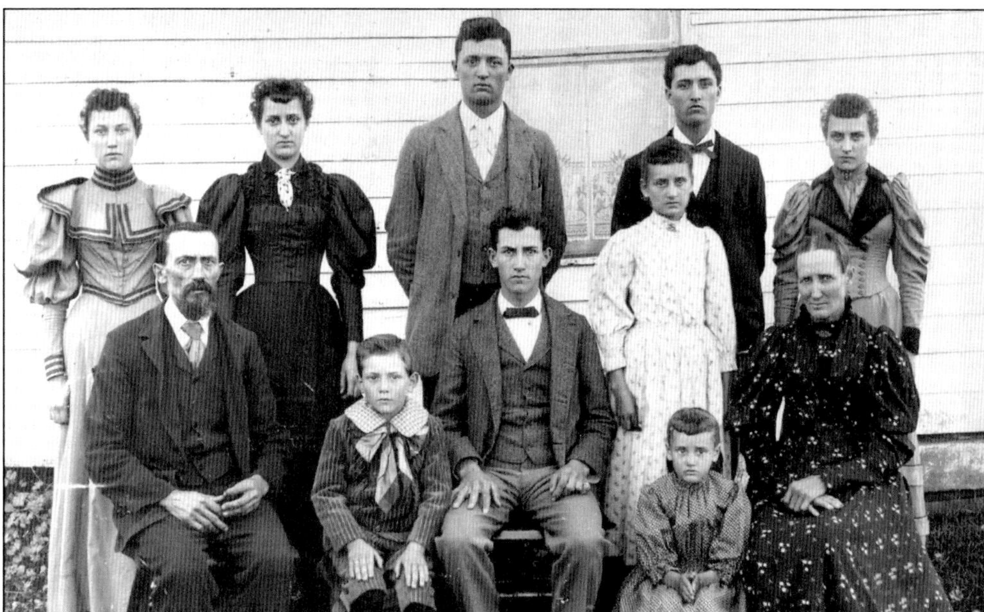

WINEMILLER FAMILY. Members of the Winemiller family pose for this 1894 picture. Sitting in front are, from left to right, Adam Winemiller, John Winemiller, Mitchell Winemiller, Elsie Winemiller, and Emaline Winemiller (née Weirick). In the back row are Edna Winemiller, Bertha Winemiller, Grant Winemiller, Harrietta Winemiller, Sherman Winemiller, and Eva Winemiller. (Courtesy of Rodney Rittenhouse.)

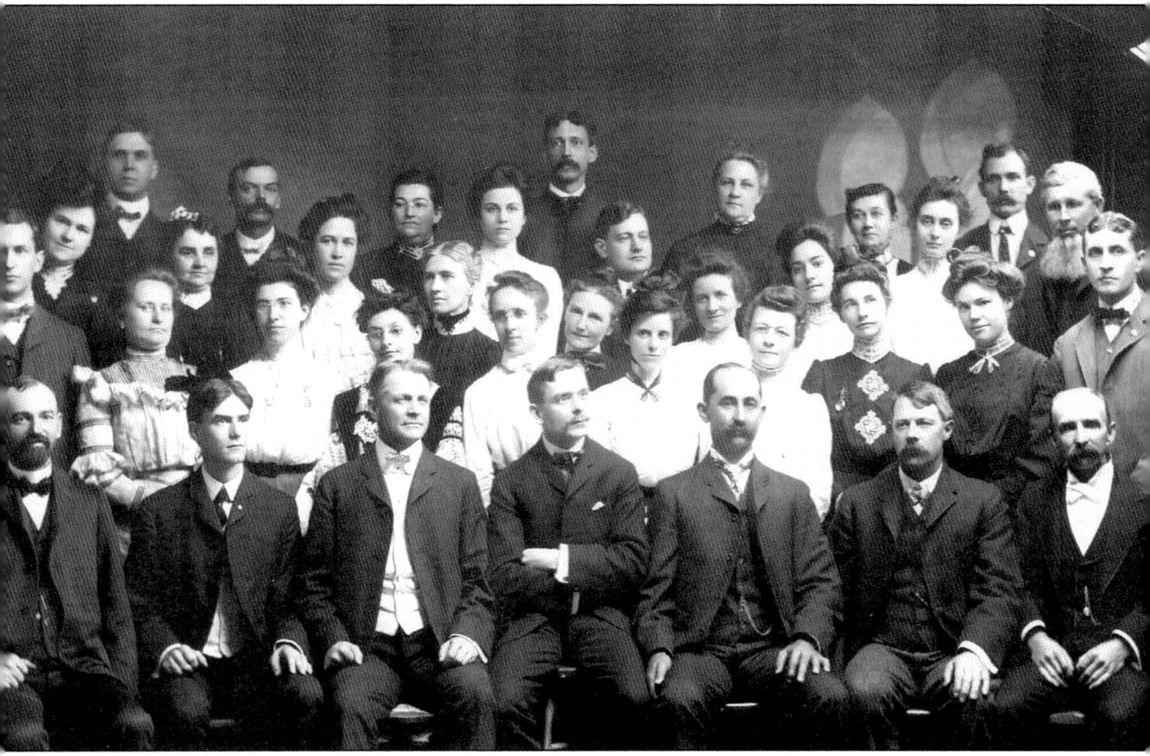

LITERATURE SOCIETY. Members of Bucyrus's literature society pose for this group image, taken in the 1890s. Identified members include (front row, seated left to right) Reverend Philpott, Jay Schell, Mr. Sarles, Dr. Hinamon, Pete Conkle, Harvey Morrow, and Madison Rogers; (second row) Edwin Beale, Mrs. Searles, Sadie Keller, Mrs. Jim Smith, Eva Dolzell, Mrs. Lictenwalter, Minnie Reese, Fairy Peters, Milli Sheckler, Mrs. Morrow, and Madison Rogers; (third row) Julia Monnett, Mrs. Shifley, Desda Heller, Susie Kramer, and Henry Sparrow on the far right side; (fourth row) Len Dozer, J. I. Smith, Mrs. Peter Conkle, Helen Tobias, Abe Sifley, Carrie Janeway Monnette, Orra Eugene Monnette, Amina Monnett Tobias, and Sula Boyer. (Courtesy of the Bucyrus Historical Society.)

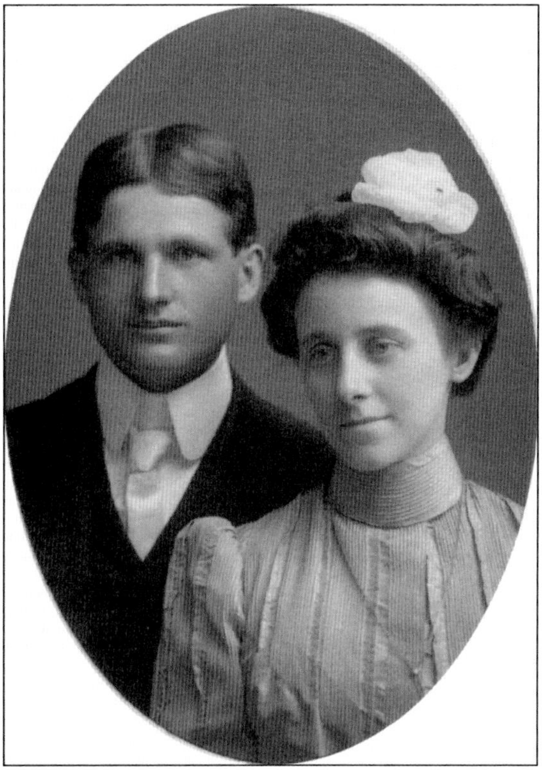

ORANGE AND BLANCHE KENNEDY. Orange Kennedy was the fourth of 12 children of Thomas and Hester Monnett Kennedy. Orange married Blanche Fink, and the couple eventually moved to Bucyrus where they operated a hatchery for many years. (Courtesy of the Holtshouse family.)

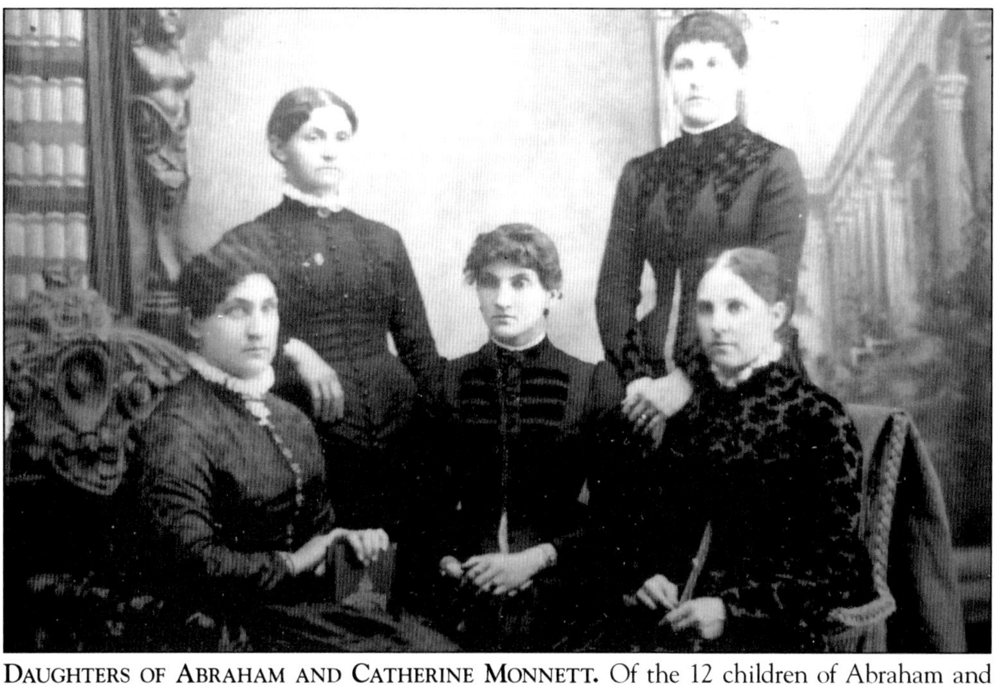

DAUGHTERS OF ABRAHAM AND CATHERINE MONNETT. Of the 12 children of Abraham and Catherine Monnett, each daughter married into well-known, established families in Crawford County. From left to right are (seated) Elsie Malcolm, Catherine Ross, and Mary Jane Hull; (standing) Martha Wright and Amina Tobias. (Courtesy of Nancy Clague.)

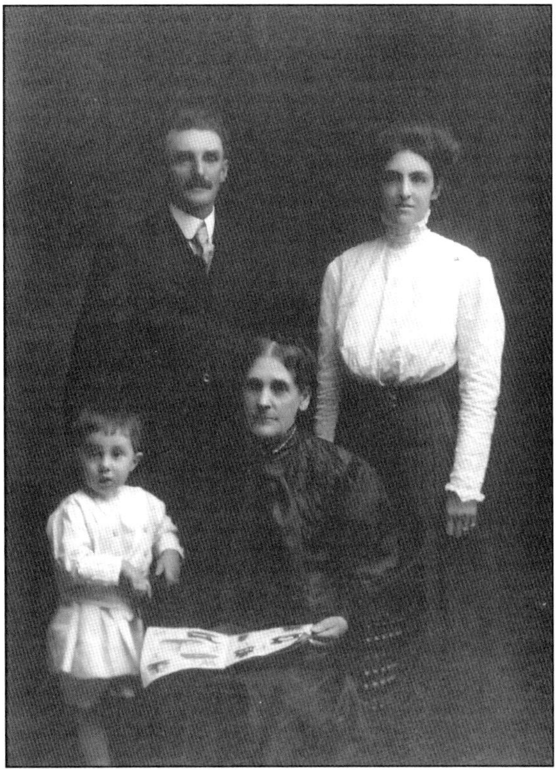

Ross Family of Bucyrus Township, c. 1909. Four generations of the Ross family sit for their portrait. Seated is Mrs. John Ross (née Lucinda Tharp), who was the daughter of Joseph Tharp and Phoebe Tharp (née Kinnear). Standing is her son, Linus High Ross, her granddaughter Nell Owen (née Ross), and great-grandson M. Ross Owen. (Courtesy of Nancy Clague.)

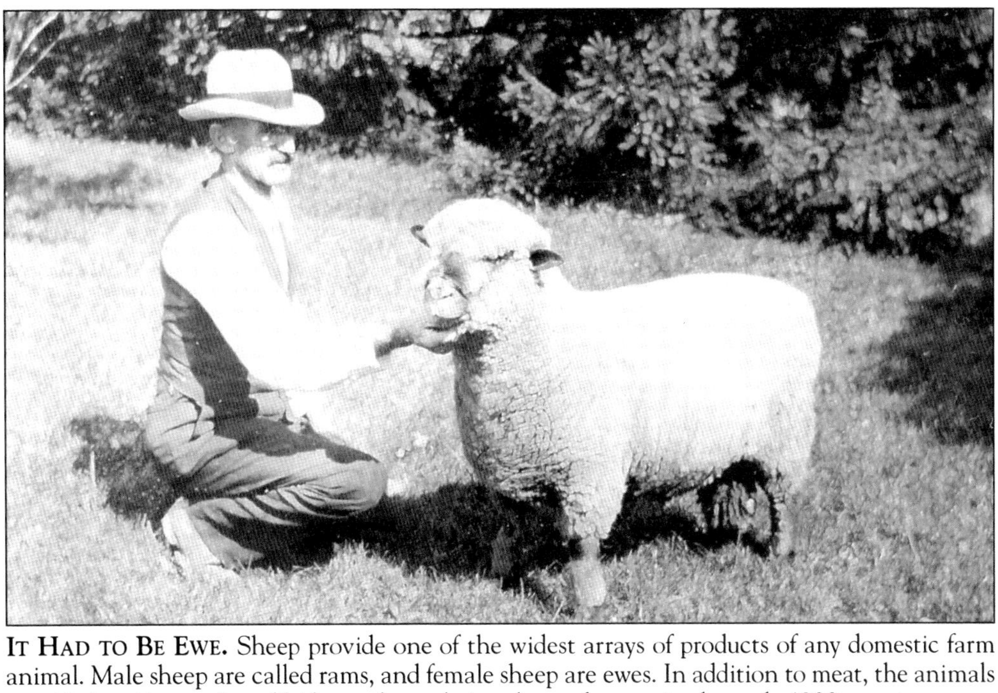

It Had to Be Ewe. Sheep provide one of the widest arrays of products of any domestic farm animal. Male sheep are called rams, and female sheep are ewes. In addition to meat, the animals provide lanolin, wool, and hide goods, so their value to farmers in the early 1900s was immense. Crawford County farmer Linus High Ross poses with his prize-winning Merino ewe in this photograph from the beginning of the 20th century. (Courtesy of Nancy Clague.)

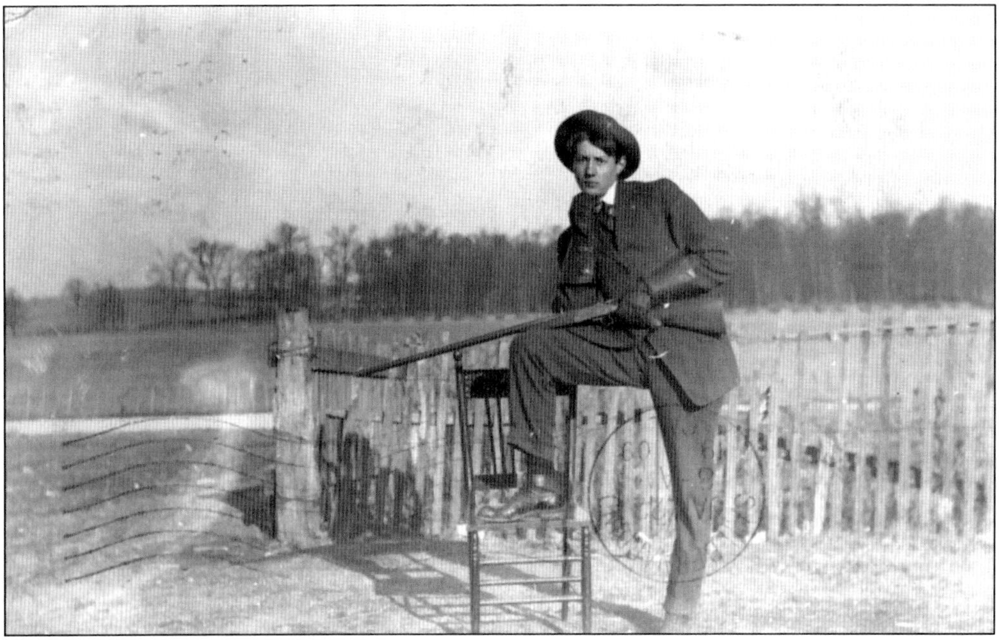

EUGENE COOK. Bucyrian Eugene Cook poses in his Sunday best, a checked suit, for this 1909 snapshot. On Cook's hands are new leather drayman's gloves, which were used for work or driving wagons in cold weather. (Courtesy of Rhea Poulster.)

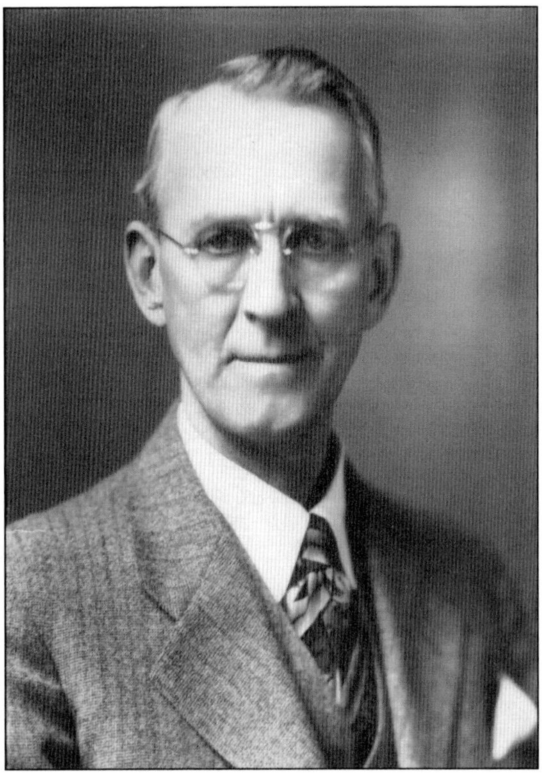

CHARLES HARRISON FRY. Serving as Crawford County Auditor from 1923 to 1930 was Charles Harrison Fry. (Courtesy of Barbara Fry.)

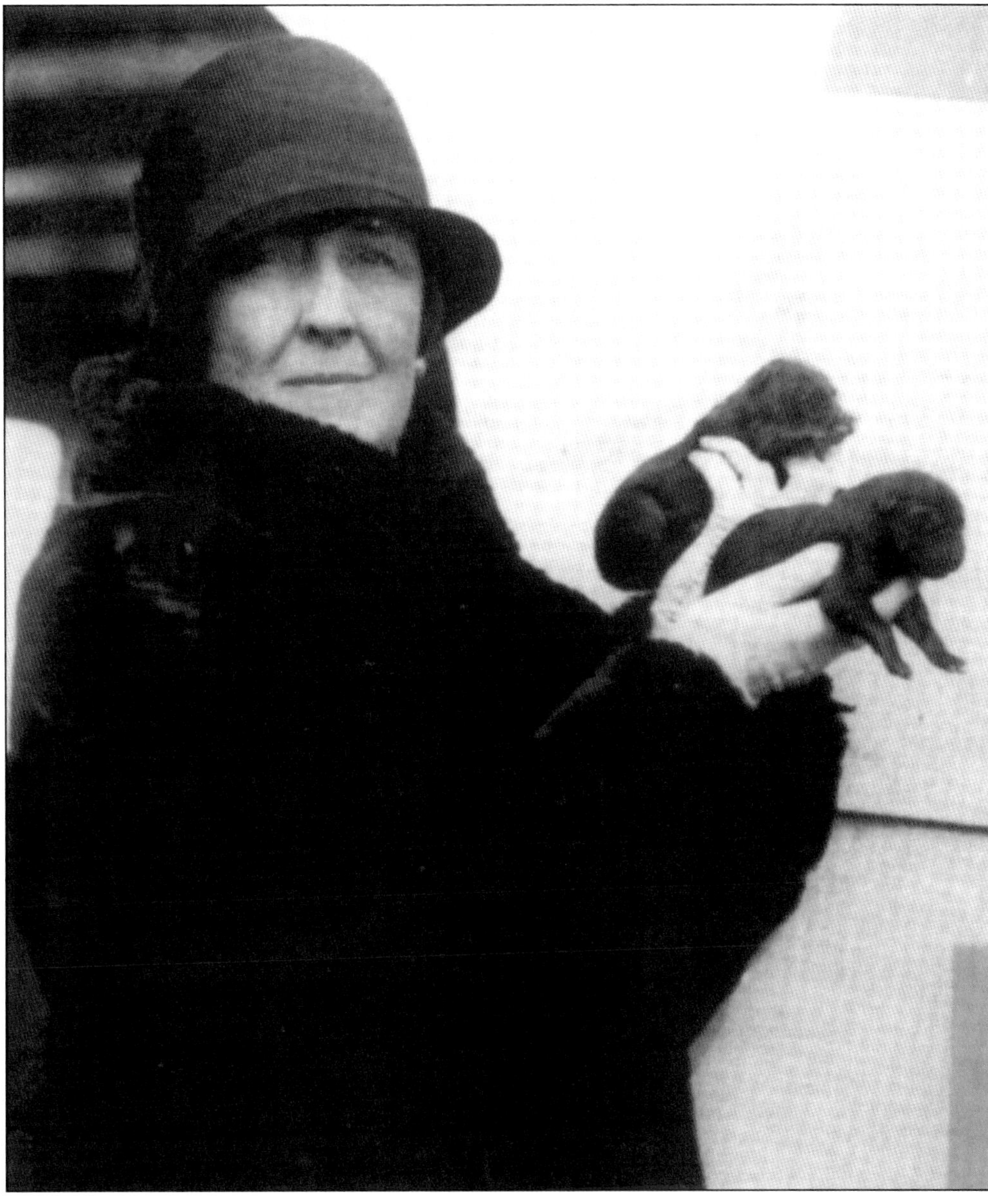

CARRIE FULTON PHILLIPS, C. 1931. Born in Bucyrus Township in 1873, Carrie Fulton was heralded as the most beautiful young woman in Crawford County. She married James Phillips, co-owner of the Uhler Phillips Store in Marion, and the couple settled there. Following the death of her infant son, James Phillips Jr., in 1903, Carrie Phillips became romantically involved with Warren G. Harding, husband of her best friend, Florence Kling Harding. Following Harding's election to the senate in 1914, Phillips attempted to blackmail him against voting on any declaration of war. When the Republican party found out about their affair, officials moved quickly to separate the two to avoid scandal, as Harding was their nominee for president. James and Carrie Phillips enjoyed an all-expense-paid grand tour of Asia in 1920–1921, courtesy of the party, and Carrie also received an annual stipend from the party for keeping her secret. According to a court ruling, the Harding-Phillips letters and correspondence will be released by the Ohio Historical Society in 2023, the 100th anniversary of Harding's death. (Courtesy of Stuart Koblentz.)

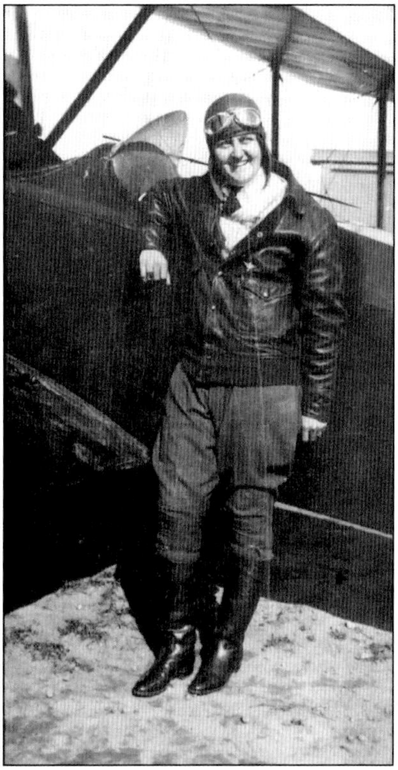

LAURETTA SCHIMMOLER, AVIATRIX. In the early days of aviation, female pilots were novelties. However, women establishing airports was unheard of, and Bucyrus's own Lauretta Schimmoler did both. Schimmoler also understood that as the military saw increasing value in the use of airplanes and aerial attacks, a deployable nursing unit would be of value. Schimmoler was not only able to convince the military of her idea, but was chosen to develop the program and train the nurses as well. In 1966, she was recognized by the air force as a pioneer in the development of air evacuation and was awarded the gold wings of the flight nurse. (Courtesy of the Bucyrus Historical Society.)

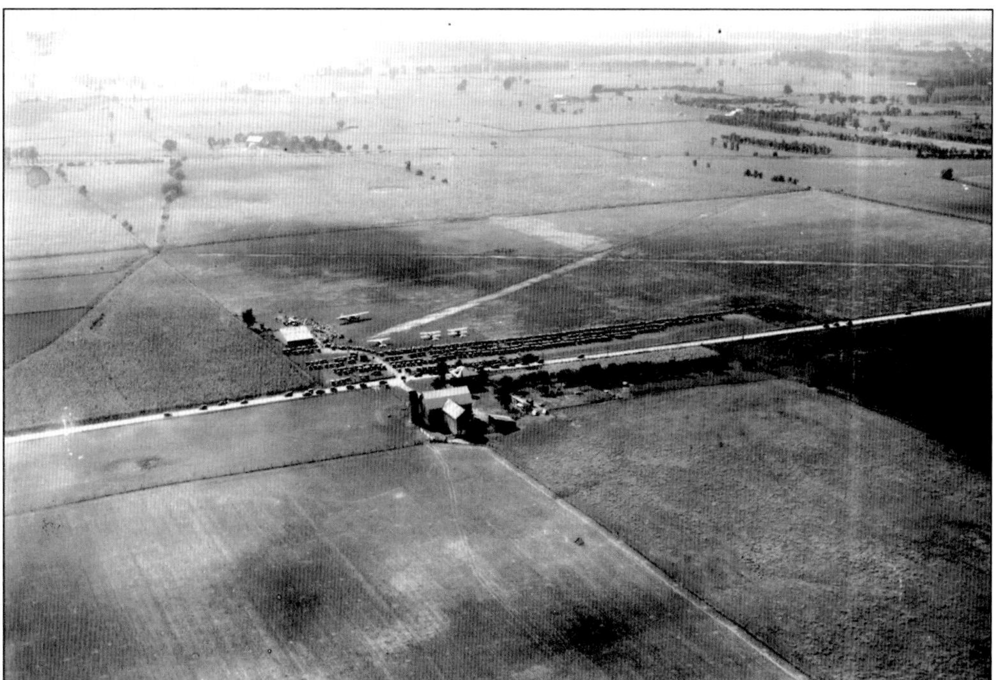

PORT BUCYRUS. Development of Port Bucyrus Airport was promoted by Lauretta Schimmoler as a training ground for pilots and a benefit for travelers. (Courtesy of the Bucyrus Historical Society.)

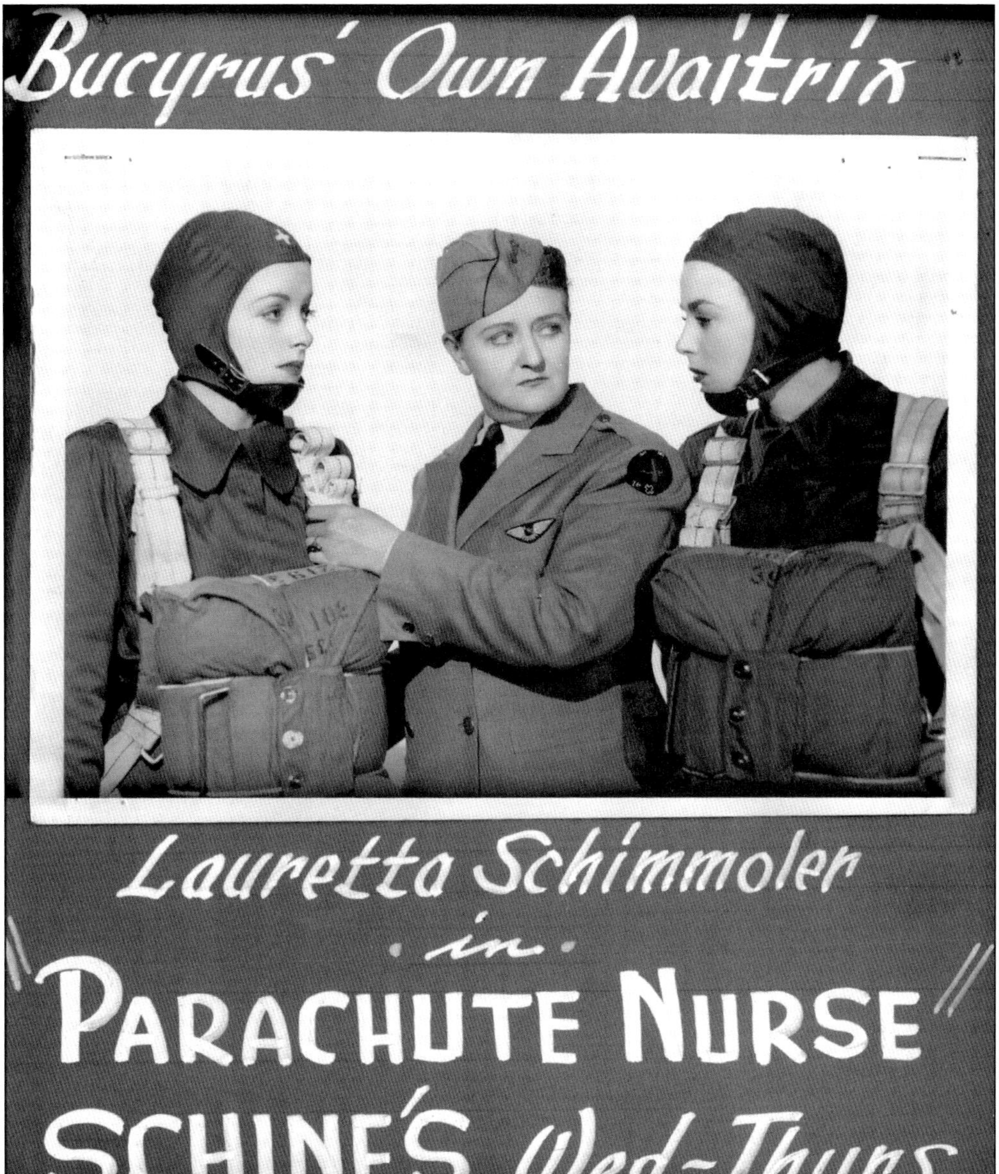

PARACHUTE NURSE. In 1930, Lauretta Schimmoler recognized a need for air nursing personnel and formed the Emergency Flight Corps, later renamed the Aerial Nurses Corps of American (ANCOA). Although her efforts to incorporate aerial nurses into the armed services were not originally supported, Schimmoler's ANCOA provided an early model for the U.S. Air Force Flight Nurses Corps. In 1942, Schimmoler was called in as a technical director for a Columbia Studios motion picture, *Parachute Nurse*. She played the pivotal role of Capt. Jane Morgan, commander of the Parachute Corps. (Courtesy of the Bucyrus Historical Society.)

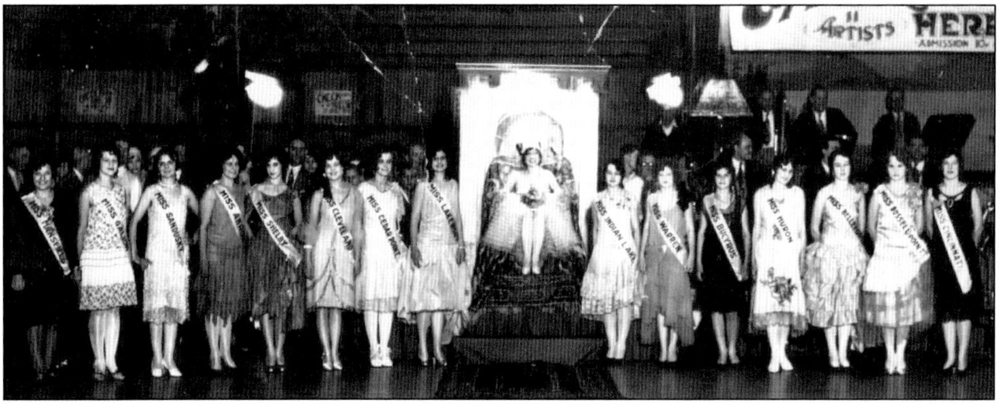

FIRST MISS OHIO PAGEANT. In the late summer of 1928, the summer community of Indian Lake, Russell's Point, hosted the first Miss Ohio Pageant. Representing Bucyrus was Norine Ehrick, whose family lived on Lucas Street. (Courtesy of the Bucyrus Historical Society.)

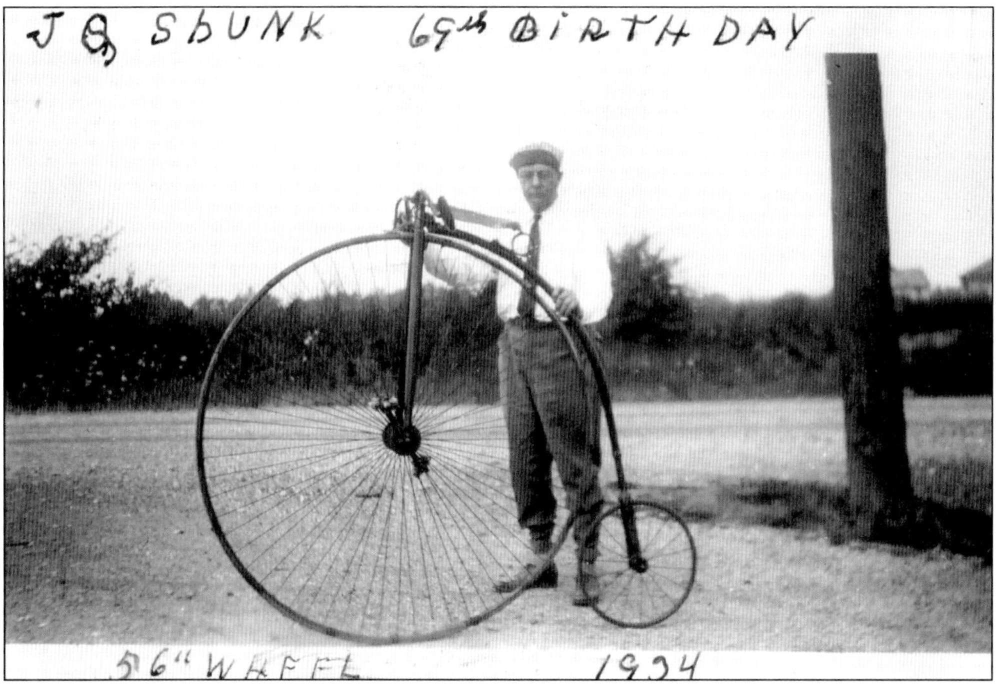

JOHN Q. SHUNK. Celebrating his 69th birthday in 1934, John Q. Shunk took his bicycle (called a Hi-Wheel) out for a ride. While the idea of riding such a bike may seem charming, getting onto and off of the bicycle took both cunning and a great deal of physical effort. The bikes were nicknamed "bone shakers" for their jarring rides atop solid rubber tires and unsprung seats; neither of which were forgiving in the event of hitting a hole or a crack while riding. (Courtesy of the Bucyrus Historical Society.)

SUSAN JACOBS ENSMINGER (1835–1938). While centenarians are a relatively common occurrence in today's world, it once was a very rare event. Such was the happy occasion on March 14, 1935, when Bucyrian Susan Jacobs Ensminger turned 100. Ensminger passed away on March 16, 1938, two days after her 103rd birthday. (Courtesy of the Bucyrus Historical Society.)

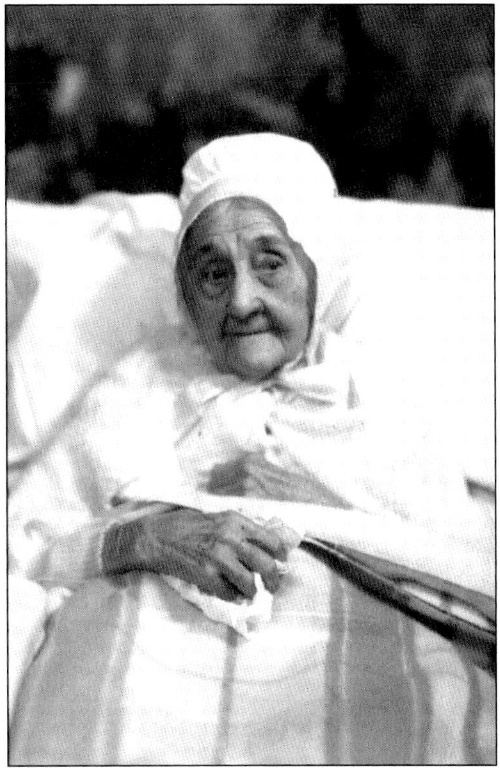

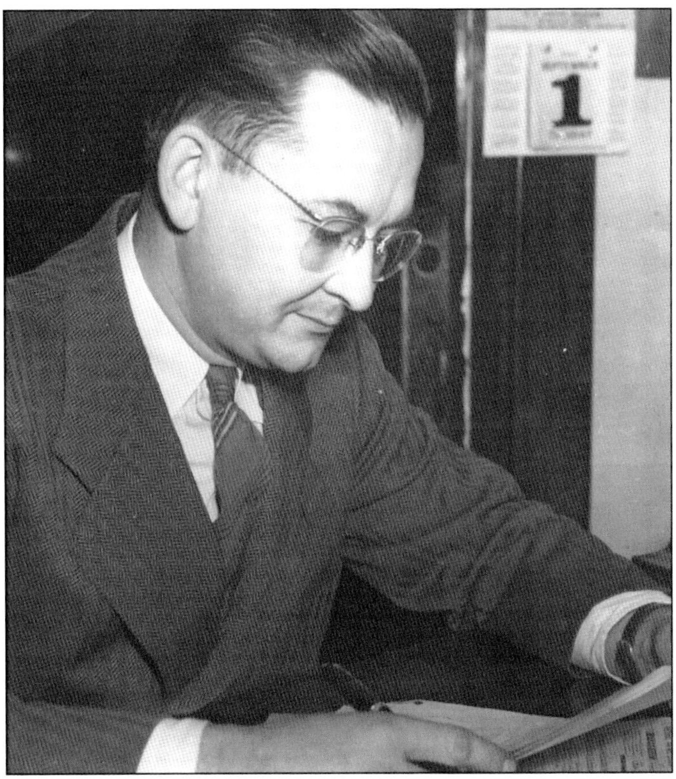

ADAM BORYCZKA. Best known for his role as the publisher of the *Bucyrus Telegraph Forum*, Adam Boryczka was also a tireless supporter of Bucyrus, helping to bring Timken and General Electric to Bucyrus, before the advent of the chamber of commerce. (Courtesy of Helen Picking Neff.)

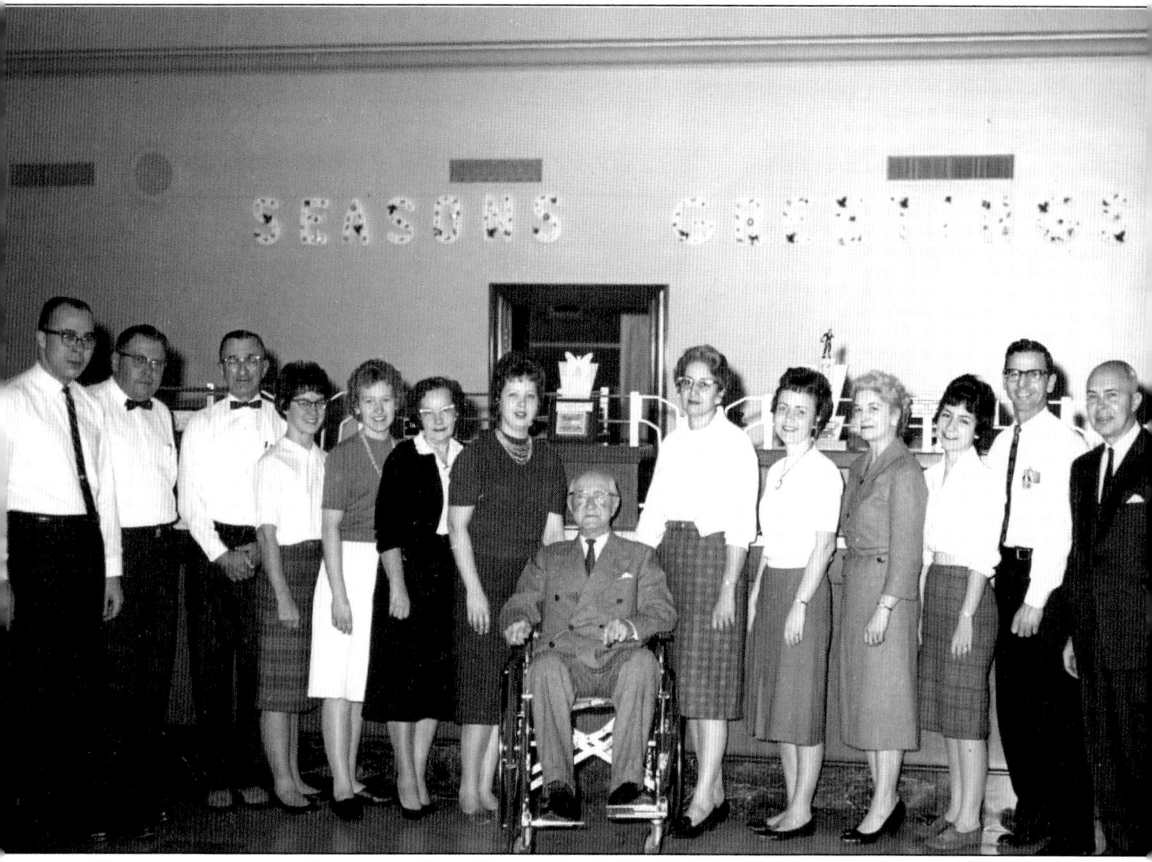

EMPLOYEES OF THE BUCYRUS CITY BANK. In 1957–1958 the Bucyrus Bank moved to its new location at the corner of Charles and South Sandusky Street. Some of the financial institution's employees posed for this photograph in the late 1950s. However, only the names of the men were recorded. The gentlemen identified are Bill Blicke, James Deaver, Roy Widman, Albert Stetzer, and Julliard Blicke (center, seated). (Courtesy of the Bucyrus Historical Society.)

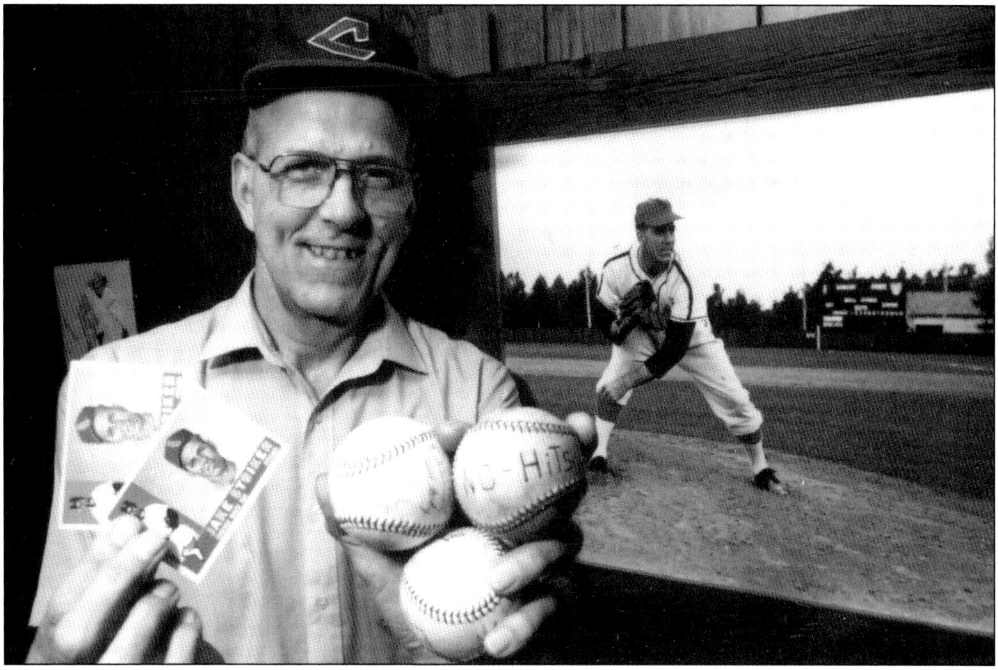

JAKE STRIKER. Bucyrus had one favorite son play major-league baseball. Jake Striker was born in New Washington in 1933. He played in the minor leagues for a time and then played for the Cleveland Indians in 1959–1960. (Courtesy of the Galion Historical Society.)

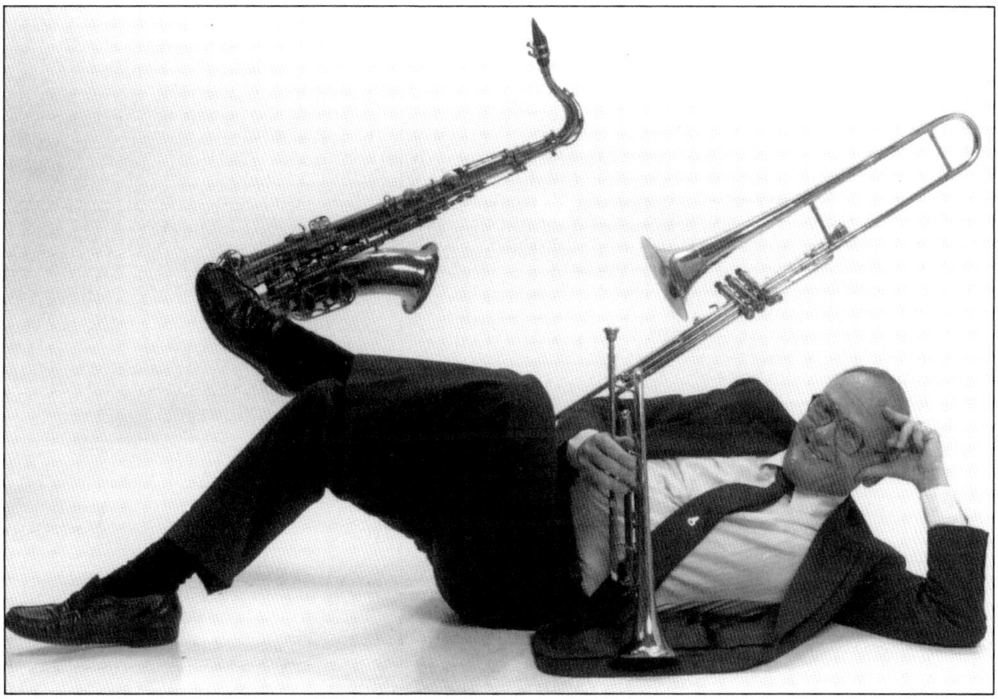

JOHN KENNEDY. Popular local bandleader John Kennedy was certainly well known after playing his share of gigs in the Bucyrus area since the 1950s. The John Kennedy Orchestra celebrated 50 years in the entertainment business on New Years Eve 2006. (Courtesy of the Galion Historical Society.)

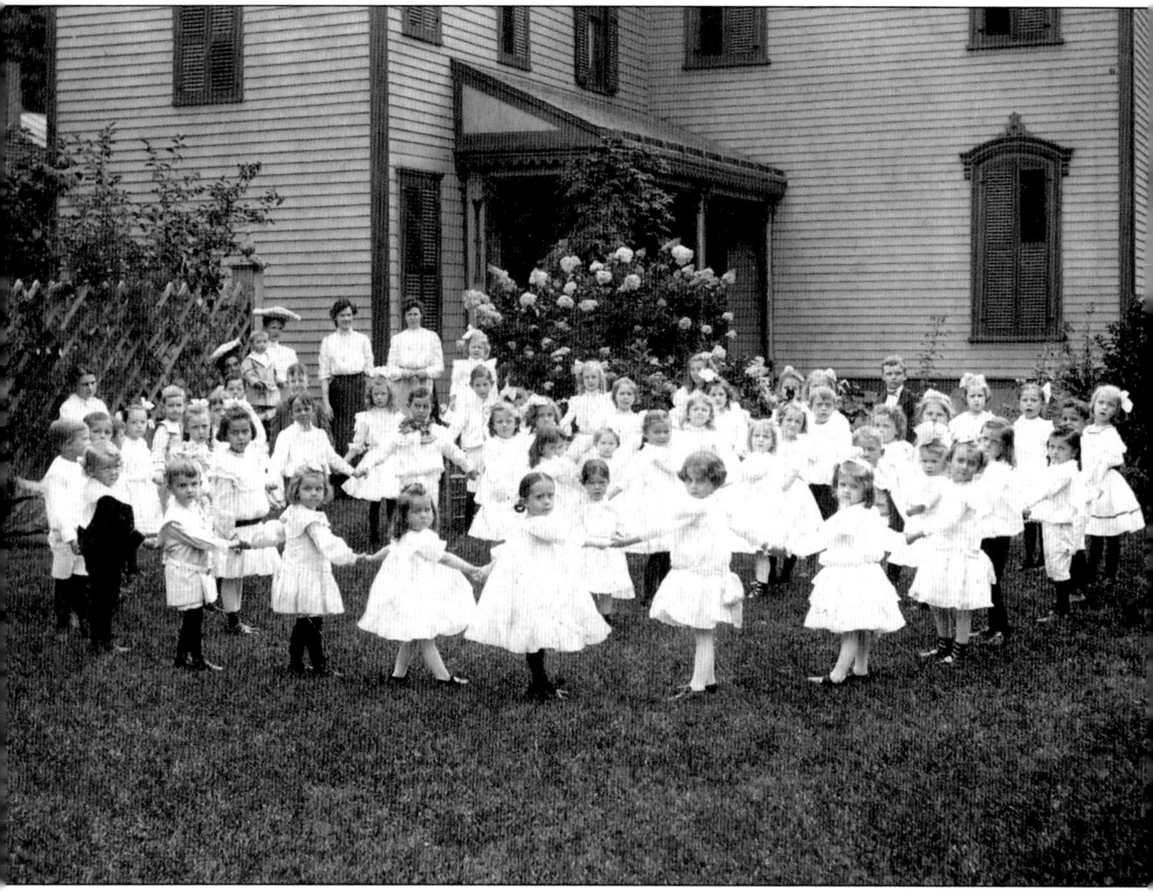

MARGARET LOUISE MONNETT'S THIRD BIRTHDAY PARTY. What was undoubtedly *the* birthday party to be seen at in 1903, the invited guests of Margaret Louise Monnett's third birthday party pose for a group picture during a game of ring-around-the-rosy outside of the Scroggs residence. Attendees included Dodge Alexander, Malcolm Aye, Daisy Baker, William Bennett, Kathryn Brink, Anna Blair, Mary Bliss, Marion Bliss, James Barth, Myrna Beal, Edith Carroll, William Colley, Alice Conklin, Josephine Cain, Robert Danley, Franklin Donnelly, Edgar Ensimmger, Marion Fraley, Clarence Gardner, George Gardner, George Hahn, Lucy Hahn, Isabel Hurr, Harriett Hurr, Inez Heinlen, Dorothy Holmes, Wilma Holmes, George Hinamon, Mary Hinamon, Dorothy Hinman, Franklin Hernicke, Charles Hernicke, Alice Kahler, Arthur Kimble, Lucille Knisley, Jeanette Knisley, James Malcolm, Katherine Malcolm, Norma Menninger, Helen Menninger, Marcella Monnett, Martha Monnett, Isabel Phillips, Niles Price, Ernestine Rowe, Richard Rowe, Helen Ruhl, William Ruhl, Mary Emily Reid, Margaret Robertson, Russell Smith, Mary Effie Stivers, Edward Vollrath, Eleanor Wise, and Virginia Wise. (Courtesy of the Bucyrus Historical Society.)

Four

THE PICKING FAMILY

While much has been written about the handcrafted copper produced by the artisans at D. Picking and Company, much less has been written about the family that has guided the company bearing the name of Daniel Picking himself. The Picking family came to Bucyrus during the city's infancy, starting out in the hardware business. The copper works were added at a later date, ultimately becoming the focus of the business itself. This chapter looks back at the Picking family.

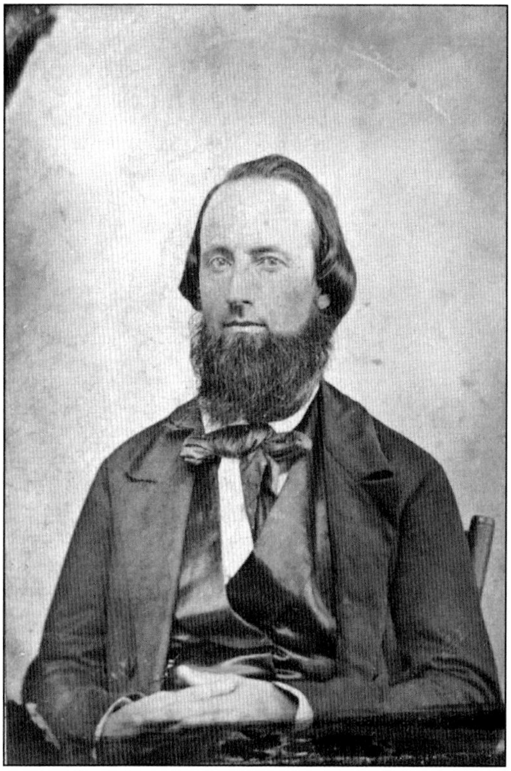

Daniel Picking. Daniel Picking immigrated to the United States from Germany as a child and was indentured to tinsmith Jacob Geiger when he was 11 years old to learn the trade. Picking learned his trade well and ultimately opened a hardware store with Geiger in Bucyrus. When the need arose for a consistent supply of copper kettles for the making of apple butter, Picking traveled to Pennsylvania and returned with coppersmiths who relocated to Bucyrus to work for him. (Courtesy of Helen Picking Neff.)

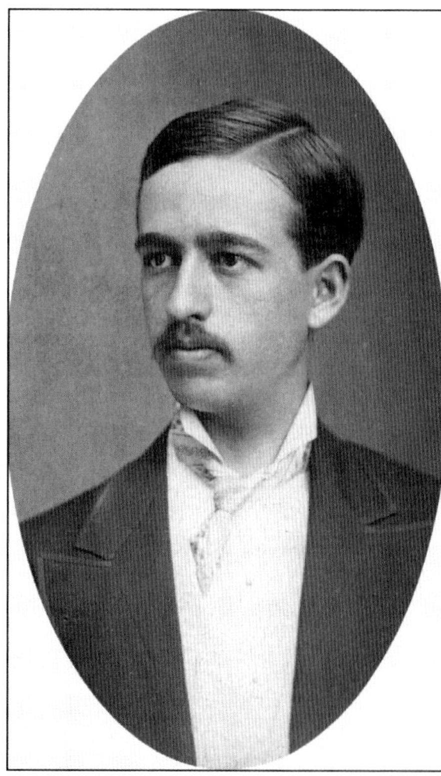

Charles Picking, 1880s. As Charles Picking came of age, the demand for apple butter kettles began to decline. Picking helped to broaden the businesses offerings to include other items, such as candy kettles and timpani drums, which are still handmade to this day. (Courtesy of Helen Picking Neff.)

LILLIE BALTZLY. When Charles Picking married, he chose Lillie Baltzly to be his bride. The couple had two sons, Robert and Wilford. (Courtesy of Helen Picking Neff.)

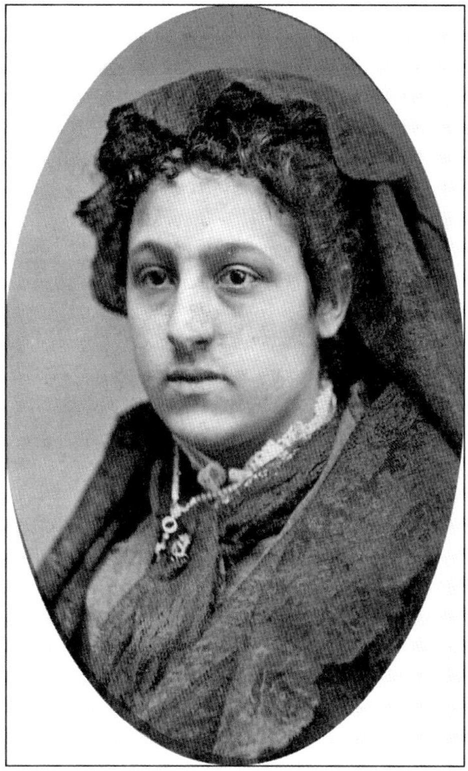

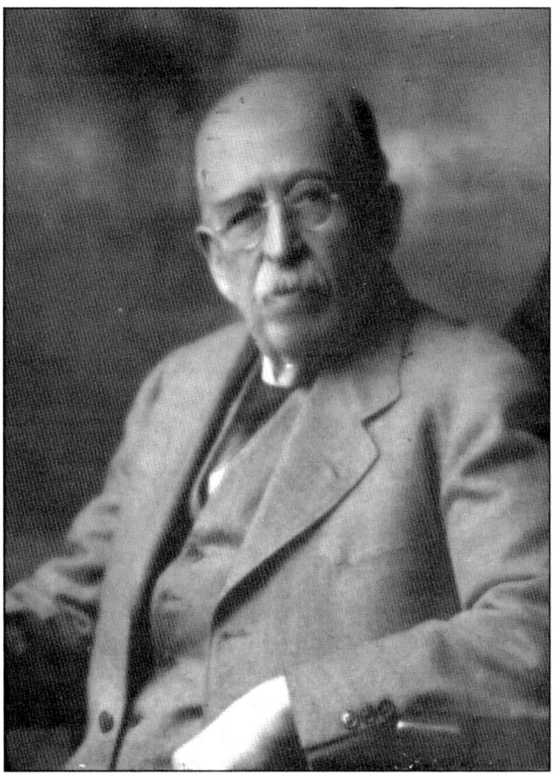

CHARLES F. PICKING. Charles F. Picking entered into the family's hardware business, and by doing so also inherited the firm's copper kettle business as well. Picking also supported the Bucyrus community by helping to charter numerous organizations and served as the city's mayor from 1922 to 1924. (Courtesy of Helen Picking Neff.)

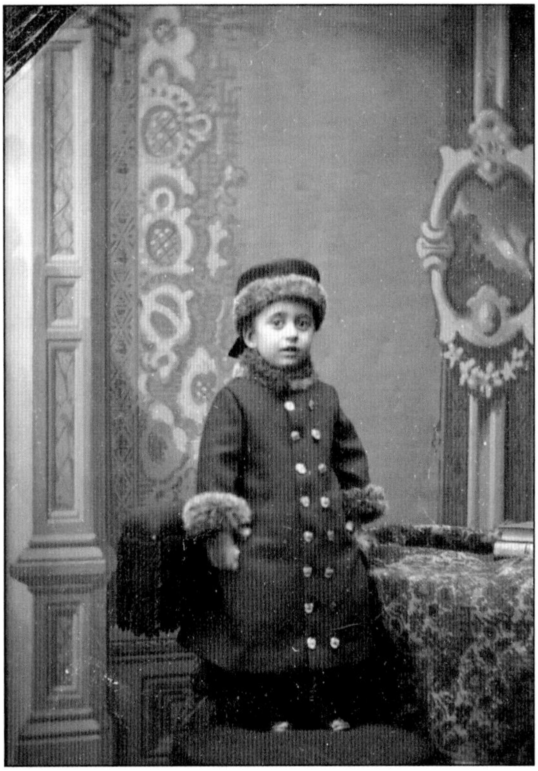

YOUNG ROBERT PICKING, C. 1882. While most Bucyrians and collectors of D. Picking's copper wares remember Robert Picking as a grown man in a business suit or as a centenarian, this photograph offers quite a different image of a young master Picking around the age of two. (Courtesy of Helen Picking Neff.)

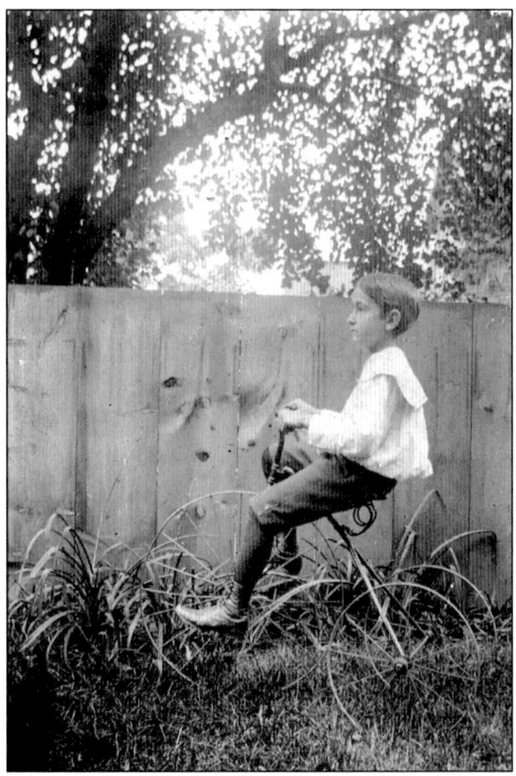

WILFORD PICKING. This is an informal photograph of Charles and Lillie Picking's son Wilford atop a tricycle. Unlike his brother Robert, Wilford did not enter into the family business. (Courtesy of Helen Picking Neff.)

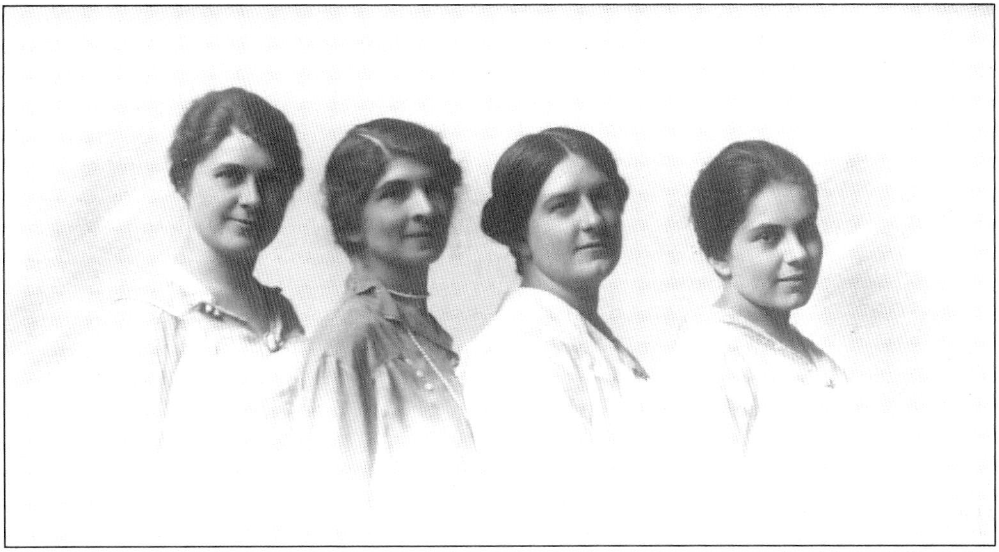

COULTER SISTERS. Robert Picking married Maude Coulter, who appears third from left in this photograph with her sisters Ethel, Blanche, and Helen (from left to right). (Courtesy of Helen Picking Neff.)

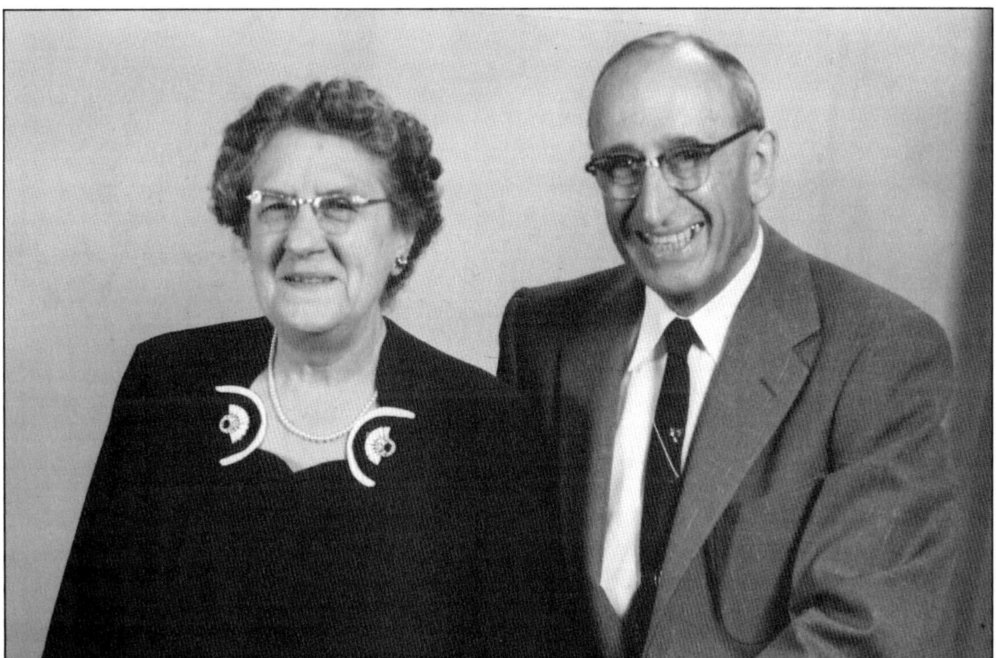

ROBERT AND MAUDE PICKING. Robert and Maude Picking were well known in Bucyrus and active in the community during their lifetimes. (Courtesy of Helen Picking Neff.)

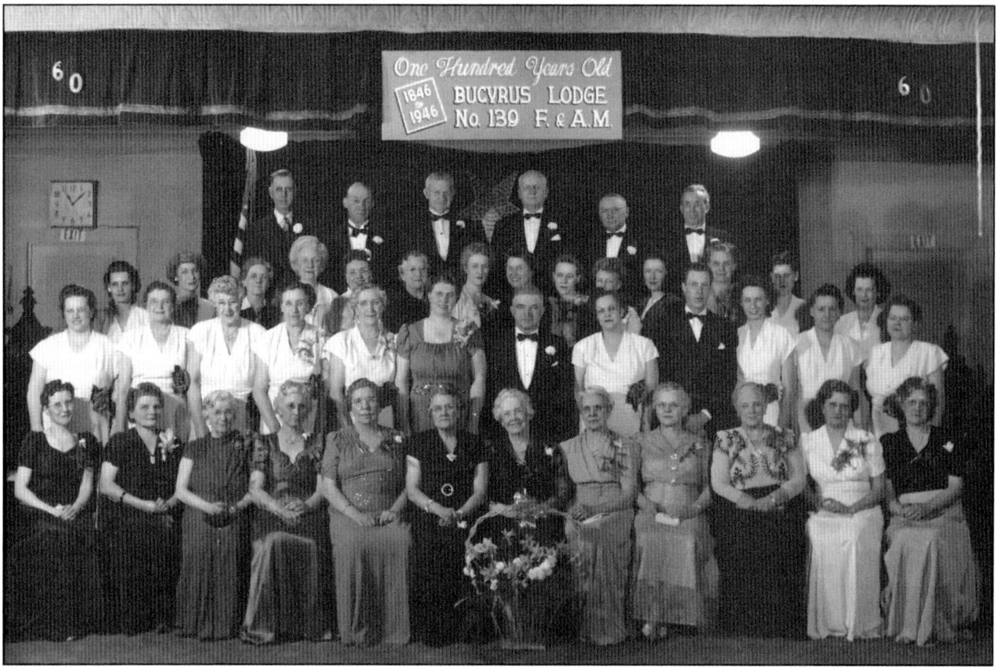

100TH ANNIVERSARY OF THE FREE AND ACCEPTED MASON, LODGE 139. Charles Picking was a Mason and enjoyed his time in the fraternal organization. He and his wife, Lillie, were among the celebrators of the Bucyrus lodge's 100th anniversary. (Courtesy of Helen Picking Neff.)

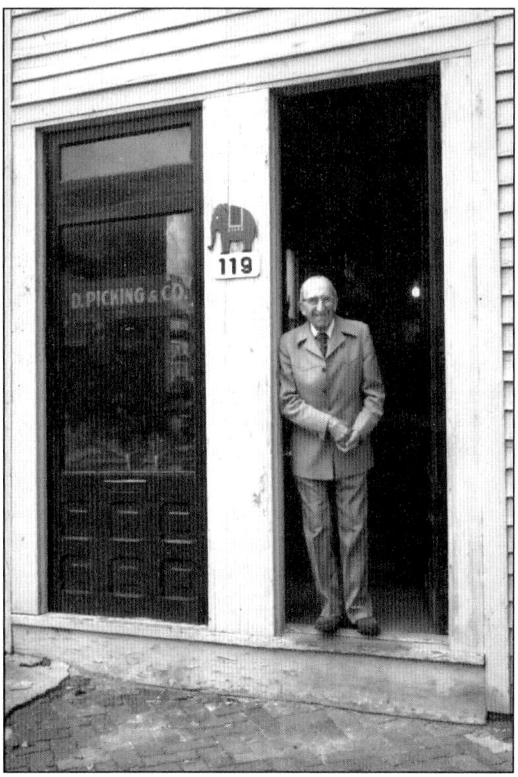

ROBERT PICKING. Robert Picking carried on the family business after his father stepped down from the day-to-day operation of D. Picking and Company. More than just a local businessman, Robert Picking also became one of the most beloved men in Bucyrus during his life. (Courtesy of Helen Picking Neff.)

HELEN PICKING NEFF. Robert Picking's daughter, Helen Picking Neff, is the fourth generation to oversee the operation of D. Picking and Company in its South Walnut Street location. The company continues to make copper kettles, timpani drums, and various other items in the tradition established by Daniel Picking in the mid-1800s. (Courtesy of Helen Picking Neff.)

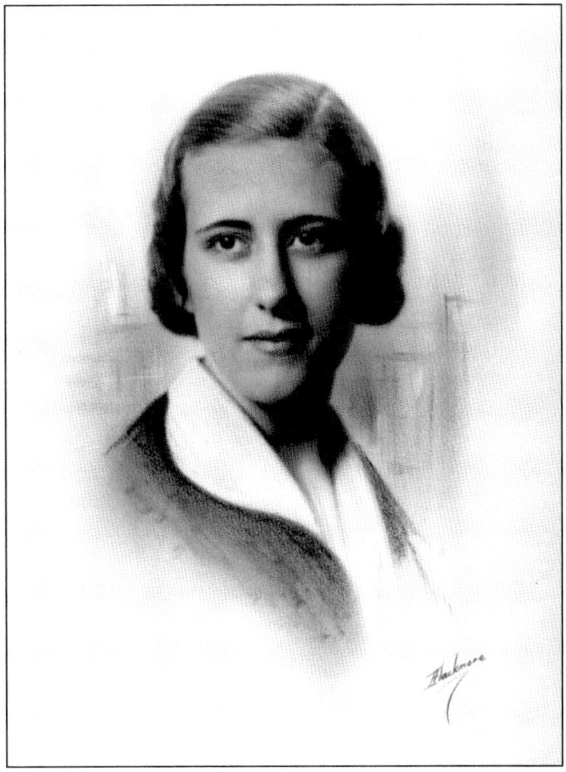

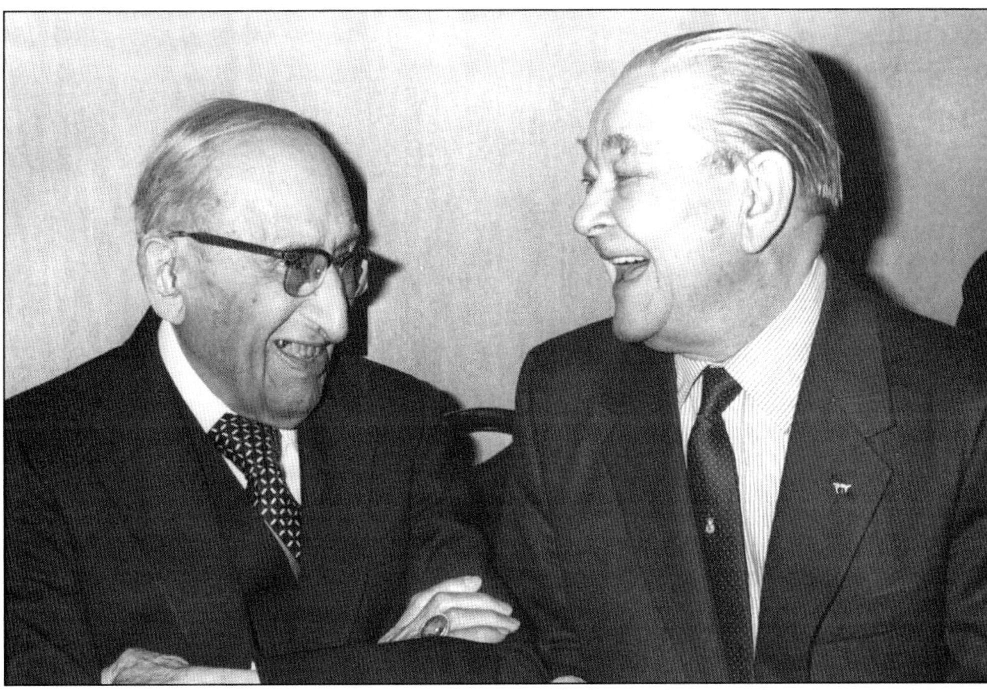

ROBERT PICKING AND ADAM BORYCZKA. Although he made many friends in his lifetime, Robert Picking especially enjoyed the long friendship that he shared with *Telegraph Forum* publisher Adam Boryczka. (Courtesy of Helen Picking Neff.)

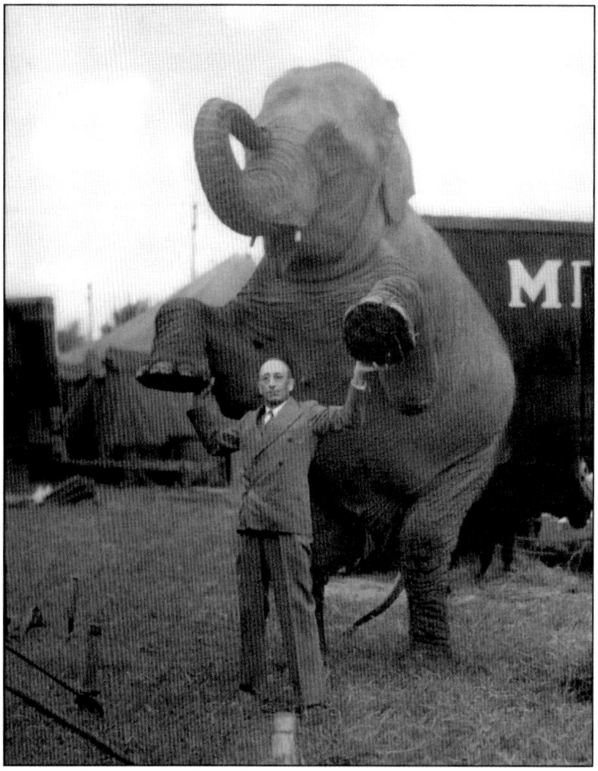

When The Circus Comes to Town. Robert Picking always ensured that a circus made the trip to Bucyrus, and he was among the first to welcome the elephants to town. The office of D. Picking and Company is proof of his love of the animals—the walls are lined with pictures of Picking atop or sometimes under the feet of the well-trained animals. (Courtesy of Helen Picking Neff.)

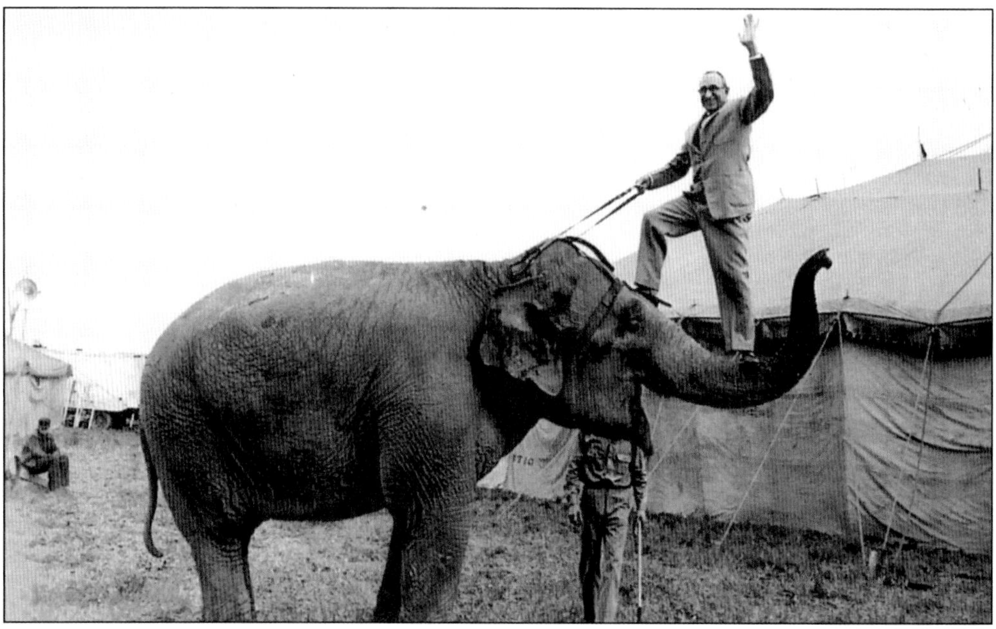

Robert Picking with Circus Elephant. As a young child, Robert Picking had an opportunity to join the circus after winning a race while riding a bicycle against a trained circus dog. When his father could not get assurances that the act would be fair to both his son and the dog, Robert stayed in Bucyrus, but his love of the circus and its elephants remained one of his life's greatest joys. (Courtesy of Helen Picking Neff.)

Five

The Monnett Family

While the modern-day residents of Bucyrus may think only of Monnett as the name of a small community in southern Crawford County, members of the Monnett family settled in Bucyrus and Bucyrus Township in August 1835 when Rev. Jeremiah Crabb Monnett and his family settled in the region. By the 1880s, the aggregate Monnett (or Monnette as some family members adopted as the spelling of the name) holdings accounted for roughly 35 square miles of real estate that stretched from Marion to Bucyrus, control of three major banks, and strategic marriages that linked them to numerous other area families. The family could claim an Ohio attorney general within its ranks, as well as the founder of Bank of America, Los Angeles. By the end of World War I, the wealth in the family had shifted to California and the Monnett name began to fade into memory.

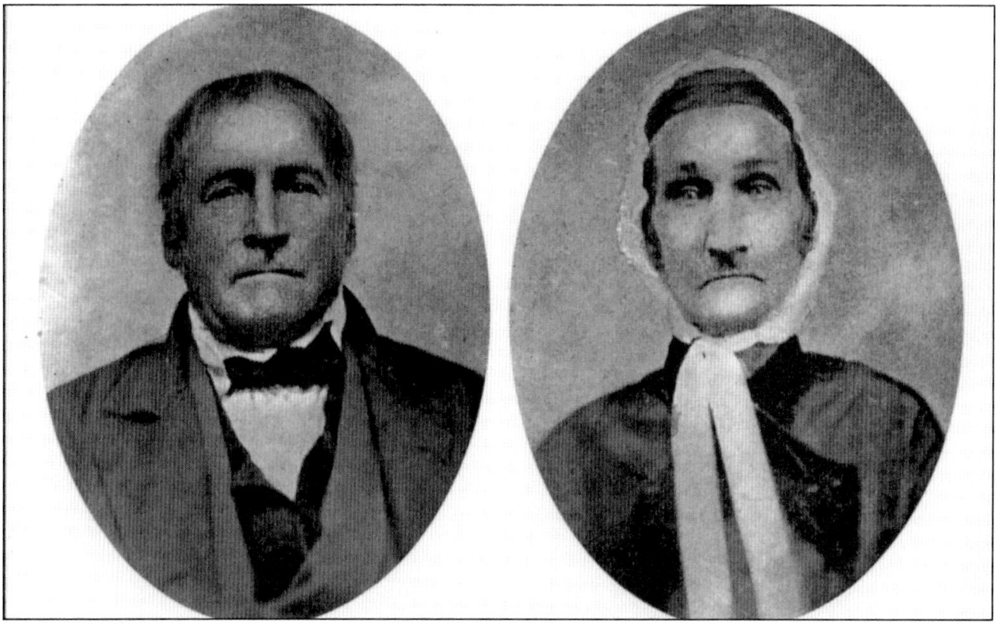

REV. AND MRS. JEREMIAH CRABB MONNETT. An itinerant minister in the Methodist Episcopal Church, the Reverend Jeremiah Crabb Monnett arrived in Crawford County in 1835, settling on what is now State Route 98 in Bucyrus Township. As a minister, he rode the circuit between Monnett Chapel, Scioto Chapel (formerly on State Route 4), and Kirkpatrick in Marion County and conducted large revivals that drew staunch Methodists from miles around. His wife, Aley, ran the farm and reared the couple's 16 children. (Courtesy of Monnett Family Genealogy.)

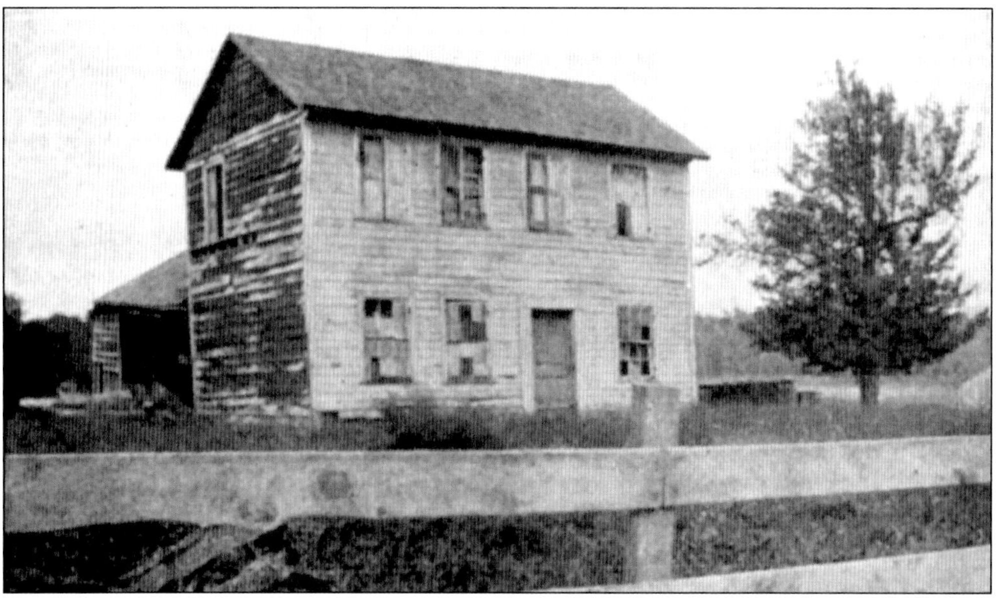

HOME OF REV. JEREMIAH CRABB MONNETT. After arriving in southern Bucyrus Township, this two-story log house was built to house the Reverend Monnett, his wife, and their 12 school-age children. Later covered in clapboards, the house was razed in the early 1900s. The site, opposite the Hord Livestock complex on State Route 98, was marked in 1935 with a small marker that remains today. (Courtesy of Monnett Family Genealogy.)

ABRAHAM MONNETT (1811–1881). After arriving and settling in Marion County's Scott Township, Abraham Monnett began using his wife Catherine's dowry to buy land in Scott and Grand Prairie townships in Marion County, and Dallas and Bucyrus Townships in Crawford County. At the height of his business career, Monnett himself would own approximately 12,000 acres of productive farmland and grazing lands. Monnett also founded the Monnett Bank, the forerunner of the Bucyrus City Bank, now United Bank of Bucyrus. (Courtesy of Barbara Metzler Dible.)

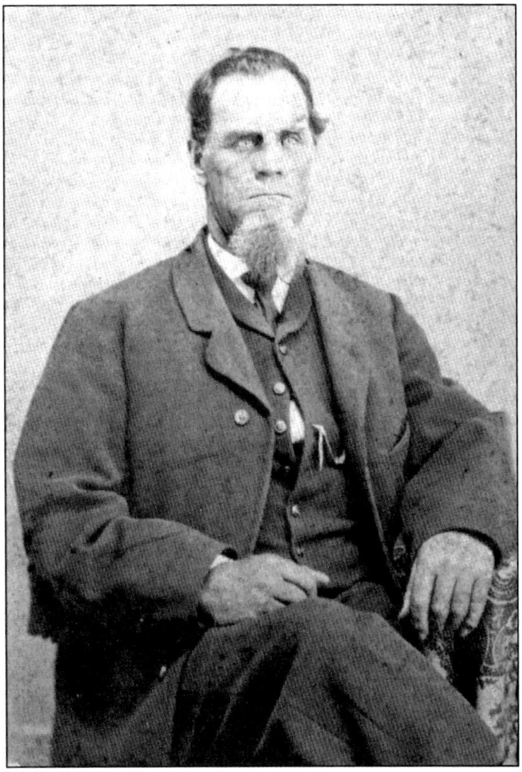

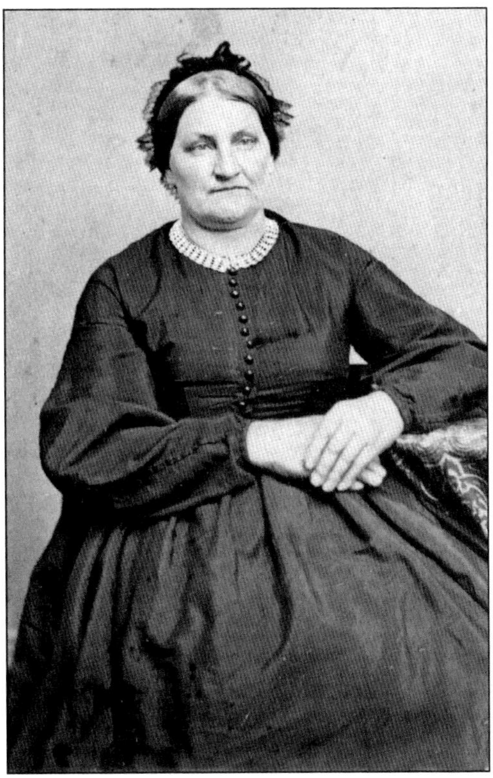

CATHERINE BRAUCHER MONNETT (1815–1875). Catherine Braucher Monnett was the mother of Abraham Monnett's 12 children. Her dowry provided the basis for her family's future wealth. She is buried in Monnett Chapel Cemetery with her husband. (Courtesy of Barbara Metzler Dible.)

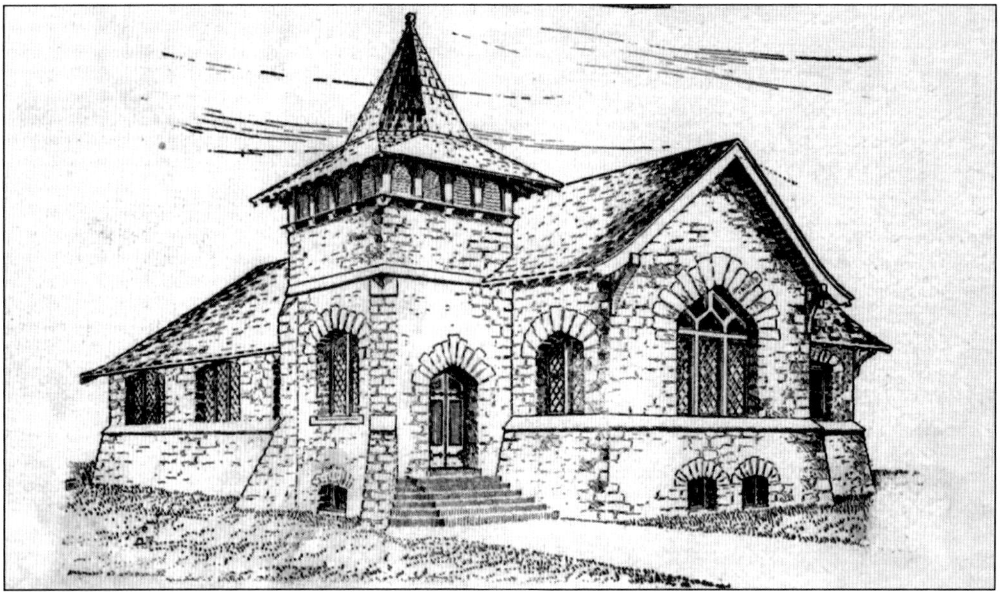

MONNETT MEMORIAL CHAPEL. In 1903, Monnett Methodist Episcopal Chapel engaged architect Frank Packard to design a chapel to replace the plank building used since 1835. The cornerstone was laid on October 18, 1903. In the 1970s, a local farmer offered to buy the building for grain storage. Monnett Memorial was added to the National Register of Historic Places in 1986. The building is still owned by Monnett family interests and has been the home of the Lighthouse Baptist Church for many years. (Courtesy of Stuart Koblentz.)

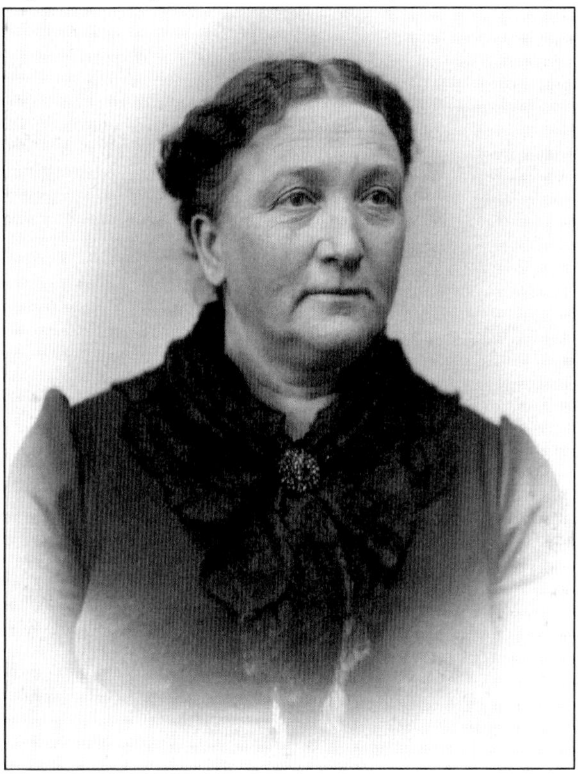

JANE LUDWIG JOHNSTON MONNETT. Born in Pennsylvania to Samuel Ludwig and his wife Elizabeth Redcah, Jane Ludwig and her family relocated to Bucyrus when she was still a toddler. Following the death of her husband, Henry D. E. Johnston in 1870, she married Abraham Monnett in 1877. The couple purchased Horace Rowse's estate, named Rose Ridge, on Rogers Street where each lived until their respective deaths. (Courtesy of Glenna Walton Kennedy.)

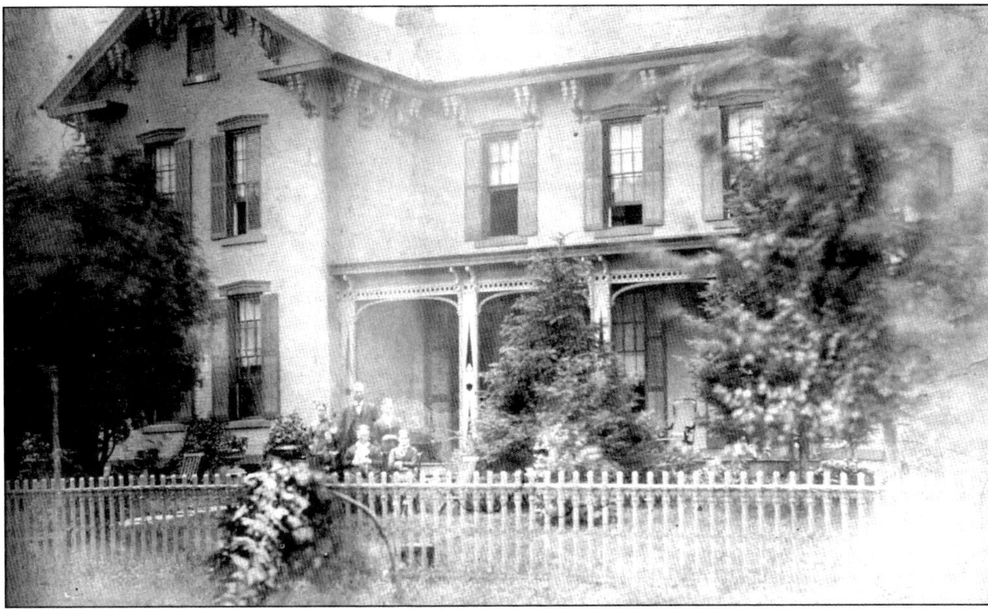

ROSE RIDGE, ROGERS STREET. Jane Monnett is seated in front of her home on Rogers Street with her daughters Nora, Zua, and Mary and their families. Built in 1868 by Horace Rowse, Rose Ridge was for many years the largest home in Bucyrus. The first floor was designed specifically for entertaining. The property hosted numerous weddings. Following the death of Jane Monnett in 1912, the home was sold to the Kings Daughters organization for institutional use. (Courtesy of Oliver Hamilton.)

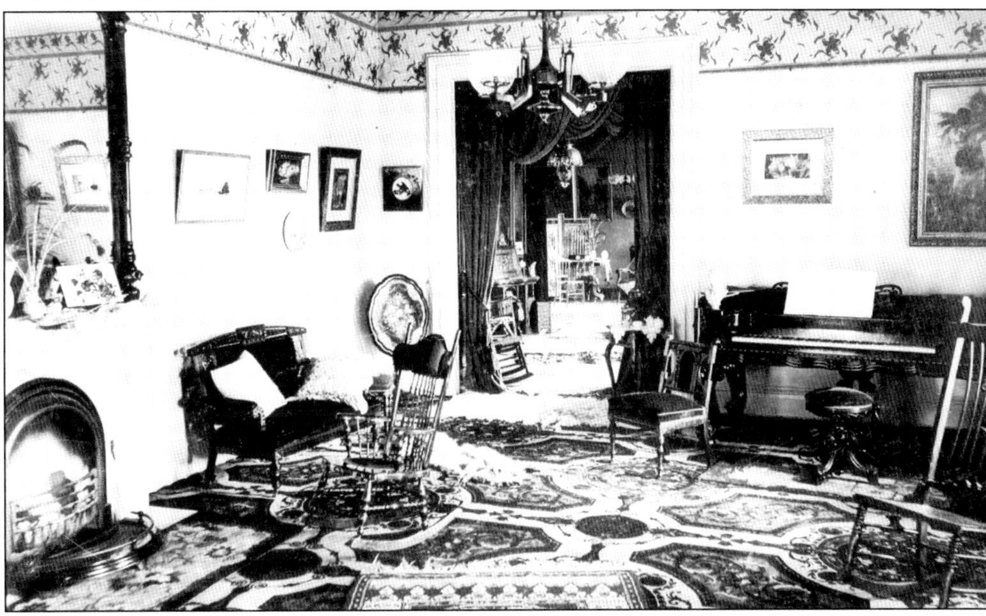

PARLOR, ROSE RIDGE. This front parlor of Rose Ridge was lavishly furnished and appointed in the fashion of its day. The room also served as an operating room when Abraham Monnett underwent surgery for the removal of bladder calculi in 1881; the same room held his body several days later prior to his funeral and burial at Monnett Chapel. (Courtesy of the Bucyrus Historical Society.)

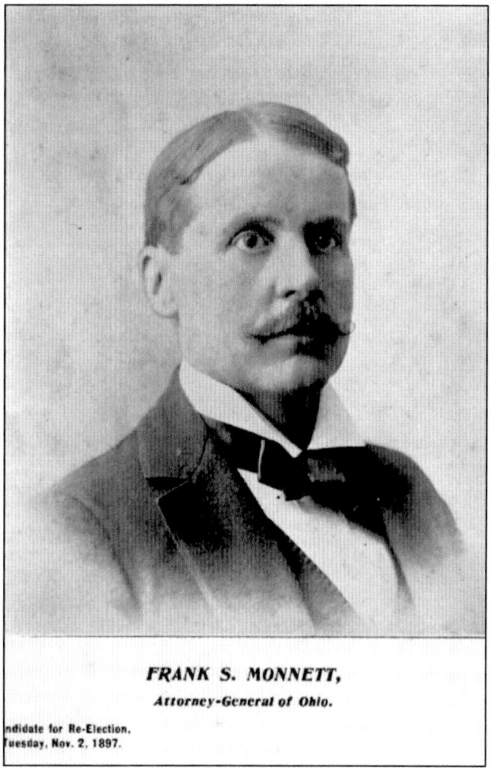

OHIO ATTORNEY GENERAL FRANK S. MONNETT. Born Francis Sylvester Monnett to the Reverend Thomas Jefferson Monnett and his first wife, Henrietta Johnston, Frank S. Monnett graduated from Bucyrus High School in 1880. After receiving his law degree in Washington, D.C., he returned to Bucyrus and established his practice in 1883. Frank was elected Ohio attorney general in 1896 and 1898, winning the first Ohio verdict against the Standard Oil Trust in 1897. In 1888, he married Ella, daughter of James and Virginia Gormely. (Courtesy of Stuart Koblentz.)

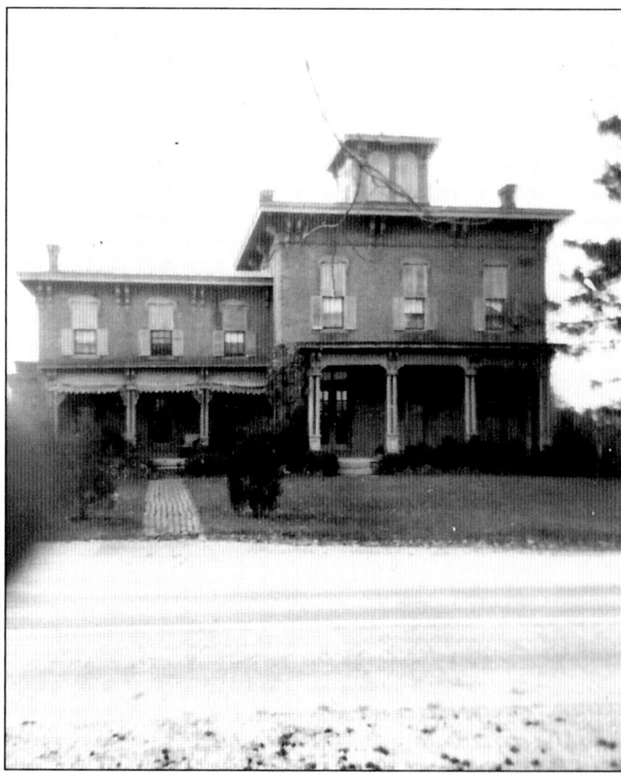

MONNETT HOMESTEAD. Built in 1866 by the Reverend Thomas Jefferson Monnett opposite his father's home on State Route 98, the massive brick Italianate villa was a local landmark until it was razed in the early 1980s. The site is now occupied by Hord Livestock's feed operations. (Courtesy of Monnett Family Genealogy.)

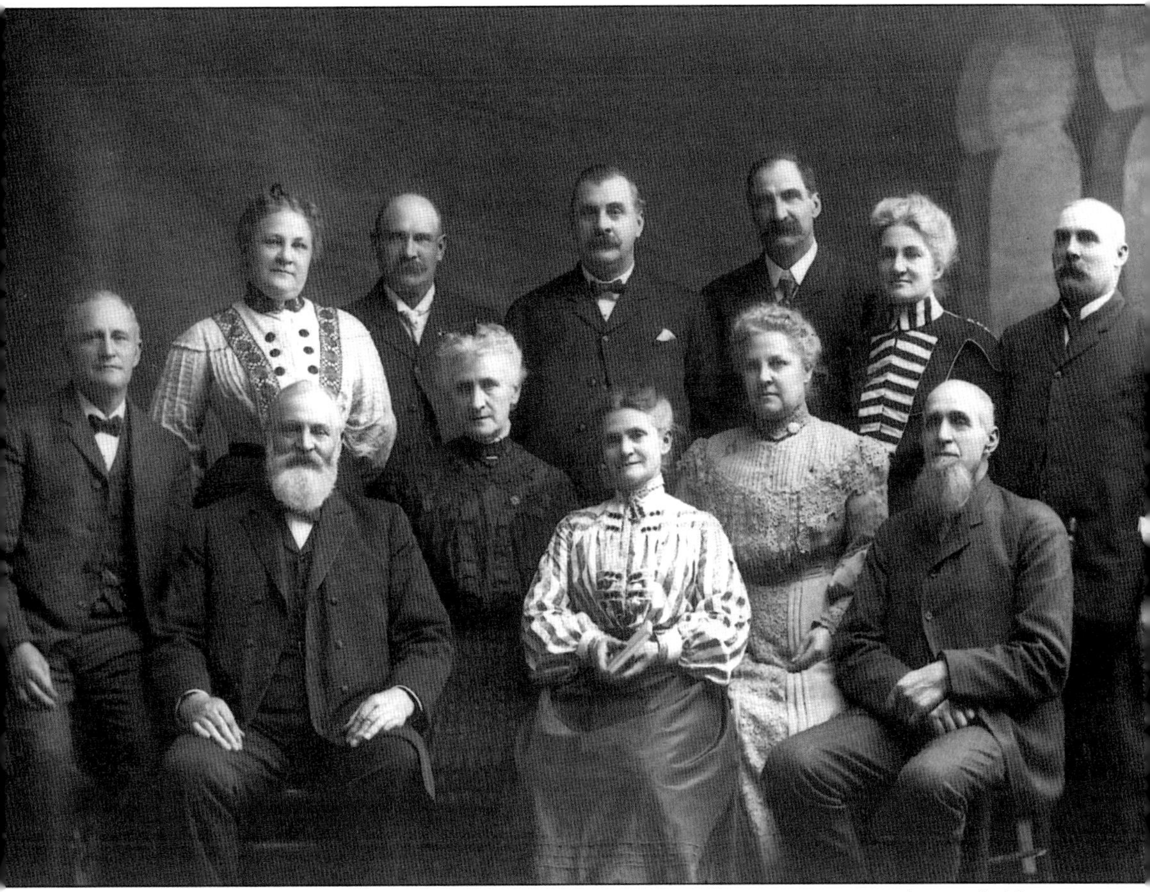

THE 12 CHILDREN OF ABRAHAM AND CATHERINE MONNETT, 1903. In 1903, the 12 children of Abraham and Catherine Monnett gathered at the Bucyrus home of their sister Elsie Monnett Malcolm for what would be their final reunion. From left to right are (seated in the first row) Ephraim Braucher Monnett, Martha Monnett Wright, and Oliver Monnett; (seated in the second row) John Thomas Monnett, Elsie Monnett Malcolm, and Mary Jan Monnett Hull; (third row) Amina Monnett Tobias, Mervin Jeremiah Monnette, Madison Welsh Monnette, Augustus Eddy Monnett, Catherine LaVendee Monnett Ross, and Melvin Monnette. (Courtesy of Stuart Koblentz.)

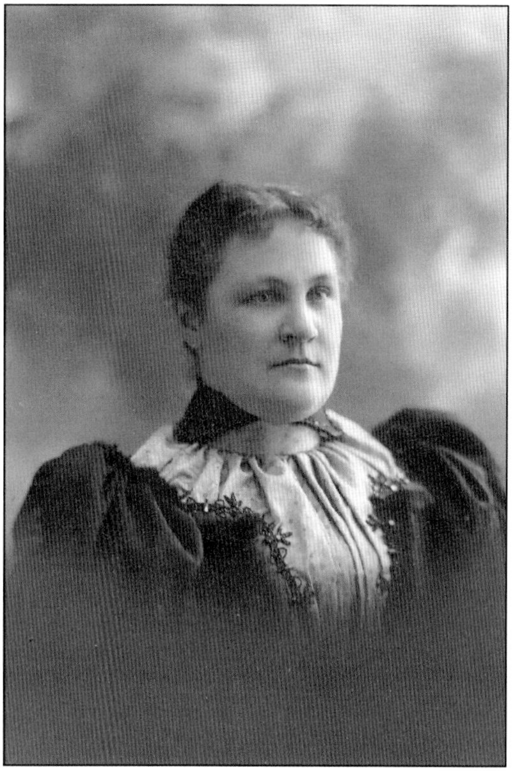

AMINA MONNETT TOBIAS. The 11th child born to Abraham and Catherine Braucher Monnett, Amina married Bucyrus attorney James Calvin Tobias in 1879 at her father's home, Rose Ridge, on Rogers Street. As a wedding present, Amina was given a farm in Marion County (known locally as Tobias Station) by her father, and a new mansion on North Sandusky Street at the top of Findlay Hill by her groom. (Courtesy of Oliver Hamilton.)

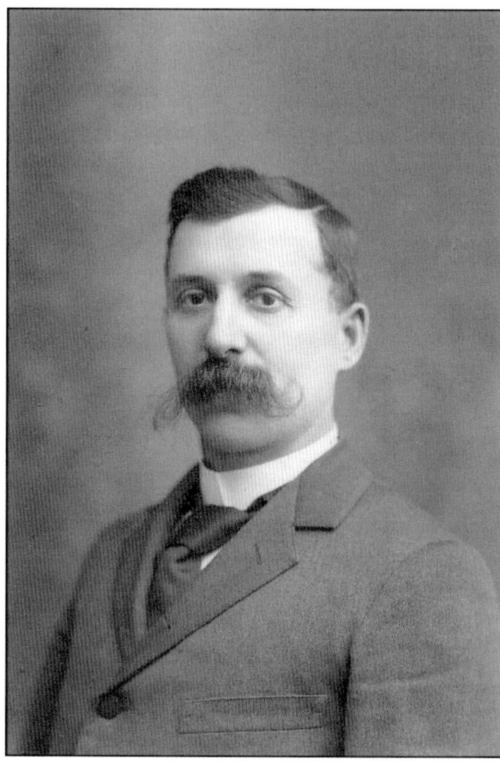

JUDGE J. C. TOBIAS. James Calvin (Cal) Tobias was elected judge of the 10th district common pleas court in 1897, a position that he retained until his retirement in 1907. During his years on the bench, he oversaw court cases in Crawford, Marion, and Wyandot Counties. Following the retirement to California, Amina Tobias's brother Mervin J. Monnette donated the Tobias residence to Bucyrus for Monnett Memorial Hospital. Cal died in Los Angeles, California, on his 50th wedding anniversary in 1929. (Courtesy of Oliver Hamilton.)

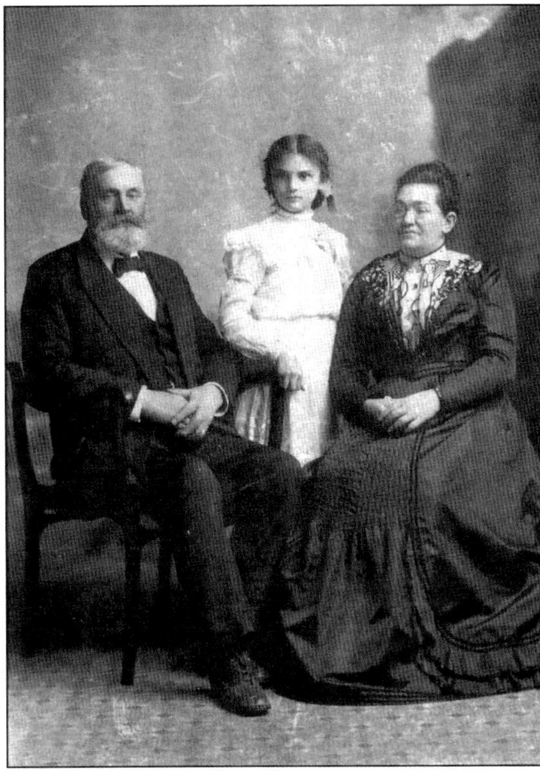

EPHRAIM MONNETT AND FAMILY. The eldest of the 12 children of Abraham and Catherine Monnett was their son Ephraim Braucher Monnett, who resided in his home on South Sandusky Street for many years. Following the death of his first wife, Ephraim married Cornelia Yost of Bucyrus. Their only child, Nellie Monnett, was raised in the family home and later married Paul Wilson Frye. Ephraim died in 1926. (Courtesy of Barbara Frye.)

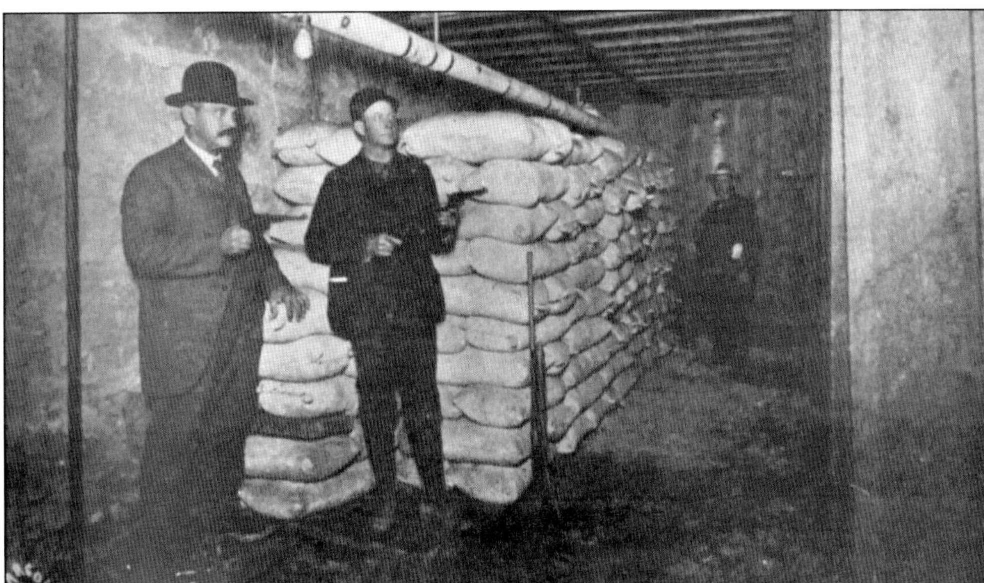

MERVIN MONNETTE, GUARDING HIS GOLD. After losing his home on Rensselaer Street, two banks, his personal savings, and possessions in the 1890 panic, Mervin J. Monnette acted on a tip from a speculator about the availability of the Mohawk Mine in Tonopah, Nevada, where he literally struck gold. This photograph was taken with Monnette (wearing the derby) and one of the guards with the first of the multimillion-dollar raw gold ore finds that took place in 1907. (Courtesy of Stuart Koblentz.)

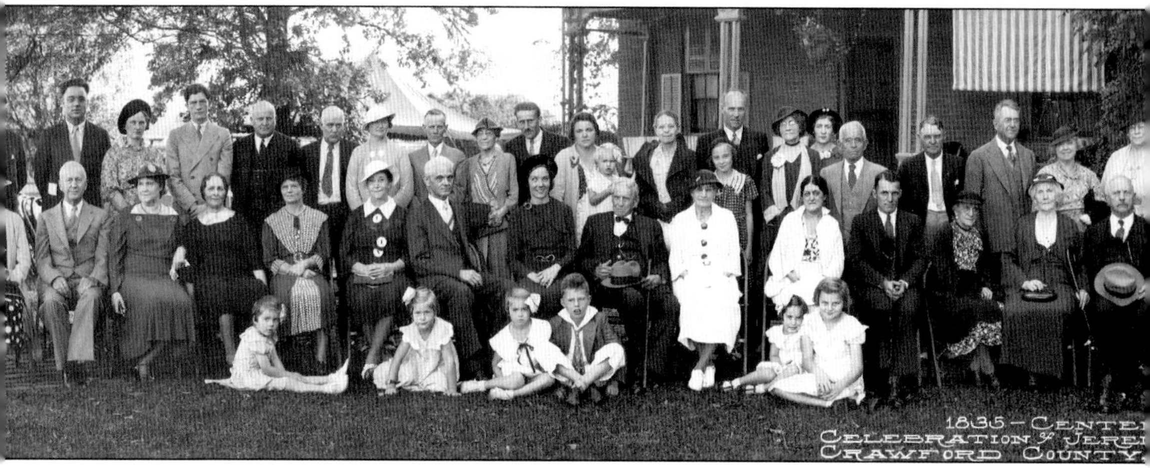

MONNETT CENTENNIAL REUNION, 1835–1935. One hundred seventy-five descendents of brothers Jeremiah Crabb Monnett, Isaac Monnett, and Thomas Monnett gathered on September 22, 1935, to mark the 100th anniversary of the family's arrival in Crawford County at the home of Fred and Charlotte (Monnett) McKnight south of Bucyrus on the Columbus Road. During the reunion, the family dedicated a bronze marker on the east side of State Route 98, at the site of the Jeremiah and Aley Monnett homestead commemorating the centennial of their settlement. Of the 102 people in this photograph, the majority were residents or natives of Crawford County at the time of the event. According to Lucille Kennedy Fullerton, a great-great-granddaughter of Thomas Monnett, the "longboy" style photograph was taken in three images, first one side, then the other, and then the middle; the final image would be assembled by Coles Studio in Columbus, Ohio. From left to right are (seated on grass) Amy Beers, Barbara Smith, Gwen Beers, Marvin Beers, Marilyn Smith, Mary Joan Kennedy, Tommy Monnett, Lucille Kennedy, Martha Monnett, and Betty Hipsher; (seated on chairs) Gertrude Wright Kling, Mrs. and Mrs. Edwin Beale, Mrs. Hull, Amy Kennedy Stump, Junie Newland Kennedy, Thomas M. Kennedy, Evelyn Kennedy Sharrock, Josephus Monnette, Melinda Carmean Monnett, Grace Monnett, Kay Monnett, Nettie Monnett, Sallie Monnett Sears, Rufus Sears, the Honorable Frank S. Monnett, Ellie Gormely Monnett, Mrs. Cyrus Austin, Ella Bliss, Charlotte McKnight, Mary

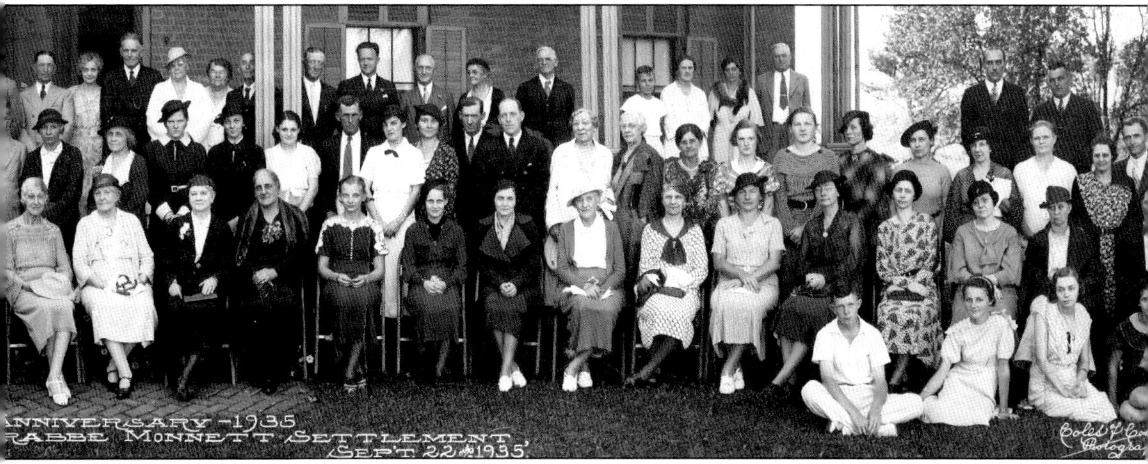

Jane Sears, Florence Monnett, Marcella Monnett, Zymilla Monnett Hamilton, Olley Monnett Lynn, Mildred Hill Kennedy, Sally Sears, Anna Sears Wiseman, Minna Monnett Knowles, and Alonzo Monnett; (standing behind the chairs) William Beers, Curtis Smith, Pauline Kennedy Smith, Sam Beers, George Wright, Clark and Hazel Wright, George Turner, Elizabeth Wright Turner, Edmund Wright Turner, Flossie Beers holding her daughter Twilia, Rosa Monnett Kellogg, George Monnette Kling (also known as Saxon Kling), Nancy Wright (standing in front of Kling), Carrie Wright McGee, Martha McGee Little, Fred Barth, James M. Hamilton, Rev. and Mrs. James Wolfe of Monnett Memorial Chapel, Lillian Osborn, unidentified, Mr. and Mrs. Hugh Bennett, Mrs. Wallace Monnett, Jane Monnett, Effie Monnett Fasching, Henrietta Monnett, Fred McKnight, Virginia Monnett, Mrs. and Mr. Ralph Kinnear, Marshall Foster, Grace High Washburn, Sue Picking, Argall Monnett Swisher, Kathryn Kennedy, Jean Kennedy, Eloise Lott Furniss, Katherine Schuller Monnett, Ada Monnett Gracely, Anna Pittman Monnett, and Zelma Swisher Lindsay and her husband; (standing on porch) Almet Kennedy, Mr. and Mrs. Edward Lewis, state senator James Hopley, Mrs. William Blicke, Mrs. Fred Barth, Floyd Knowles, Sam Stump, Rev. David Roller, William Blicke, unidentified, unidentified, unidentified, unidentified, Hattie Mae Holmes Monnett, Orrin Kay Monnett, Ray Furniss, and Harold Monnette. (Courtesy of the Bucyrus Historical Society.)

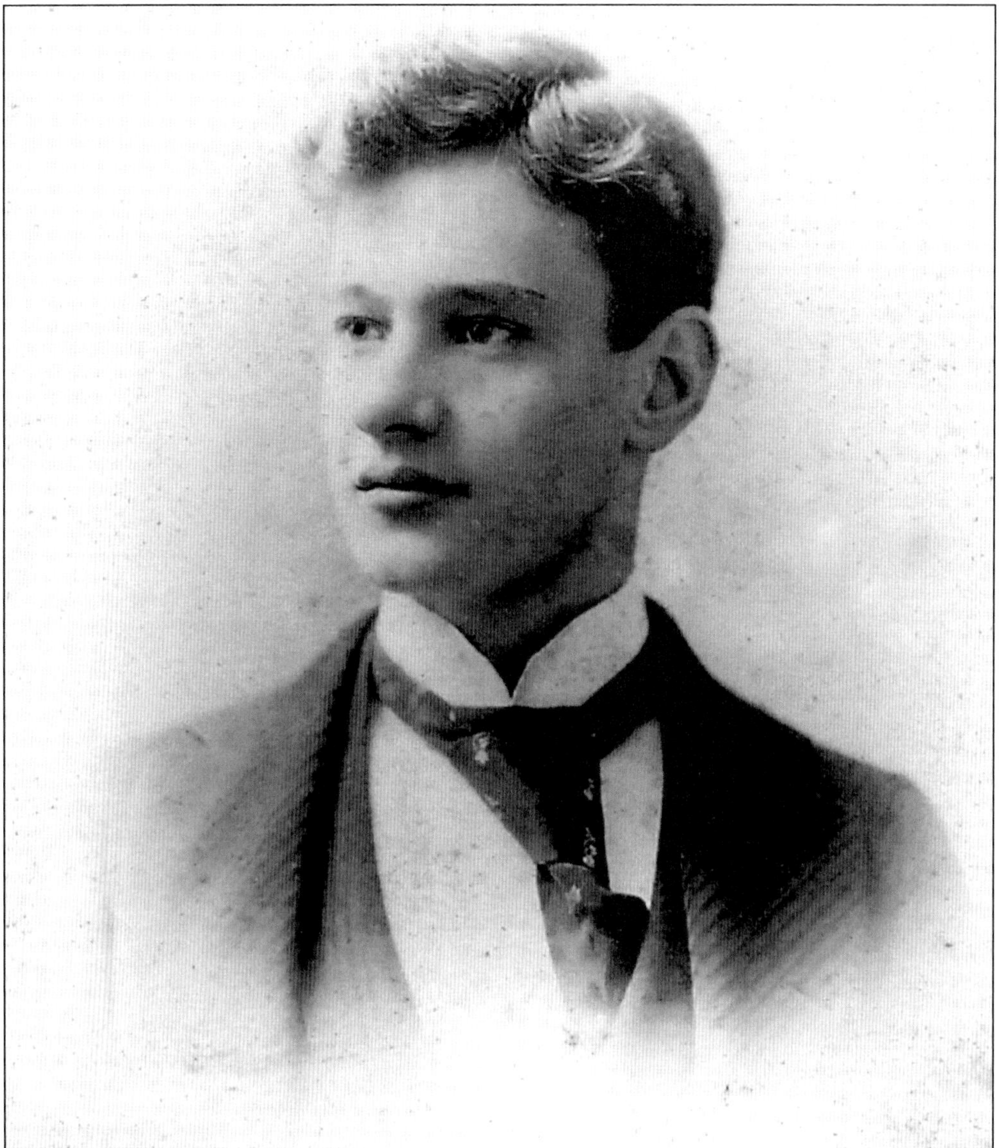

ORRA E. MONNETTE. The son of Mervin J. Monnette and his first wife, Olive Hull, Orra E. Monnette practiced law in Bucyrus for a number of years. Following his father's successful gold strike at the Mohawk Mine in Tonopah, Nevada, Orra moved to Los Angeles to help the investment and oversight of the windfall profits. Their first acquisition was controlling interest in the American National Bank of Los Angeles. After four additional banking acquisitions and mergers, Orra emerged as chairman of one of the largest bank holding companies in southern California, which was renamed the Bank of America, Los Angeles. Orra continued to grow the bank holding company through the efficient use of modern bank branches. In 1929, Amadeo Giannini, founder of the Bank of Italy (San Francisco) proposed a merger of the two financial intuitions, forming what is now known as the Bank of America, with Gianni and Orra co-chairing the Bank of America Board. Orra also served as the chairman of the Los Angeles Public Library System and is recognized as the founder of its branch library system. Orra died in Los Angeles in 1936. (Courtesy of Oliver Hamilton.)

Six

Industry

Bucyrus has a proud history of industrial production. Initially industrial production was not seen as something of value by early city leaders. However, seeing benefits accrued by communities with manufacturing capabilities, the attitude quickly changed. At its production height following World War II, plants in Bucyrus made road equipment and produced steel and other durable goods that were shipped around the world. This chapter looks back on three such companies, Hadfield-Penfield Steel Company, W. A. Riddell Company, and Timken.

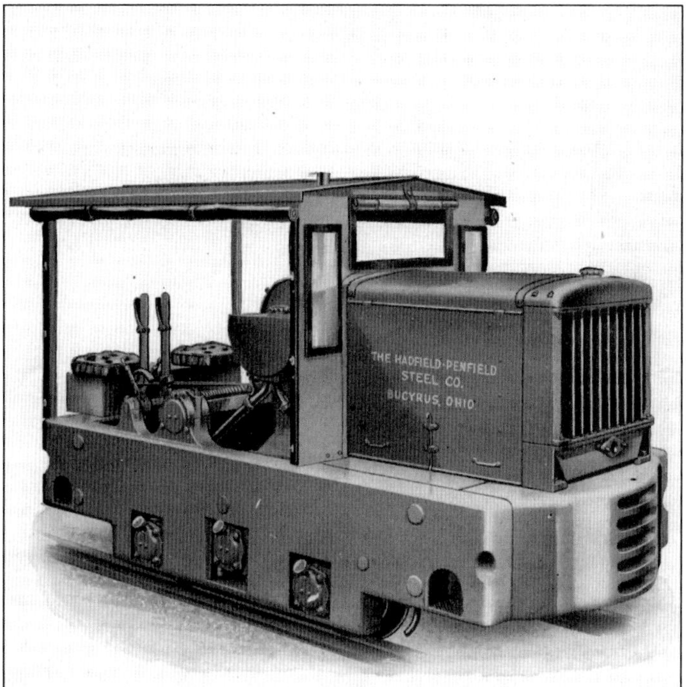

Four Ton Model OZ American Gasoline Locomotive, Cab Type

AMERICAN GASOLINE LOCOMOTIVE, MODEL OZ. Before the acceptance of trucks in mining and quarrying operations, vehicles such as Hadfield-Pennfield's American gasoline locomotive were used on narrow-gauge tracks to haul materials. While inexpensive to operate, their reliance on fixed tracks limited their appeal as truck design became more refined. (Courtesy of the Marion County Historical Society.)

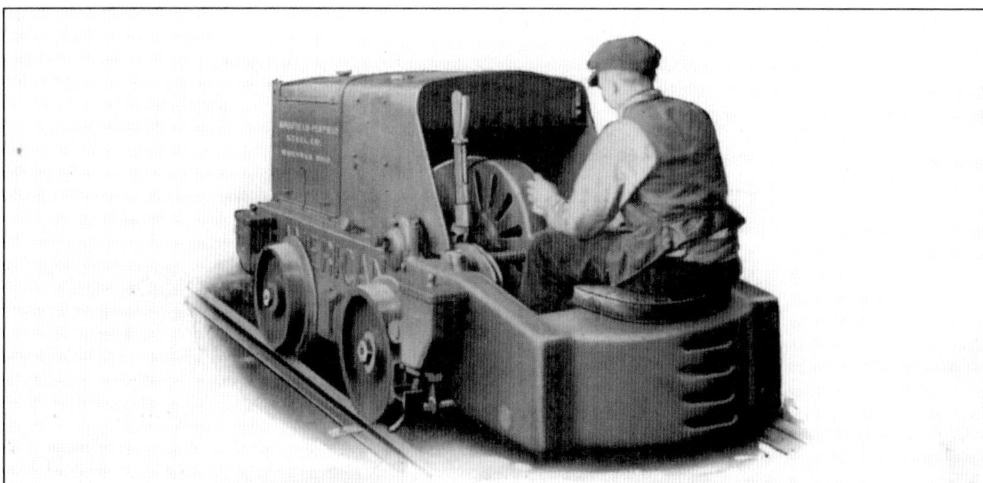

Four Ton Model OZA Low Down Type American Gasoline Locomotive

AMERICAN GASOLINE LOCOMOTIVE, MODEL OZA. For underground mining operation, Hadfield-Penfield built the model OZA, designed specifically for low-clearance tunnels. (Courtesy of the Marion County Historical Society.)

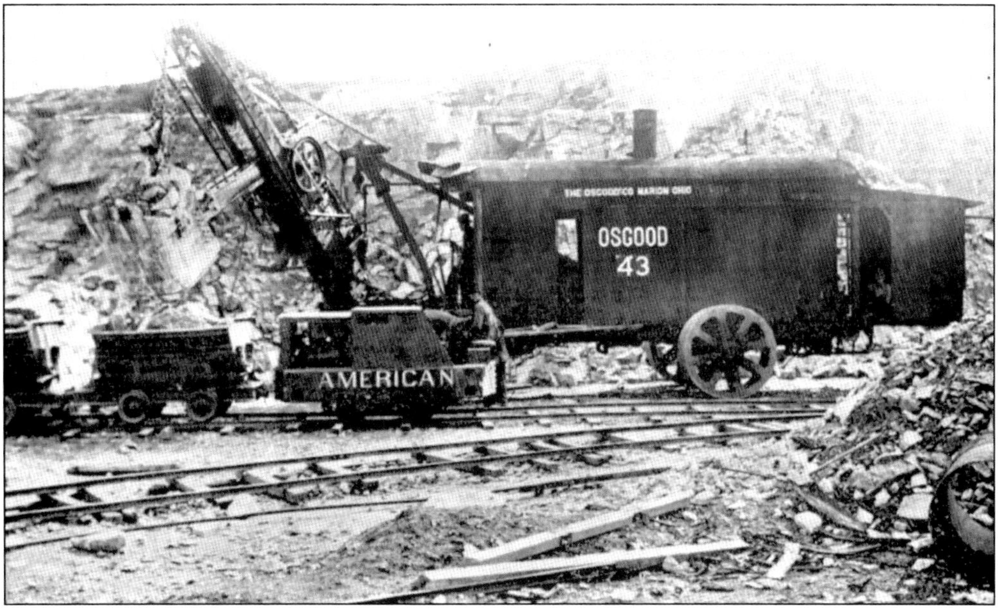

EVANS STONE QUARRY, OUTSIDE MARION, OHIO. This catalog photograph shows a Model OZ at work in the Evans Limestone Quarry in Marion, Ohio. Next to it is an Osgood steam shovel. Now a lake, the area is part of Quarry Park and operated by the Marion Department of Parks and Recreation. (Courtesy of the Marion County Historical Society.)

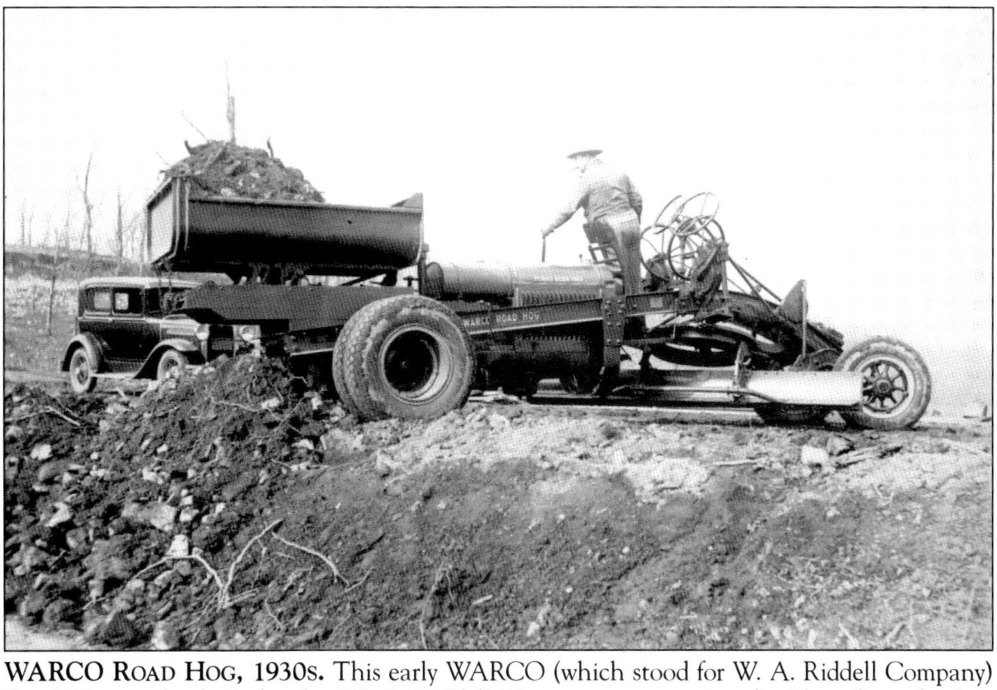

WARCO ROAD HOG, 1930S. This early WARCO (which stood for W. A. Riddell Company) Road Hog grader built by the W. A. Riddell Company was equipped with a dump bucket, allowing it to not only grade surface area, but also transport fill and other material. (Courtesy of the Bucyrus Historical Society.)

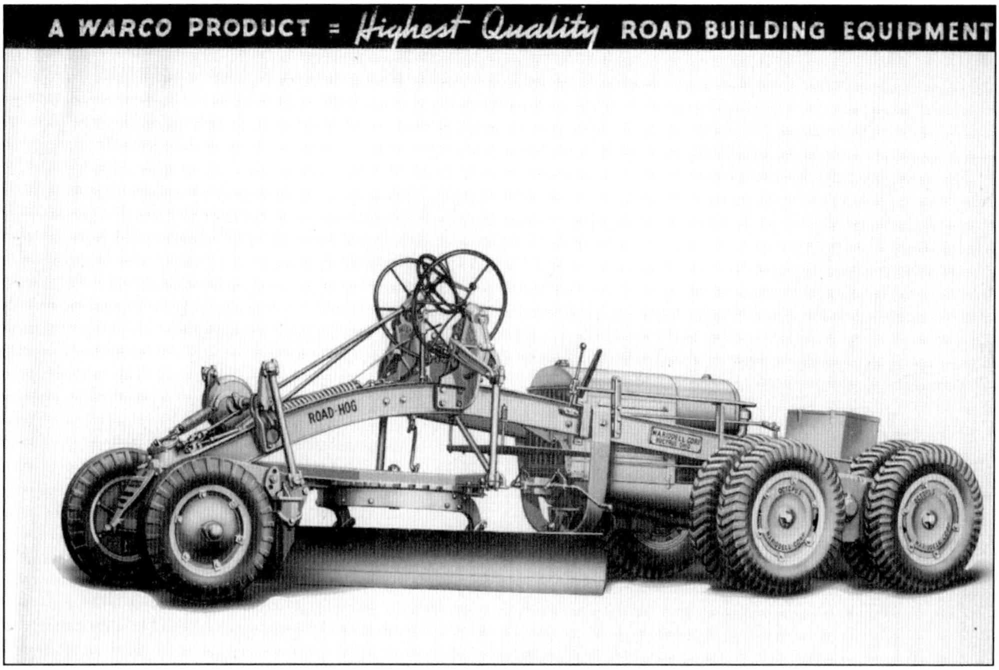

WARCO MODEL H GRADER. In 1947, the W. A. Riddell Company facility in Bucyrus employed 172 local workers and was frequently cited as one of the safest Ohio heavy manufacturing plants to work in. (Courtesy of the Marion County Historical Society.)

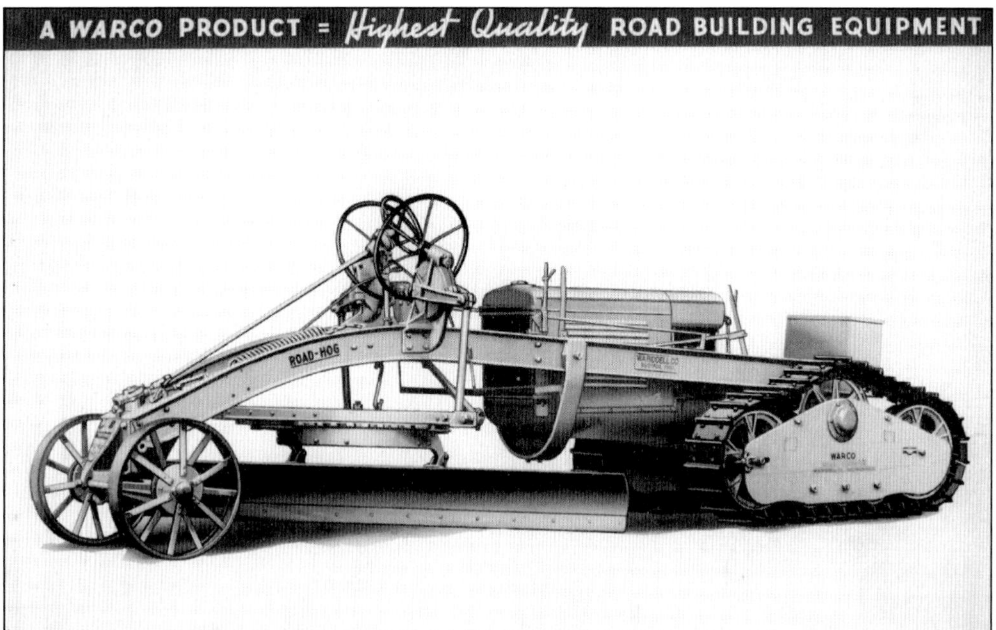

WARCO MODEL H HALF-TRACK. The W. A. Riddell Company line was flexible and could be outfitted with either half-track or 20-inch wheels. Products bearing the trade name Road Hog first appeared in the 1920s, playing upon the machinery's ability to cut wide swaths in a single pass. (Courtesy of the Marion County Historical Society.)

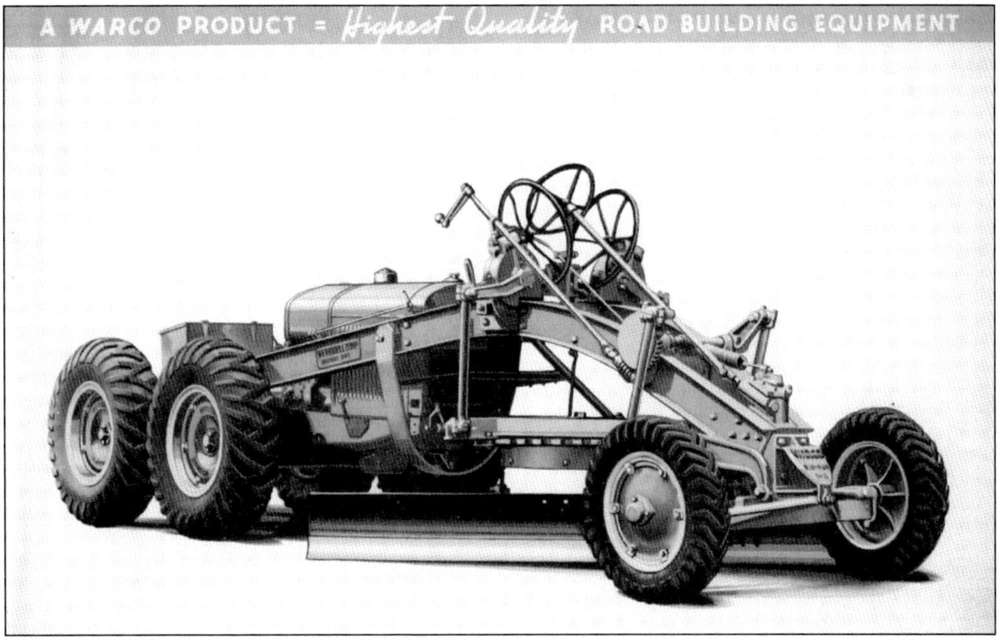

WARCO MODEL S GRADER. Built by the W. A. Riddell Corporation, W. A. Riddell Company–brand graders represented high quality and value for the price. The Model S grader was approximately 21 feet in length. Oliver, General Motors, or International Harvester engines were fitted to the machines for power and were also equipped with Lockheed hydraulic brakes. (Courtesy of the Marion County Historical Society.)

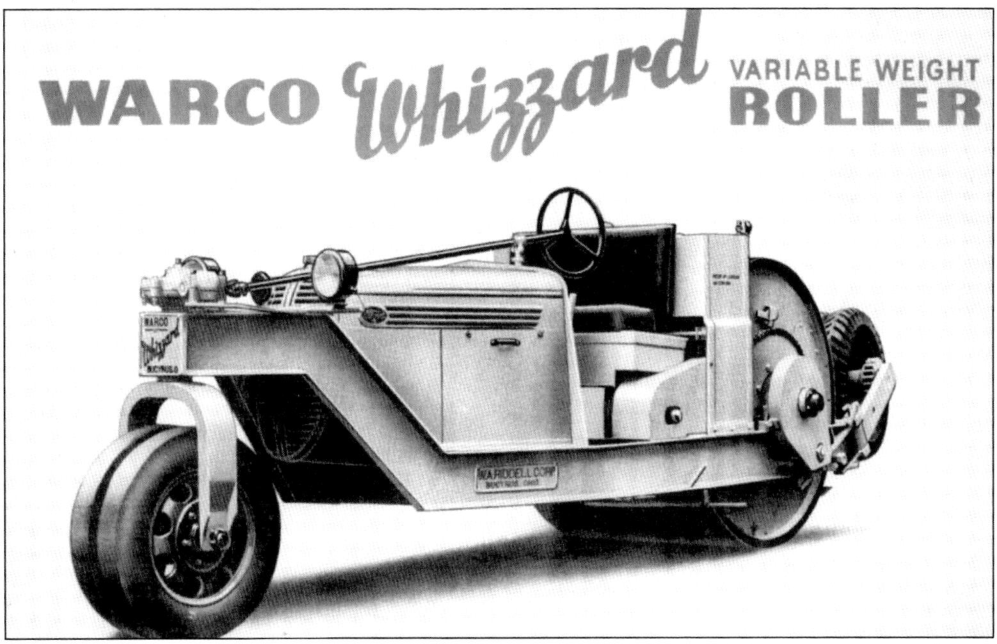

WARCO WHIZZARD. The W. A. Riddell Company fulfilled a need for a medium-sized road roller with the introduction of its Whizzard line. The Ford V8-powered Whizzard was unique in that it was also equipped with a trailing drive system, enabling it to reach highway speeds of 20 miles per hour for transport purposes. (Courtesy of the Marion County Historical Society.)

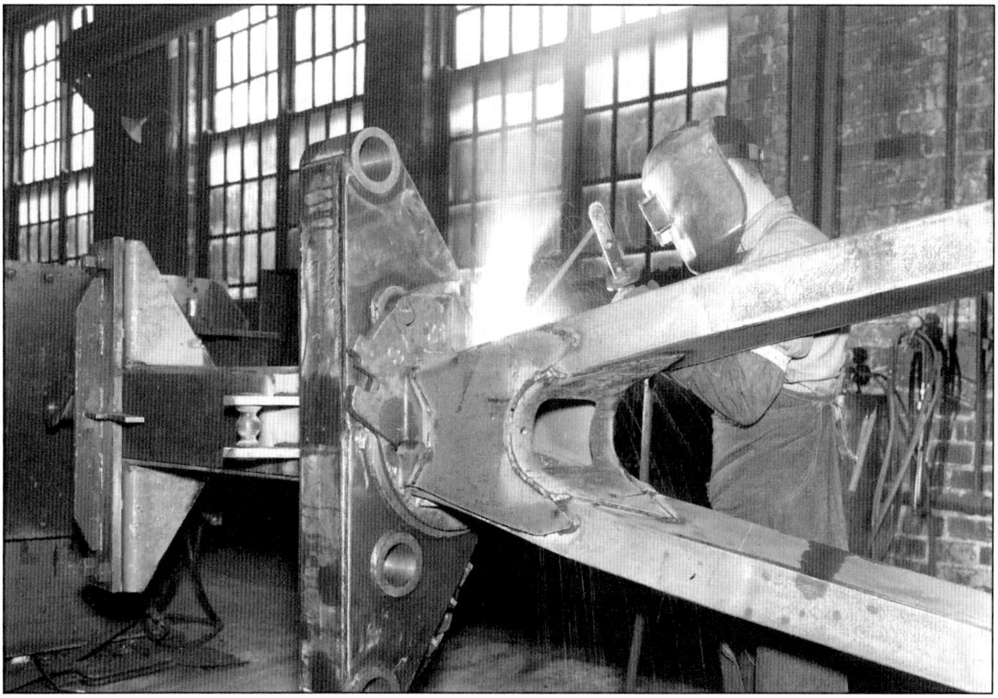

Welding. An unidentified W. A. Riddell Company employee is shown welding the structural chassis of a grader in the Bucyrus plant. (Courtesy of the Marion County Historical Society.)

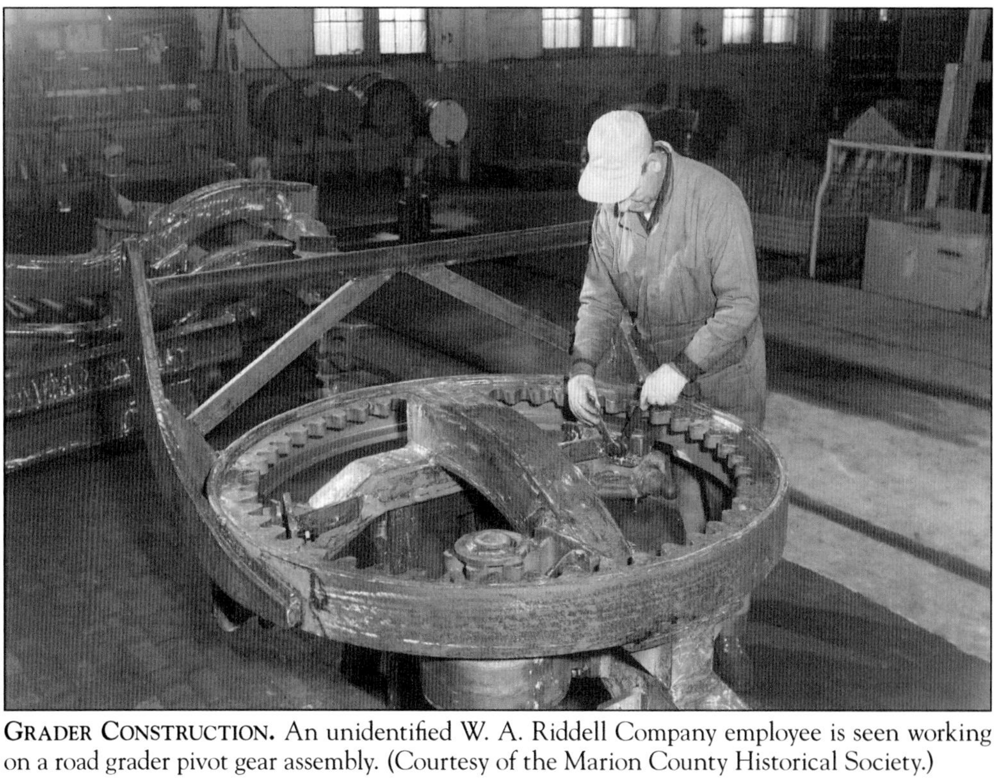

Grader Construction. An unidentified W. A. Riddell Company employee is seen working on a road grader pivot gear assembly. (Courtesy of the Marion County Historical Society.)

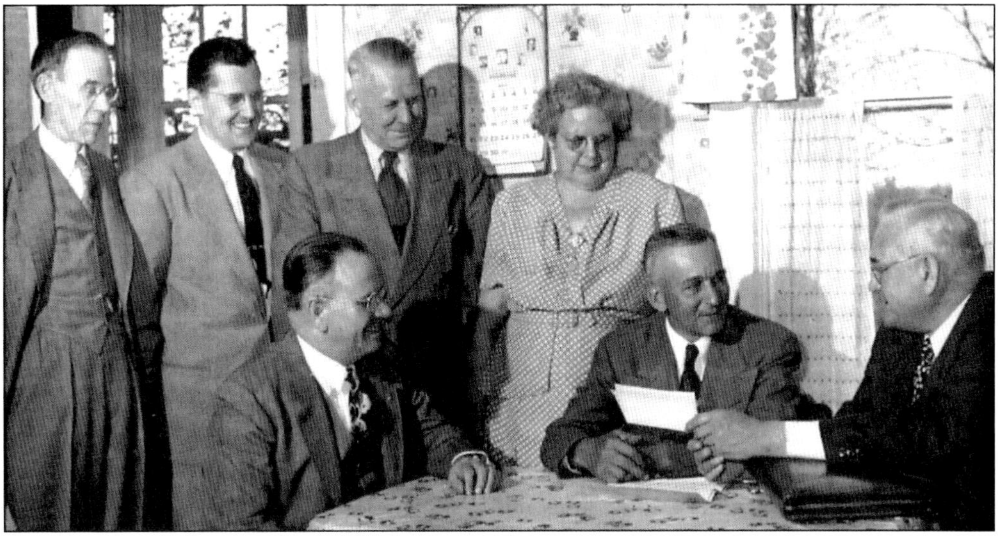

THE YAUSSEYS SELLING THE FARM TO THE TIMKEN ROLLER BEARING COMPANY. The Timken Roller Bearing Company selected and purchased the Yaussey farm for its Bucyrus facility. Standing are, from left to right, C. M. Maratta; Russell Fowler; H. M. Richey, representing the Timken Company; and Mrs. Yaussey. Seated is Bucyrus mayor F. P. Sitler, Austin C. Yaussey, and F. K. Domer, head of real estate for the Timken Company. (Courtesy of the Timken Company.)

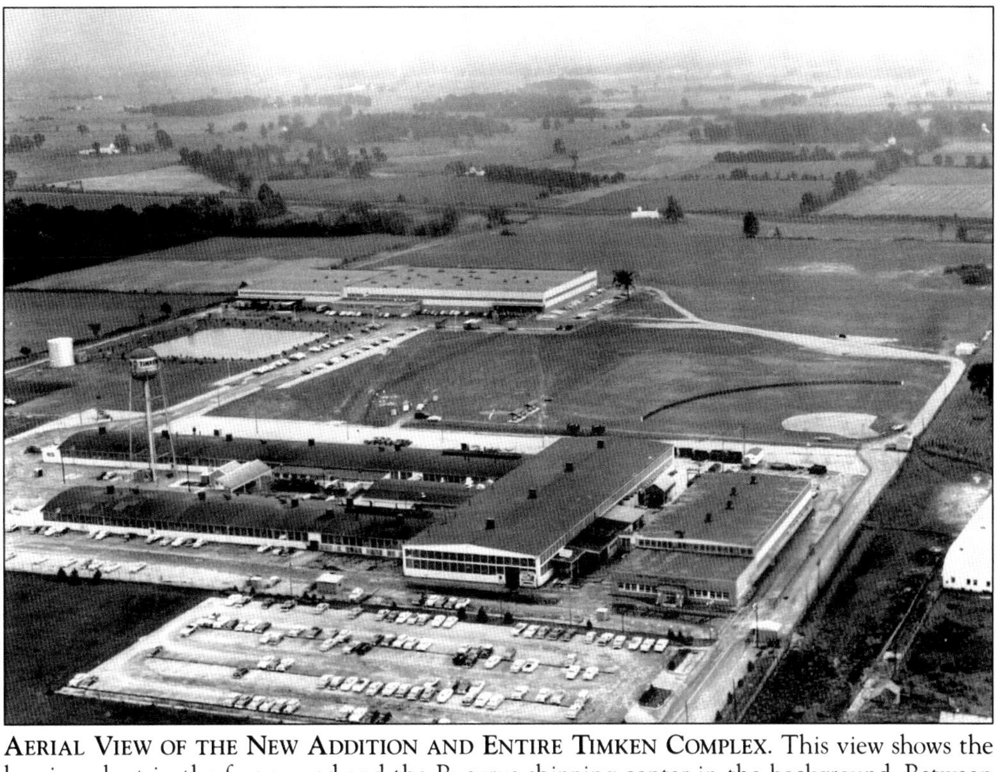

AERIAL VIEW OF THE NEW ADDITION AND ENTIRE TIMKEN COMPLEX. This view shows the bearing plant in the foreground and the Bucyrus shipping center in the background. Between the two plants is the recreation area. The Timken Company invested nearly $12 million in the construction of the entire complex. (Courtesy of the Timken Company.)

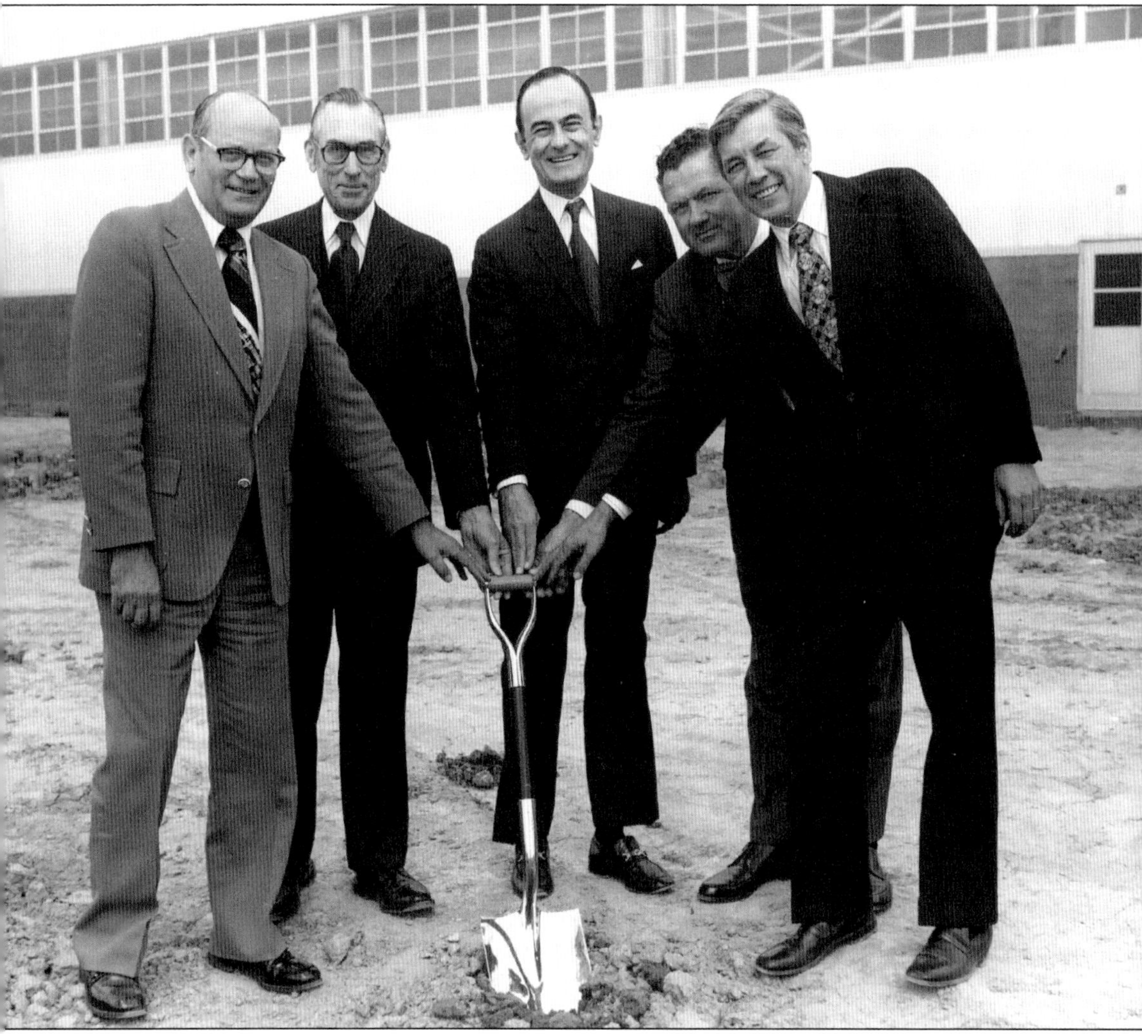

GROUNDBREAKING FOR TIMKEN ADDITION. Shortly after the Bucyrus facility was completed, ground was broken for expansion of the plant. Groundbreaking for the plant addition was attended by Timken and Bucyrus city officials. (Courtesy of the Timken Company.)

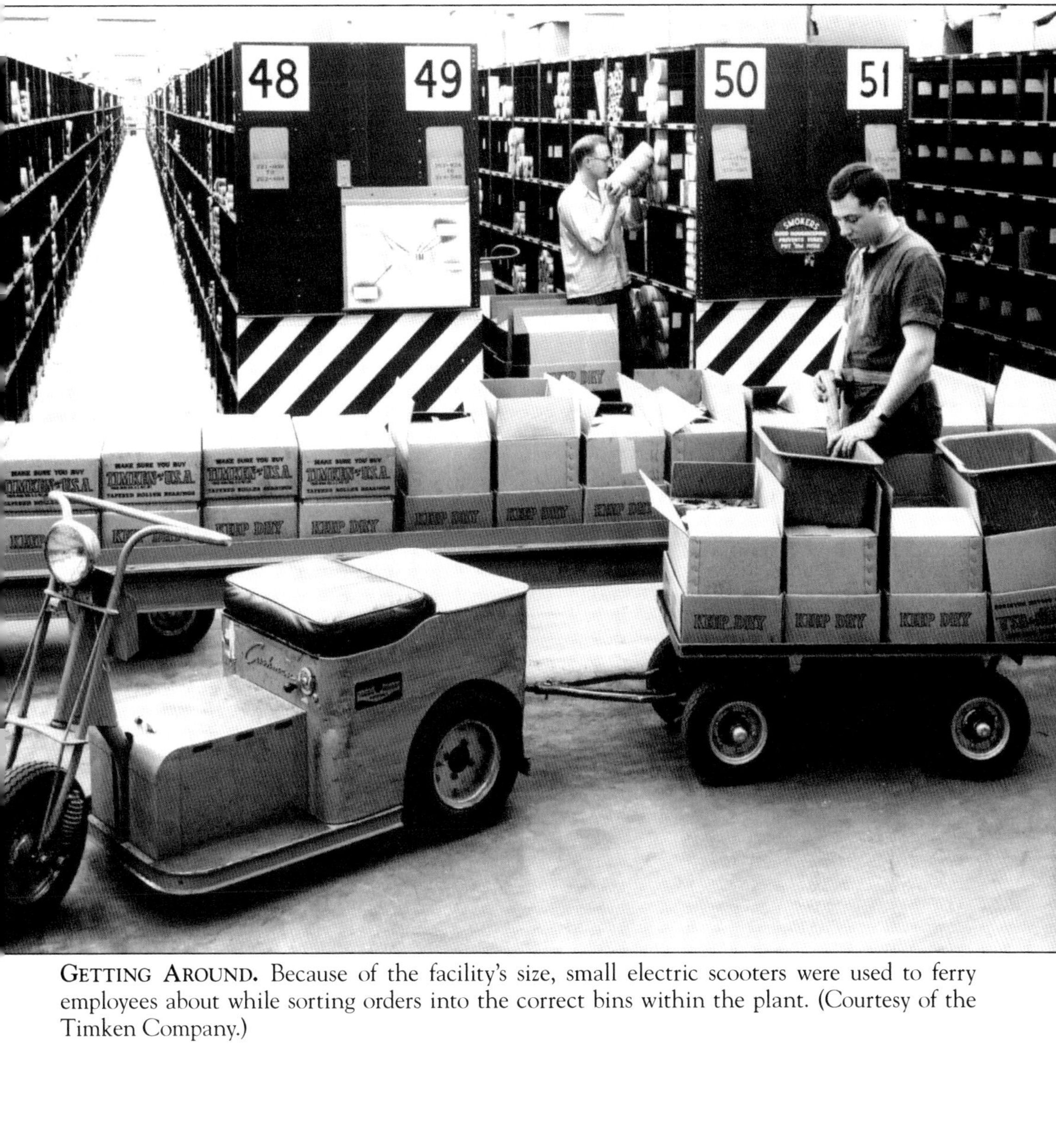

GETTING AROUND. Because of the facility's size, small electric scooters were used to ferry employees about while sorting orders into the correct bins within the plant. (Courtesy of the Timken Company.)

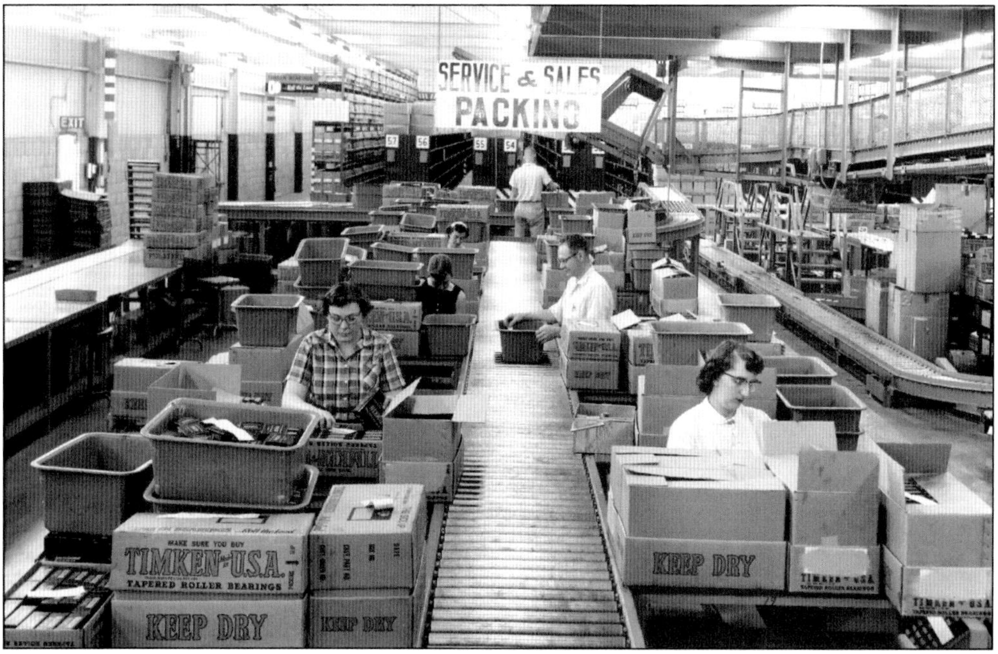

EMPLOYEES IN THE PACKING AND SHIPPING DEPARTMENT. When built, Timken's Bucyrus facility allowed for the integration of new technology for the deployment of roller bearing products. The facility's early success led to additions that increased its size and efficiency. (Courtesy of the Timken Company.)

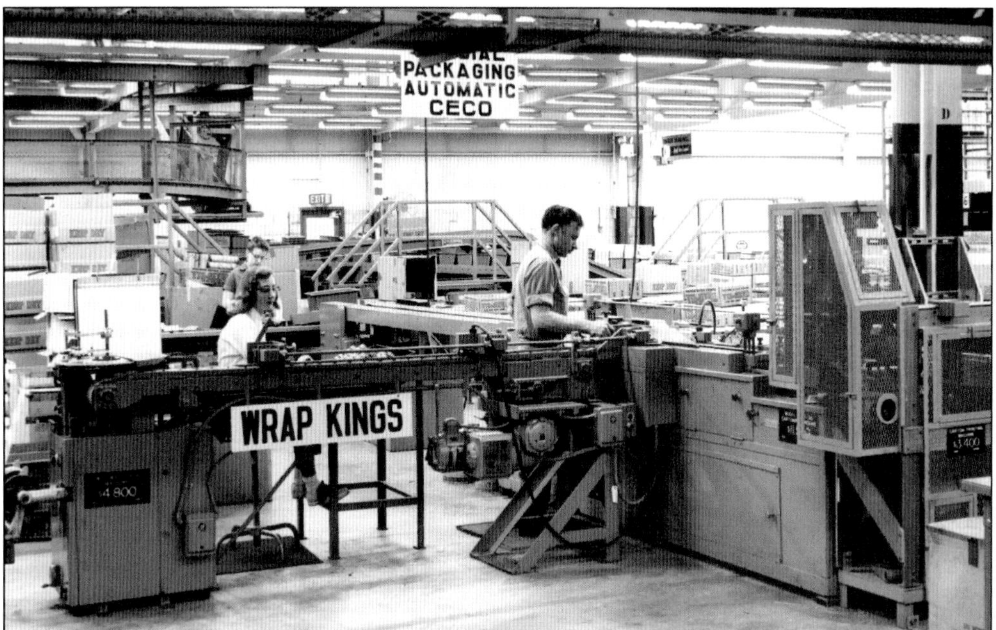

PRODUCT PACKAGING AND SHIPPING. Employees in the shipping plant with the sophisticated shipping machines could wrap and heat-seal the product, imprint the Timken part number, insert the product into a carton, and seal the carton. During an eight-hour shift, the machine could package 15,000 bearings. (Courtesy of the Timken Company.)

Seven

THE BEST OF THE 'WURST

To those outside of Crawford County, perhaps no other event is as well known as the Bucyrus Bratwurst Festival. Since August 1967, the community has celebrated its German heritage through the annual event. The Bratwurst Festival is an annual three-day event that helps different local organizations, school groups, and the community raise money for their respective groups while having a bit of fun in the process. There are many activities to keep all entertained. There are daily parades, live entertainment, contests, an auction, and, of course, the food.

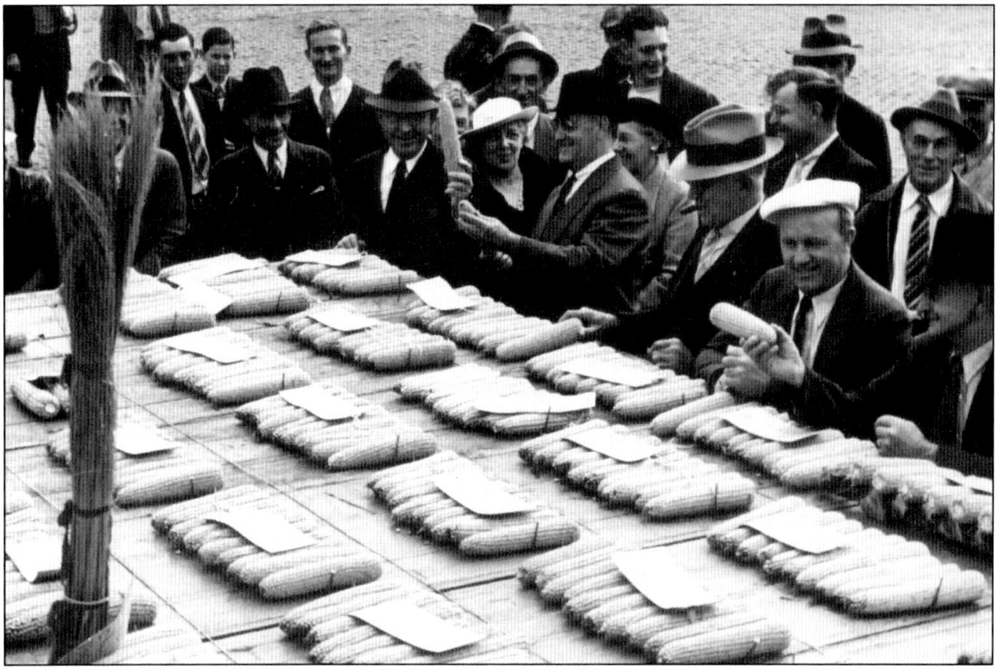

CORN SHOW, C. 1940S. Prior to the first Bratwurst Festival in 1967, Bucyrus held the Corn Show, then Colonel Crawford Day's celebration. During the Corn Show era, corn was judged on color, sugar content, and uniformity for the seed type. (Courtesy of the Bucyrus Historical Society.)

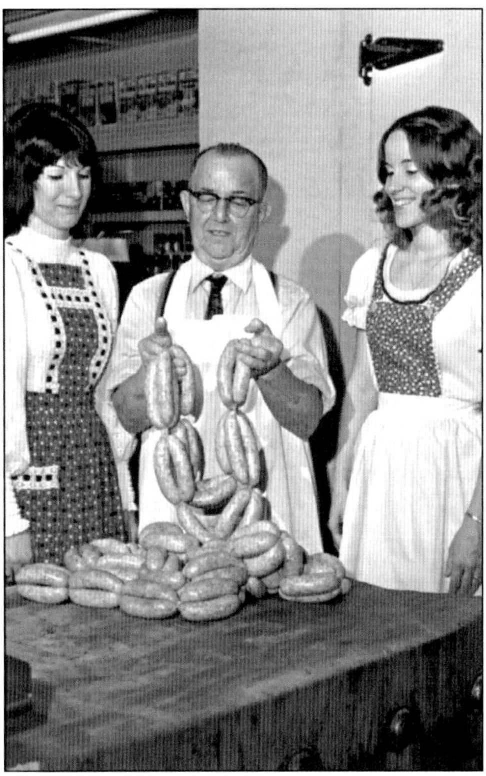

BUCYRUS, BEAUTIES, AND BRATWURST, C. 1969. This photograph was used on postcards to promote Bucyrus as the bratwurst capital of the world in the late 1960s and early 1970s. (Courtesy of the Bucyrus Bratwurst Festival Committee.)

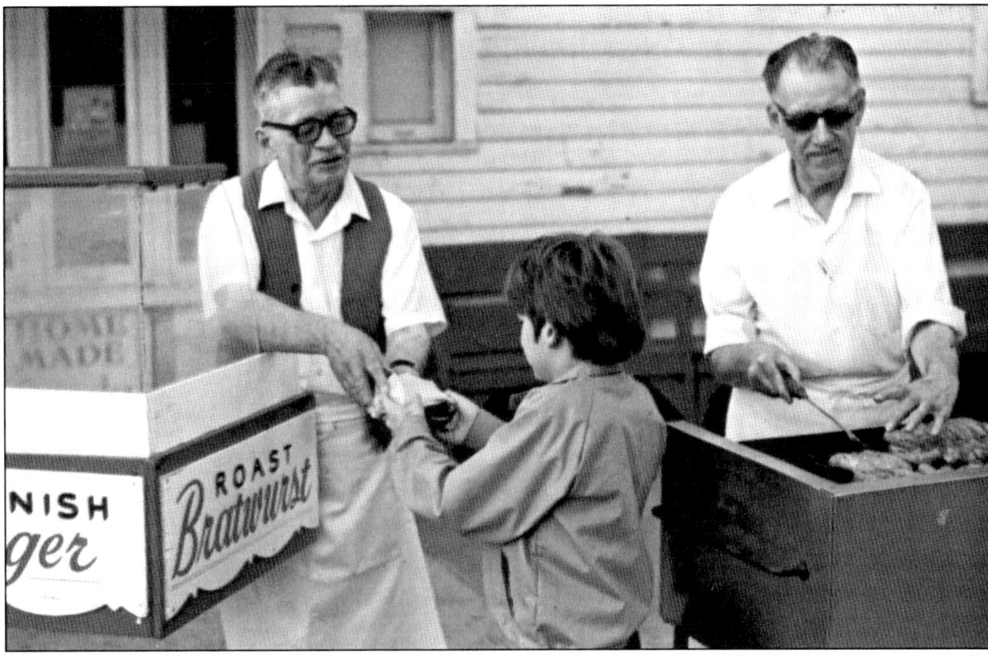

BRATWURST PROMOTIONAL PHOTOGRAPH, 1970S. According to the dictionary, *bratwurst* is the old high German word for "fresh pork sausage for frying." Entomologically, the word breaks down as *brat*, "meat without waste," and *wurst*, "sausage." It is pronounced in Bucyrus as "brāt-wurst." (Courtesy of the Bucyrus Bratwurst Festival Committee.)

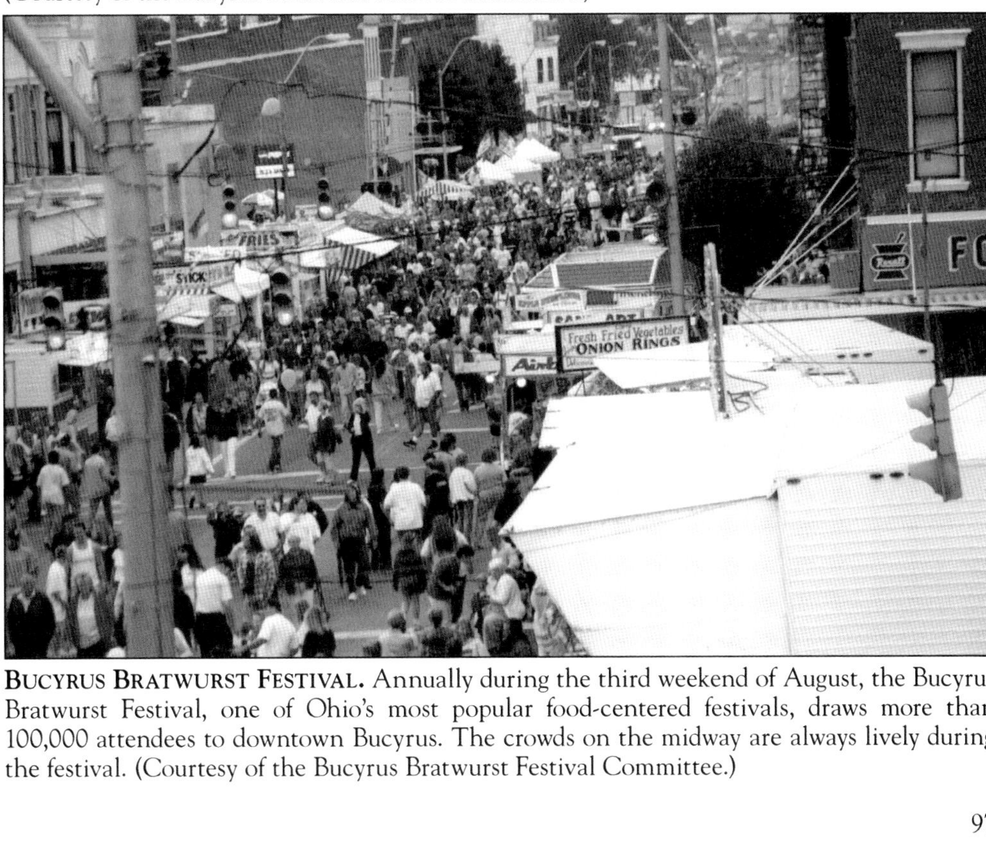

BUCYRUS BRATWURST FESTIVAL. Annually during the third weekend of August, the Bucyrus Bratwurst Festival, one of Ohio's most popular food-centered festivals, draws more than 100,000 attendees to downtown Bucyrus. The crowds on the midway are always lively during the festival. (Courtesy of the Bucyrus Bratwurst Festival Committee.)

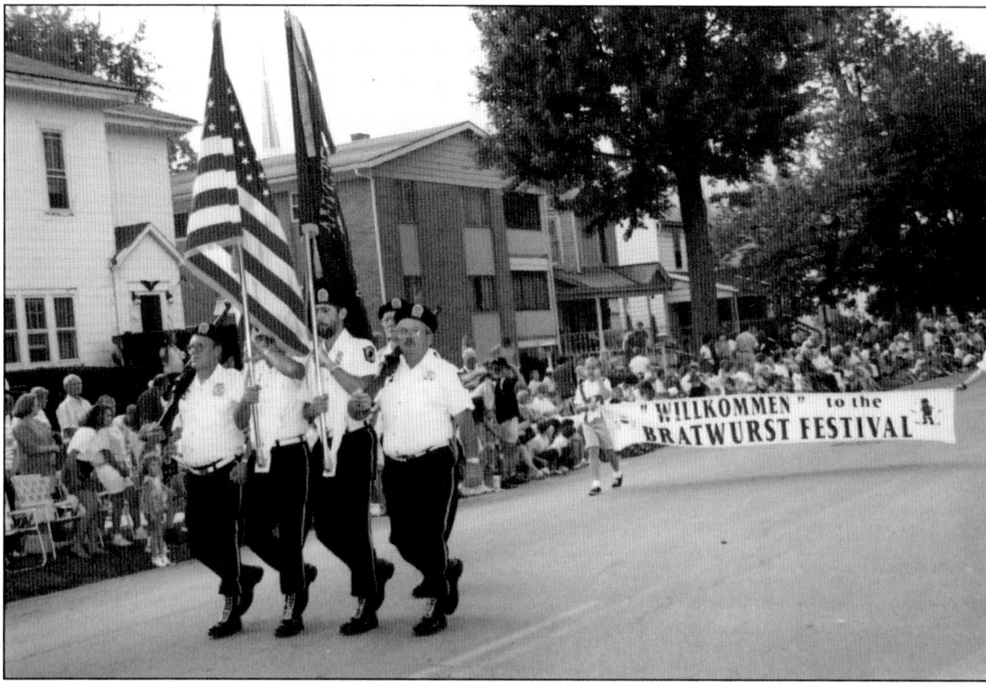

COLOR GUARD KICKING OFF THE PARADE. The flags and color guard welcome the start of the Bratwurst Festival parade. The parade is one of the longest in the state and kicks off the annual event on the third Thursday of August. (Courtesy of the Bucyrus Bratwurst Festival Committee.)

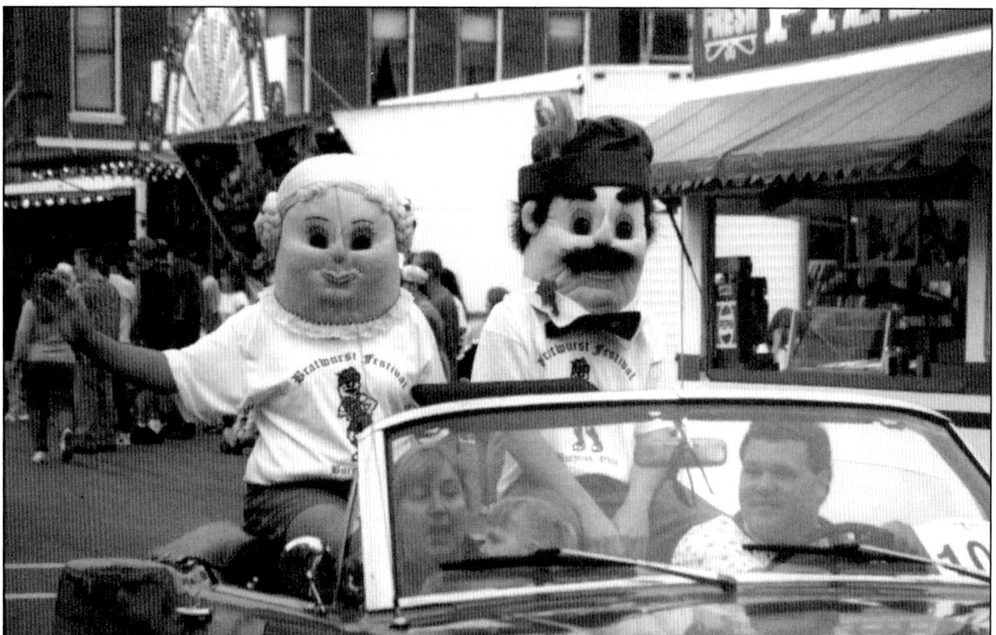

BRATTY AND BRATINA. The mascots of the Bucyrus Bratwurst Festival are Bratty and Bratina, who appear in event advertising, the parade, and other festival-sponsored events. Bratty and Bratina were even married one year during the festival. (Courtesy of the Bucyrus Bratwurst Festival Committee.)

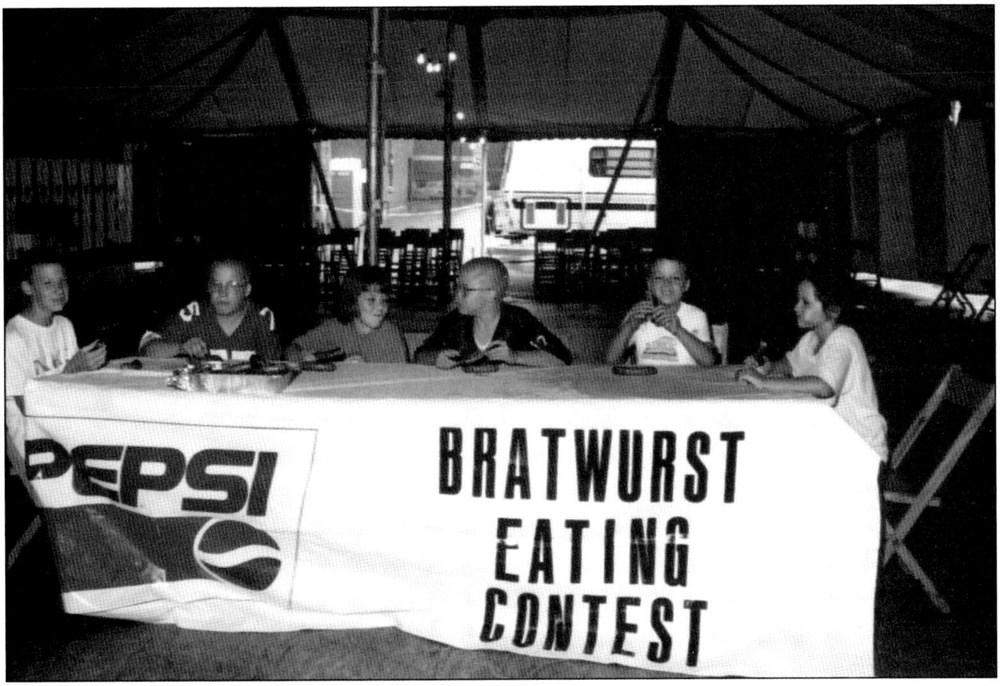

BRATWURST EATING CONTEST. Contestants prepare for the junior division bratwurst sandwich eating contest. Many recipes using bratwurst are made during the festival, but the favorite has always been the round sausage. (Courtesy of the Bucyrus Bratwurst Festival Committee.)

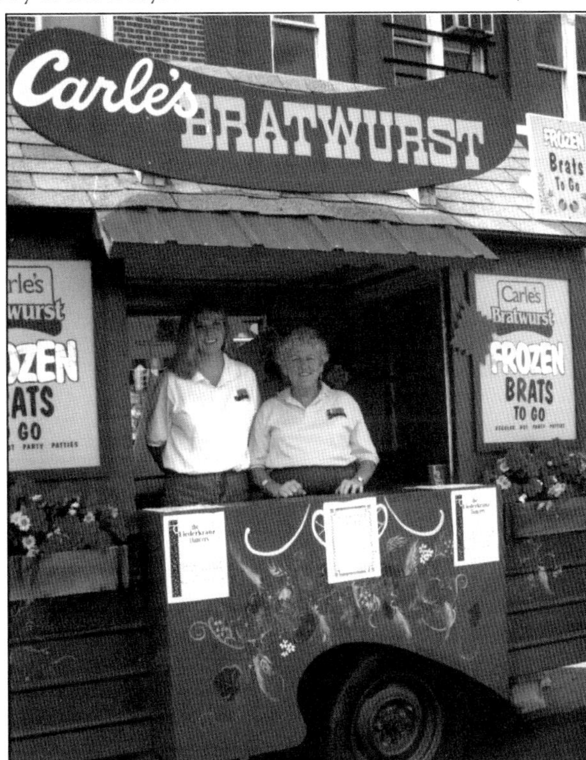

CARLE'S BRATWURST WAGON. Carle's Bratwurst, one of the remaining original Bucyrus bratwurst makers, draws its own fans to the festival. This bratwurst wagon is a mainstay at the festival. What makes each brand of bratwurst unique is its maker's blend of ingredients and seasonings. Ruth Carle Spiegle is standing on the right. (Courtesy of the Bucyrus Bratwurst Festival Committee.)

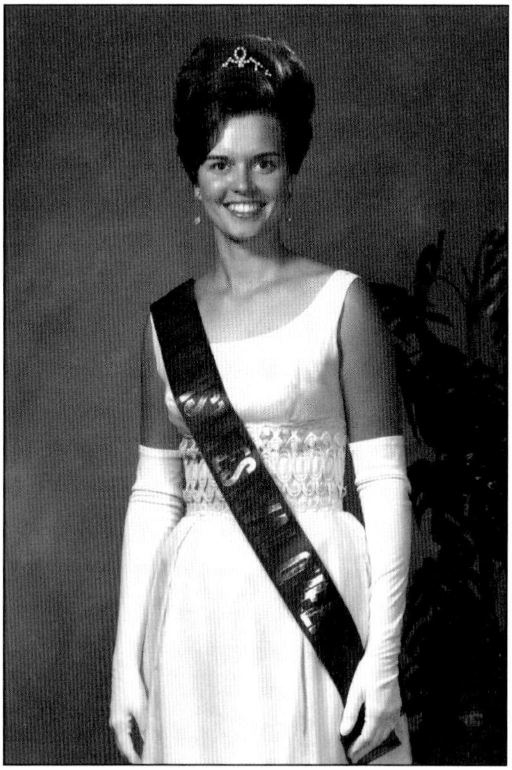

BRATWURST QUEEN KATHY FETTER. Each year, a bratwurst queen is chosen to preside over the festivities and represent the Bratwurst Festival at Ohio's other festivals. The lovely Kathy Fetter was the first Bratwurst Festival Queen in 1968. (Courtesy of the Bratwurst Festival Committee.)

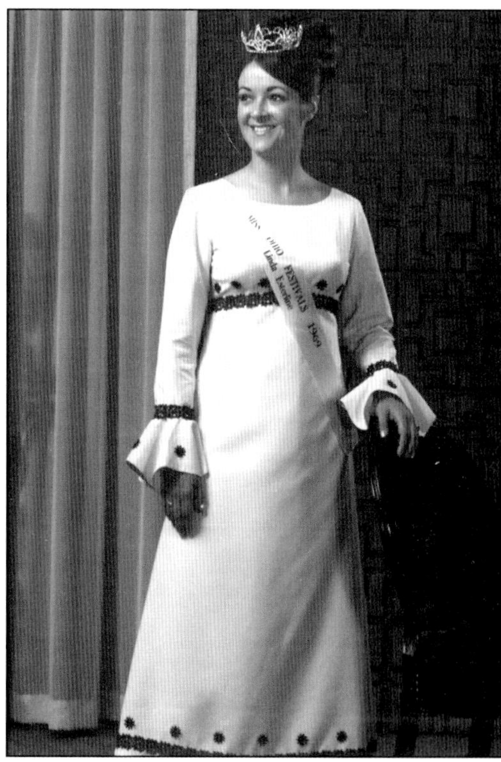

BRATWURST QUEEN LINDA ESTERLINE. Linda Esterline Durtschi was named bratwurst queen in 1974. She competed in the Ohio Festivals Queen contest, winning that title as well. Linda still lives and works in Bucyrus. (Courtesy of the Bucyrus Bratwurst Festival Committee.)

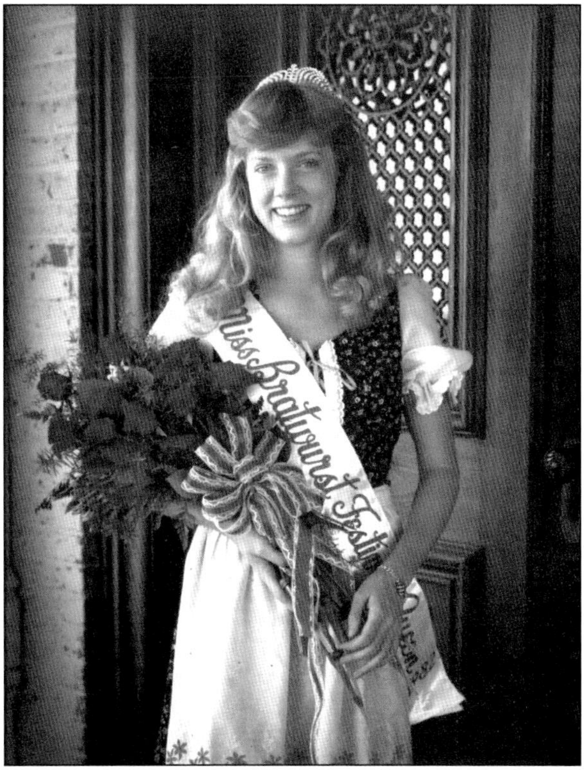

BRATWURST QUEEN KATHY BAKER. Another beautiful festival queen was Kathy Baker, who posed in front of the Bucyrus Historical Society in 1982. (Courtesy of the Bucyrus Bratwurst Festival Committee.)

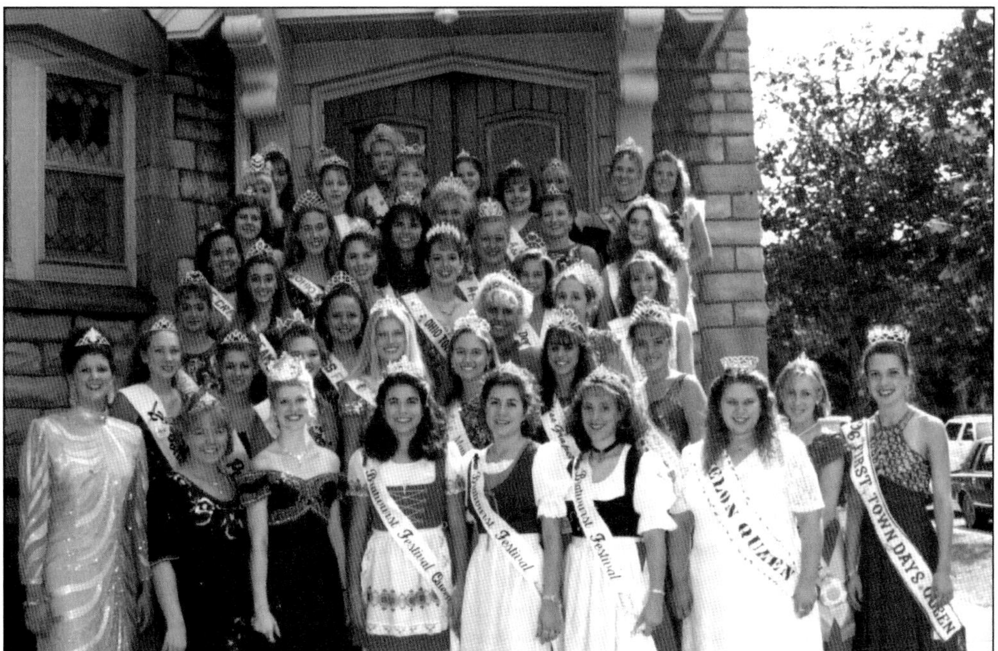

OHIO'S FESTIVAL QUEENS. For each Ohio festival, there is a festival queen who not only oversees her sponsoring festival, but also acts as a goodwill ambassador by attending other festivals held during her reign. (Courtesy of the Bucyrus Bratwurst Festival Committee.)

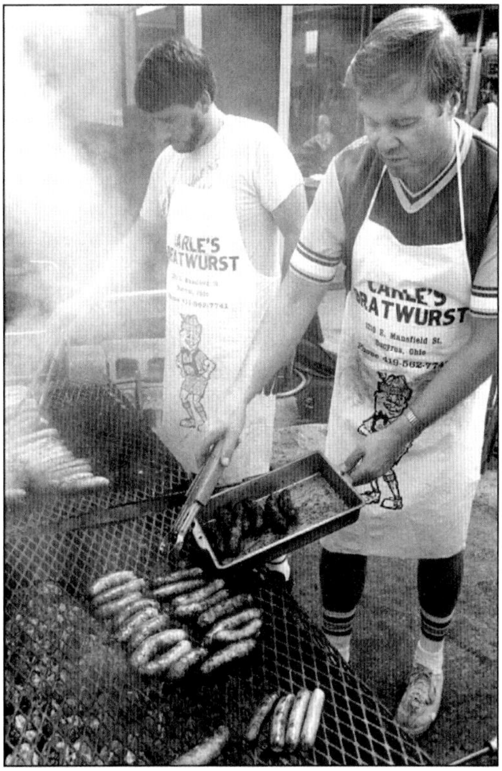

FOOD FOR THE FESTIVE. Part of the sights and sounds of any festival is the preparation of the honored food. During the Bratwurst Festival, vendors grill in the open air. Bratwurst can be served by itself, in a sausage bun, or cut in half, filleted, and then served on a hamburger bun. (Courtesy of the Bucyrus Bratwurst Festival Committee.)

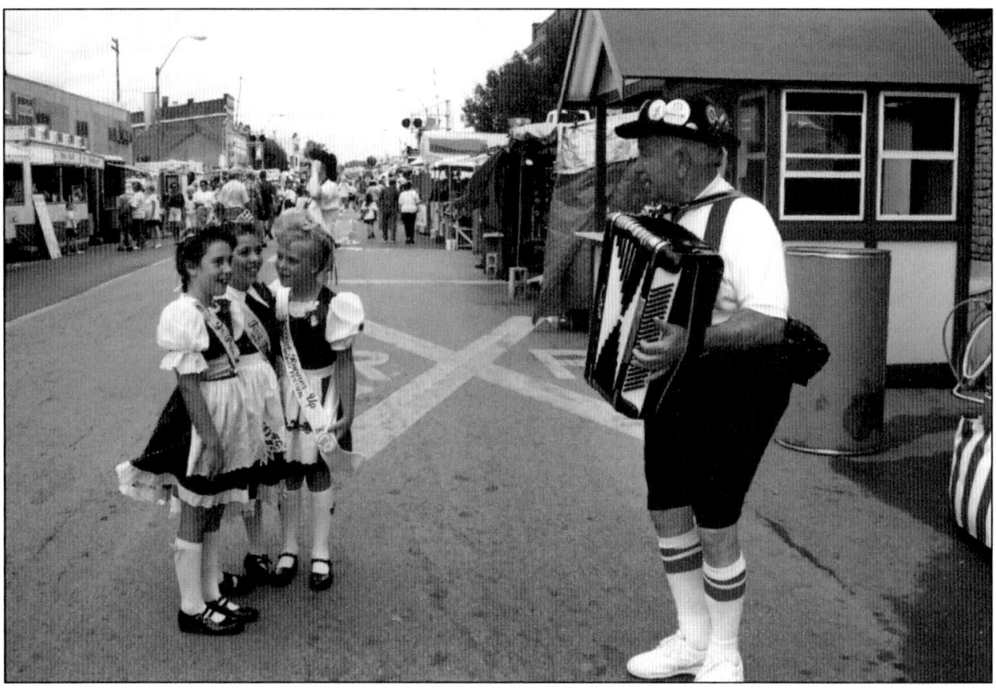

OOMPAH. The junior bratwurst festival queen shares the spotlight with her court and strikes a pose for the German accordion player on the midway. (Courtesy of the Bucyrus Bratwurst Festival Committee.)

Eight

Greetings from Bucyrus

In the early 1900s, the least expense and preferred method of communication with those who lived far away was the penny postcard. Introduced as private mailing cards in the 1890s, postcards provided just enough space for writing a short note, and with the efficient mail system using passenger trains available at the time, it was possible for a person to in Bucyrus to write a postcard, mail it in the morning to Mansfield, and have a reply delivered that same night. Postcards could be location specific or contain other sentiments such as birthday, Easter, or Christmas greetings. As long-distance telephone calls became less expensive, the penny postcard's popularity declined, and postcards are now sent by vacationers, often with the note "Wish you were here."

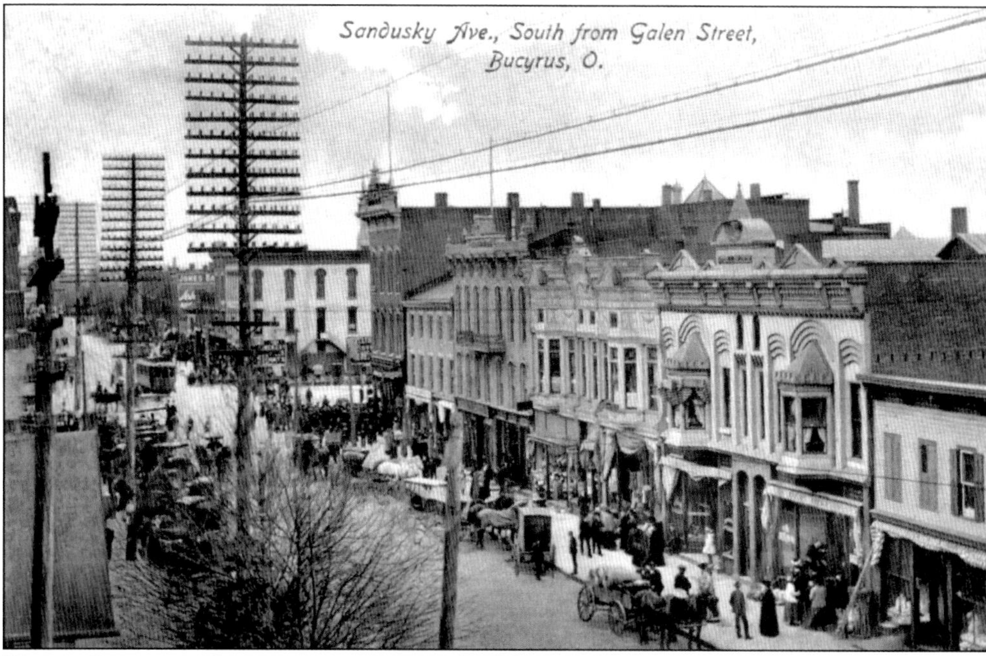

NORTH SANDUSKY STREET, 1909. Postcards of the era that were community centered, as this one is for North Sandusky Street, tried to show bustling scenes of commerce. The massive 12-rack telephone poles had room enough to carry 120 wires, but wires have been erased from the image to make the view more pleasant. (Courtesy of the Charles Spiegle collection.)

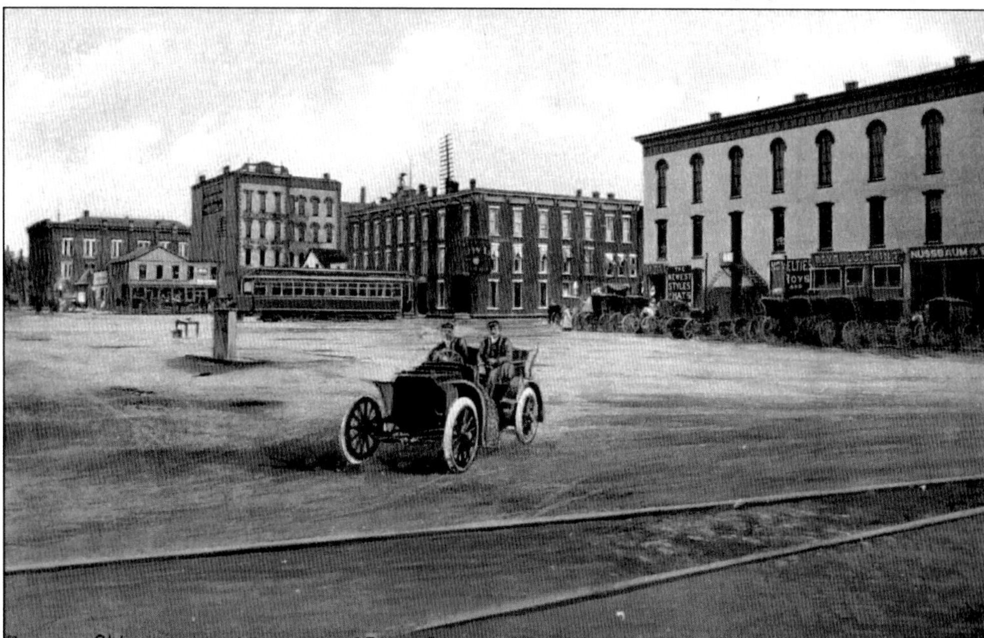

LOOKING SOUTH EAST ON WASHINGTON SQUARE, 1906. Sometimes penny postcards were doctored to include images that did not appear in the original. In this case, the automobile —still a rarity in 1906—was added to the postcard to provide additional interest to the picture. (Courtesy of Stuart Koblentz.)

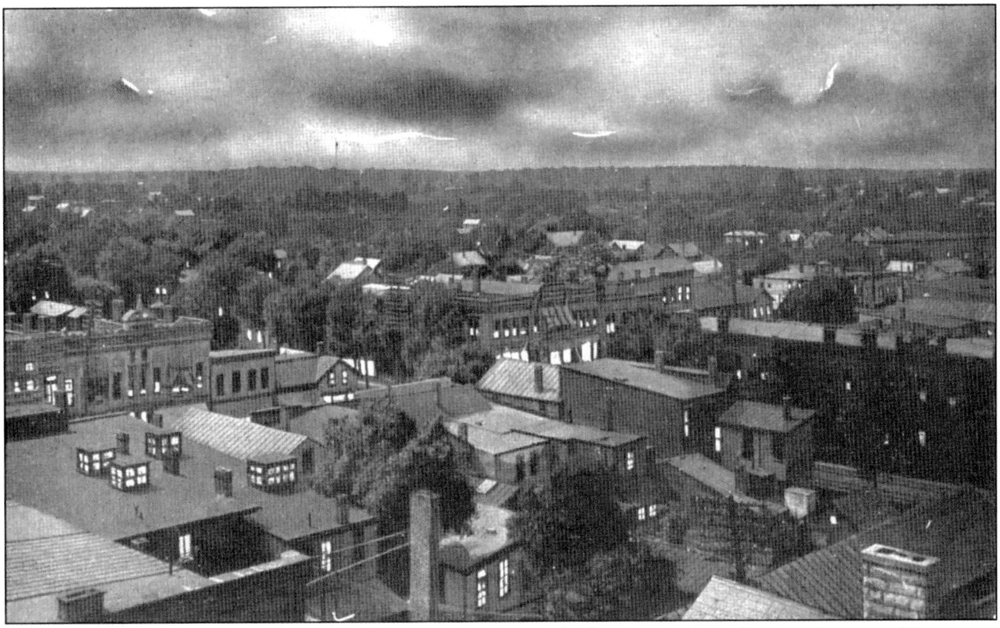

LOOKING NORTHWEST. As with the previous postcard, this is another doctored view of Bucyrus. Instructions from the postcard company to the printer of the cards in Germany stated that this was to be a nighttime view when color was applied to the original photograph, which was taken in the morning from atop the steeple of the Methodist church on Walnut Street. (Courtesy of Stuart Koblentz.)

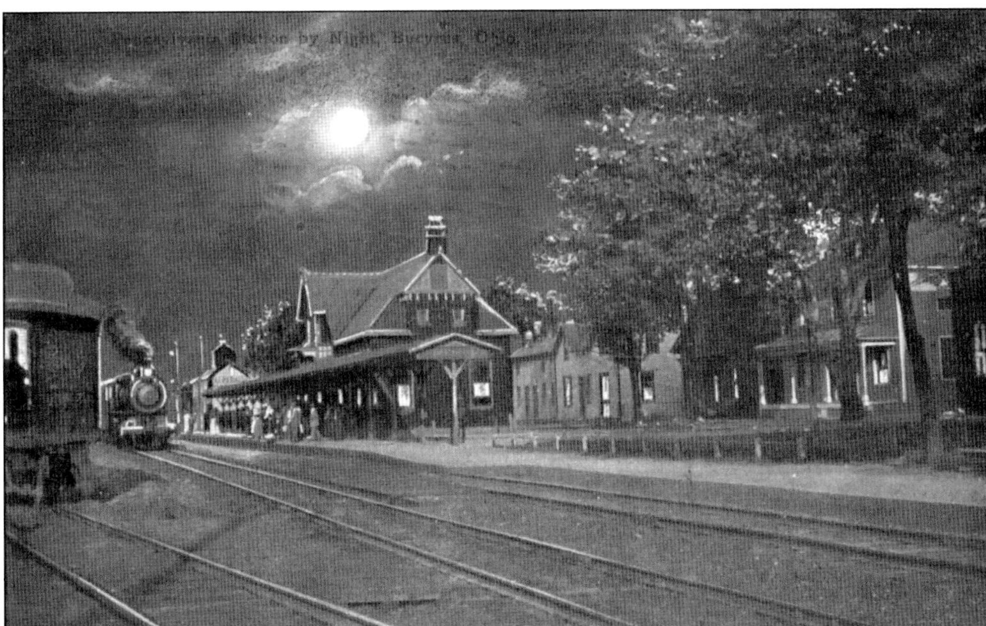

PENNSYLVANIA RAILROAD STATION. The Pennsylvania Railroad Station was located off Sandusky Street, along Railroad Street, which for many years was known as the home of Bucyrus's houses of ill fame. (Courtesy of Stuart Koblentz.)

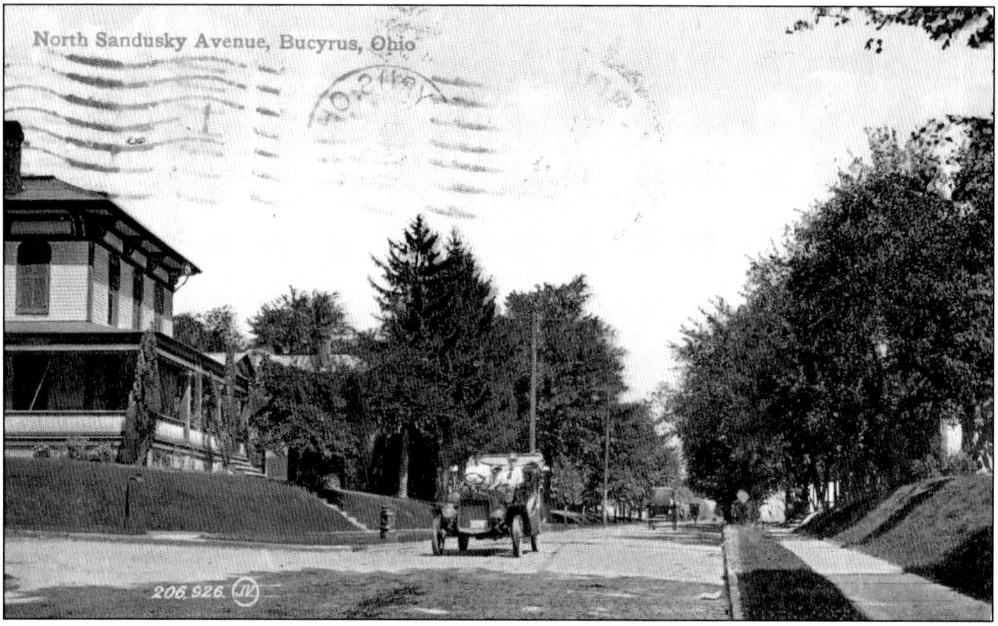

North Sandusky Avenue. Perhaps one of the most widely circulated postcards of the pre-World War I era was this view of North Sandusky "Avenue" at Hill Street, back when the area was primarily a residential neighborhood. Cards like this were produced in Germany because of the vivid dyes and color systems developed by the Germans just before the late 1800s. (Courtesy of Stuart Koblentz.)

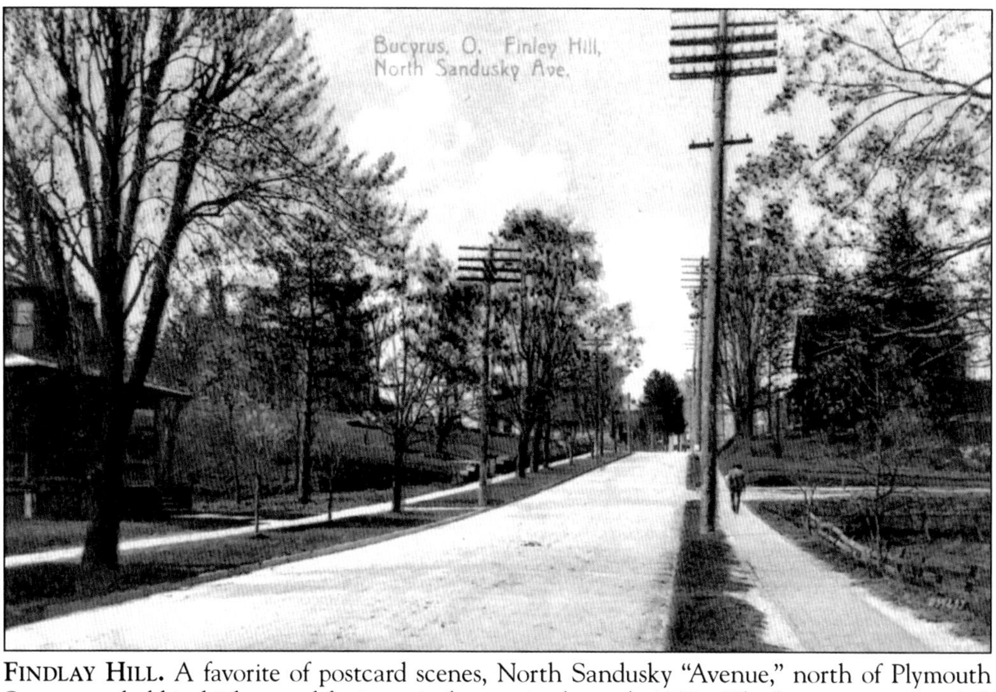

Findlay Hill. A favorite of postcard scenes, North Sandusky "Avenue," north of Plymouth Street, was held in high regard for its quiet beauty in the early 1900s. The low stone wall to left of the road marked the Tobias property, which is now the site of Bucyrus Community Hospital. (Courtesy of Don and Mary Ellen Lust.)

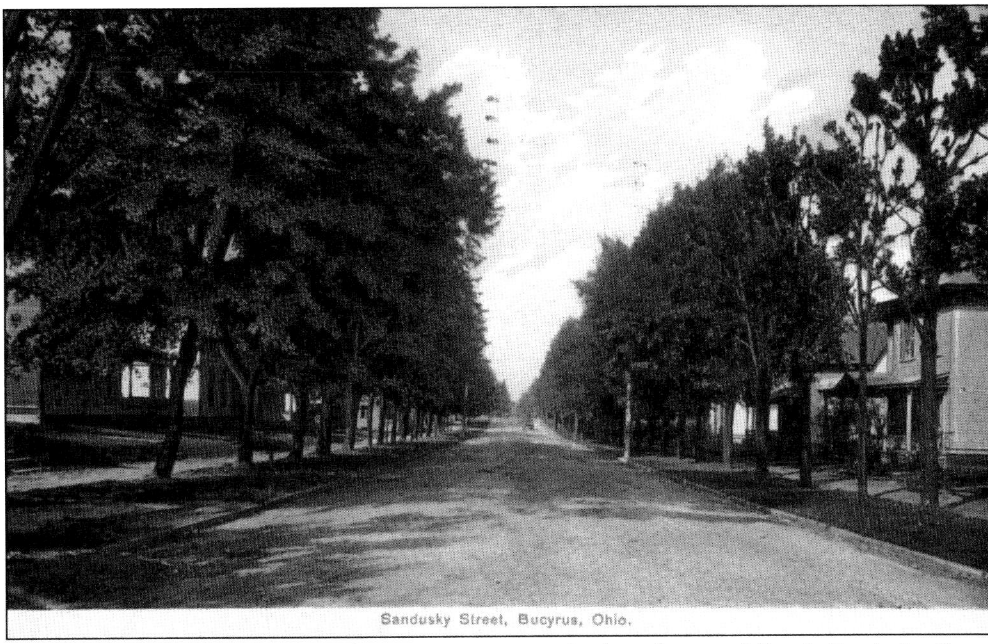

SOUTH SANDUSKY STREET. No less impressive was the broad vista of South Sandusky Street from Charles Street. Bucyrus planners wisely set aside broad street beds. Today this road is heavily traveled and designated State Routes 4 and 98. (Courtesy of Don and Mary Ellen Lust.)

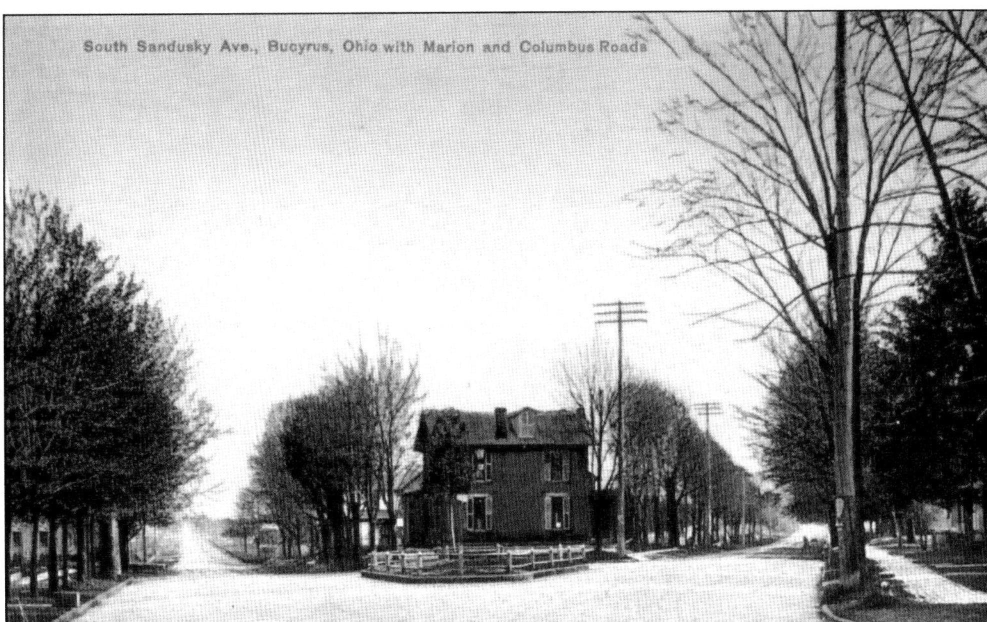

THE POINT. It is hard to imagine that there once was a time that the point where State Routes 4 and 98 merge was ever a bucolic country scene as captured in this photograph. The rail-split fence is gone, as is the small home. The First Federal Community Bank now stands on the point, and the roads are busy with traffic. (Courtesy of Stuart Koblentz.)

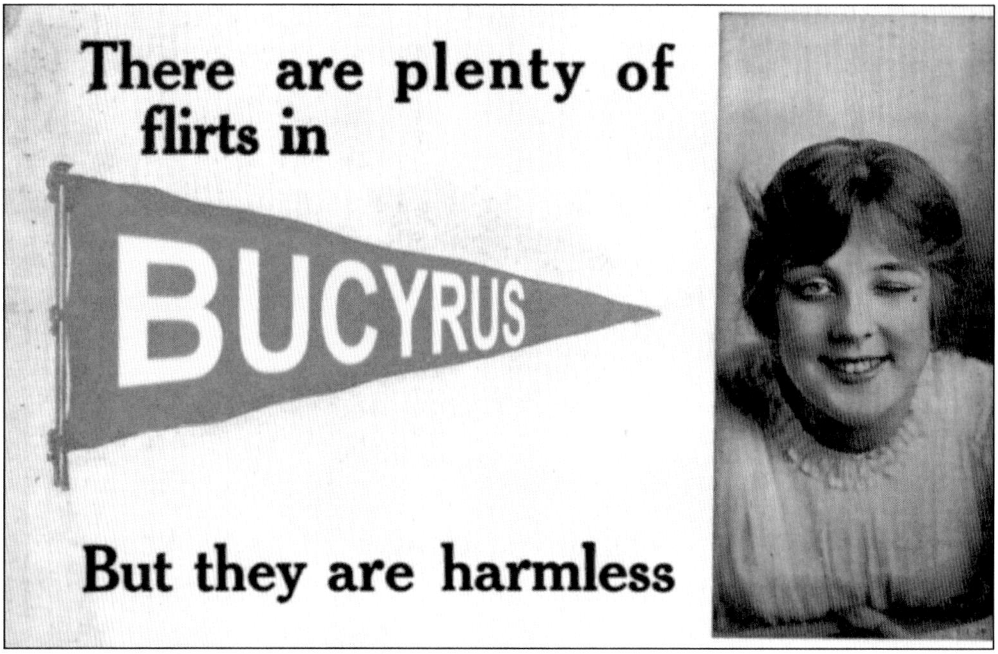

FLIRT ALERT! This is an example of a generic postcard that was customized in 1915 for sale in Bucyrus and was about as racy as they came in those days. Similar cards were sold in Marion, Columbus, and Findlay. Still, it does beg the question are there still plenty of flirts in Bucyrus? (Courtesy of Stuart Koblentz.)

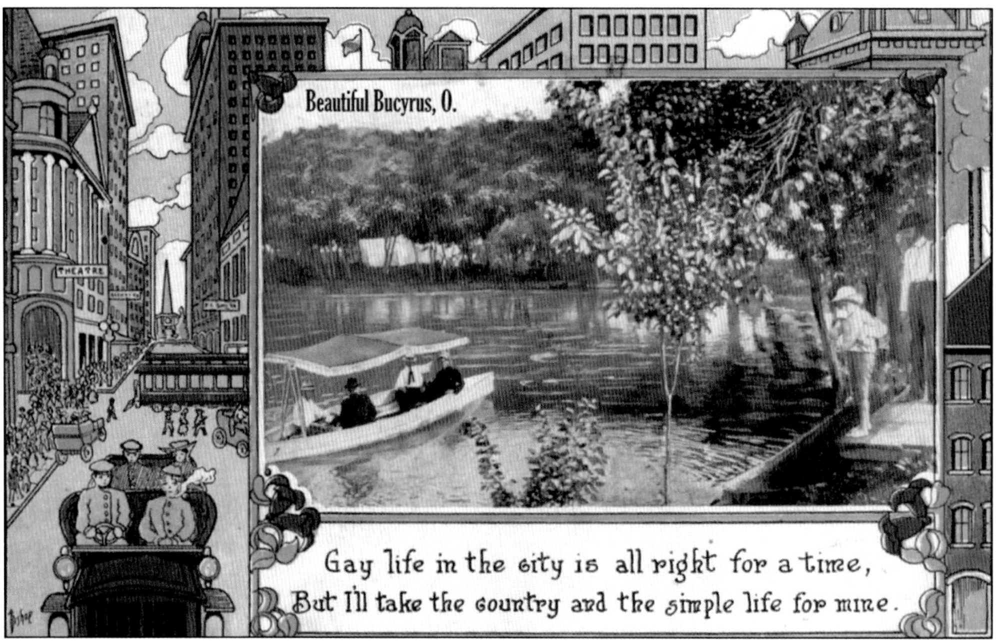

BEAUTIFUL BUCYRUS. Another generic card customized for Bucyrus shows a tranquil water scene. This card, published in 1909, also includes ornate line drawings. Note that the man and woman in the car are wearing dusters. (Courtesy of Stuart Koblentz.)

Nine

At Home in Bucyrus

For some people, an old house is just a building, something to tear down for a cinder block building and other forms of bland progress. For others, the houses of yesteryear capture the eye and the imagination of days gone by—a time when a home could truly be as unique as the person who lived in it. In some cases, such as the Monnette-Fisher mansion, it is too late. But Bucyrus is blessed with many examples of architecture that are second to none. Understanding these structures will lend itself to their future preservation for generations to come.

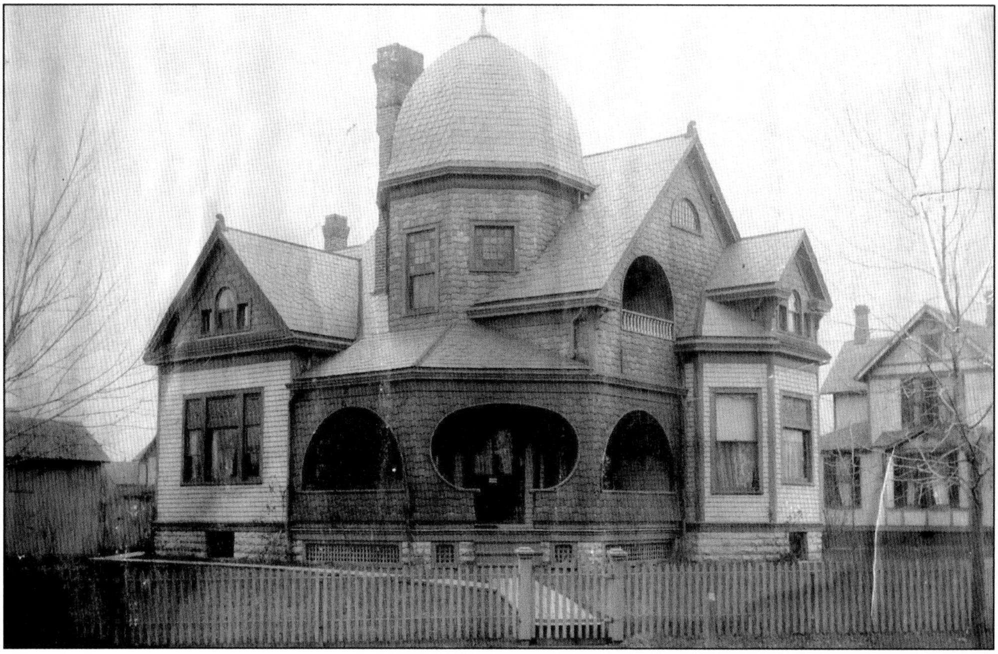

SMITH W. BENNETT RESIDENCE. Perhaps one of the best examples of the Queen Ann shingle style of Victorian architecture in Bucyrus is the S. W. Bennett home. Designed to fit the lot with maximized exposures, this charming cottage is still stands at 432 Hopley Avenue. (Courtesy of the Bucyrus Historical Society.)

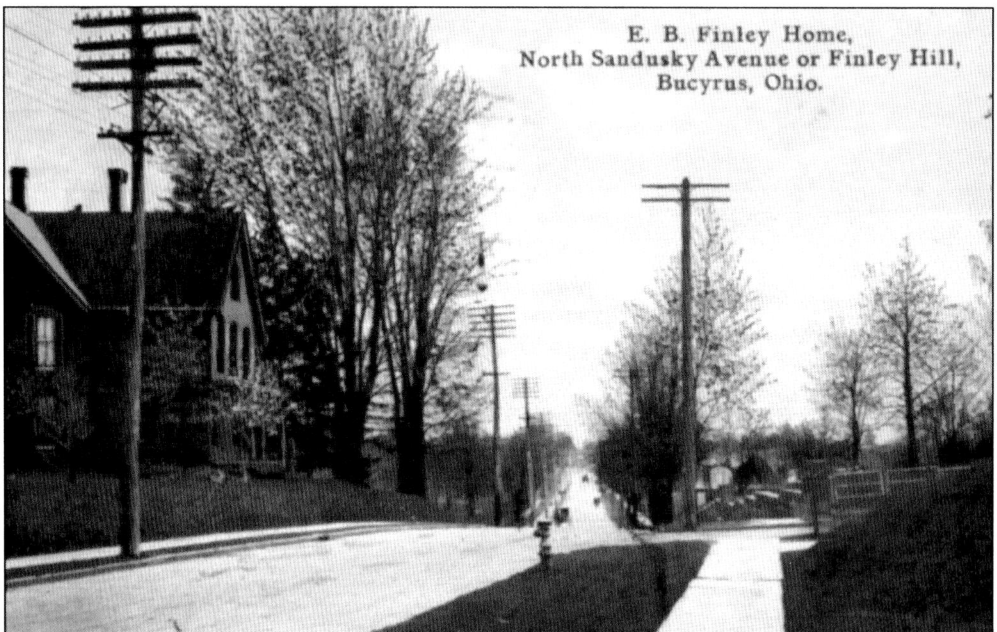

FINLEY RESIDENCE. The Finley residence once stood on the hill of the same name where North Sandusky and Plymouth Streets intersect. The Gothic style brick house was razed for commercial development, and at one time the site housed Bucyrus's Borden Burger Food-A-Rama fast-food restaurant. (Courtesy of Don and Mary Ellen Lust.)

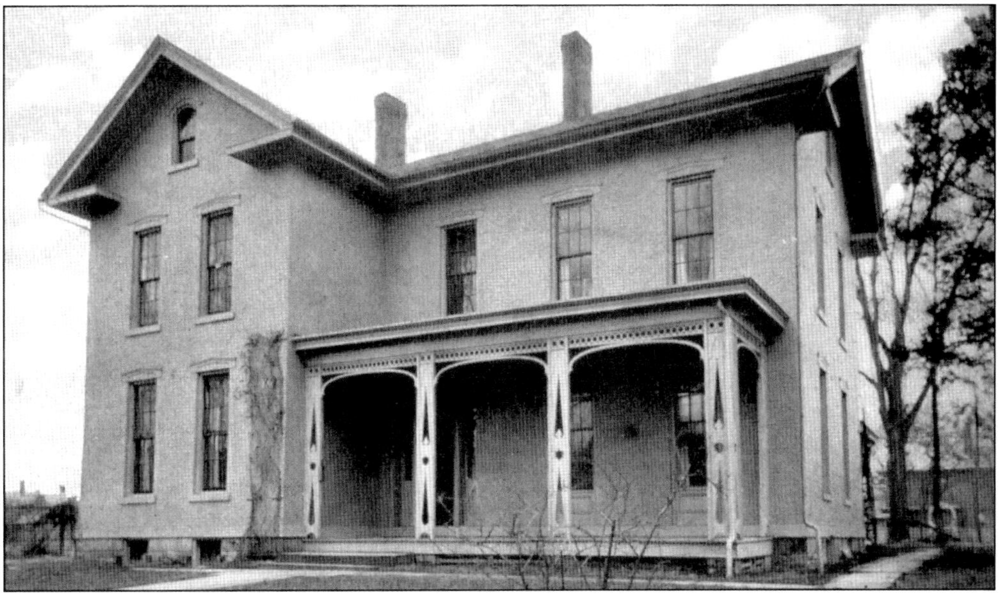

KINGS DAUGHTERS HOME, ROGERS STREET. Originally built by Horace Rouse, and later known as Rose Ridge, this large brick home was chosen by the In As Much Circle of Kings Daughters, a charitable organization, for its children's home because of its size. One uncommon feature about the house was its delicate carpenter Gothic porch supports, which were designed to be beautiful in themselves and to cast interesting shadows on the porch as the sunshine passed over them each morning. (Courtesy of Stuart Koblentz.)

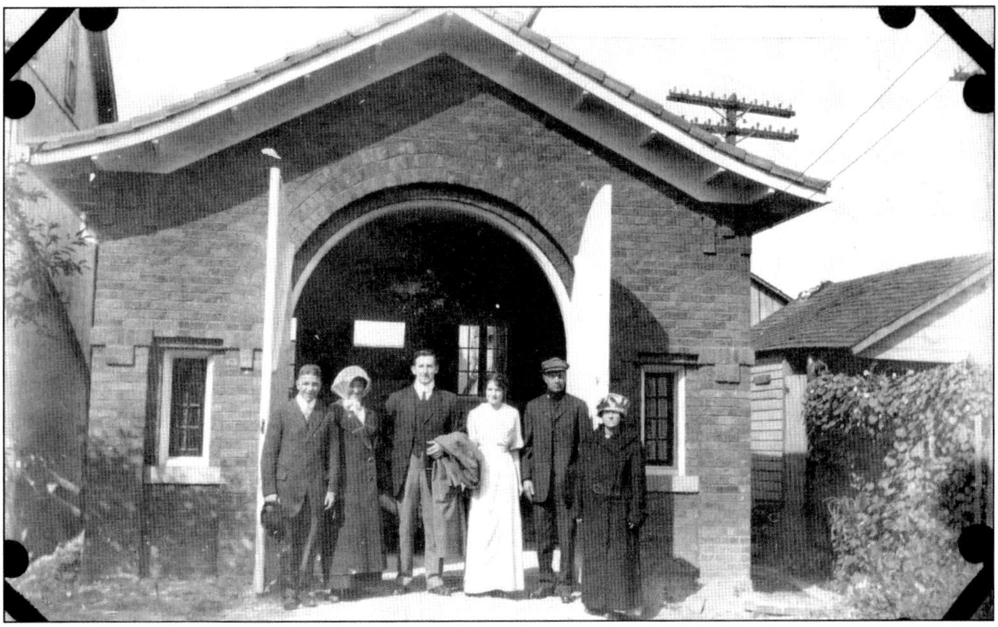

SHUNK STABLES, EAST MANSFIELD STREET. Members of the Shunk Family pose outside of their home's stable, once located to the rear of their property on East Mansfield Street. The Shunk's were avid early motorists, traveling on unimproved roads as far away as Prospect to picnic during the summer. The family ultimately replaced the stables with a more usable garage when automobiles became the norm rather than the exception. (Courtesy of the Bucyrus Historical Society.)

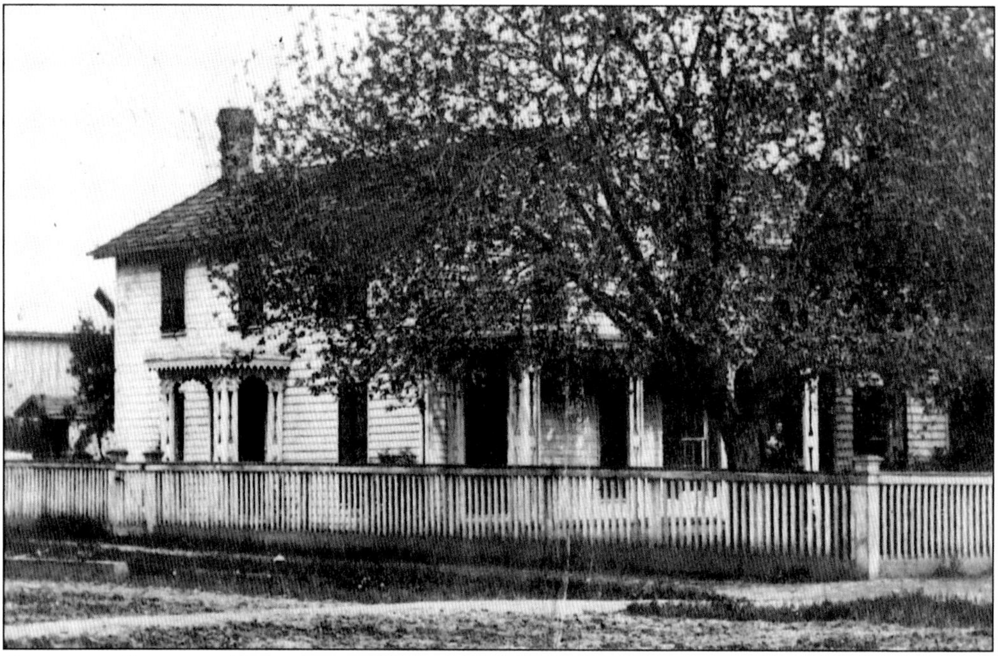

ORIGINAL SCROGGS RESIDENCE. While best known as the spacious home of the Bucyrus Historical Society, the Scroggs house was originally much smaller than the current structure. The house was enlarged after the Civil War; part of the original house was kept as the kitchen wing of the current structure. (Courtesy of the Bucyrus Historical Society.)

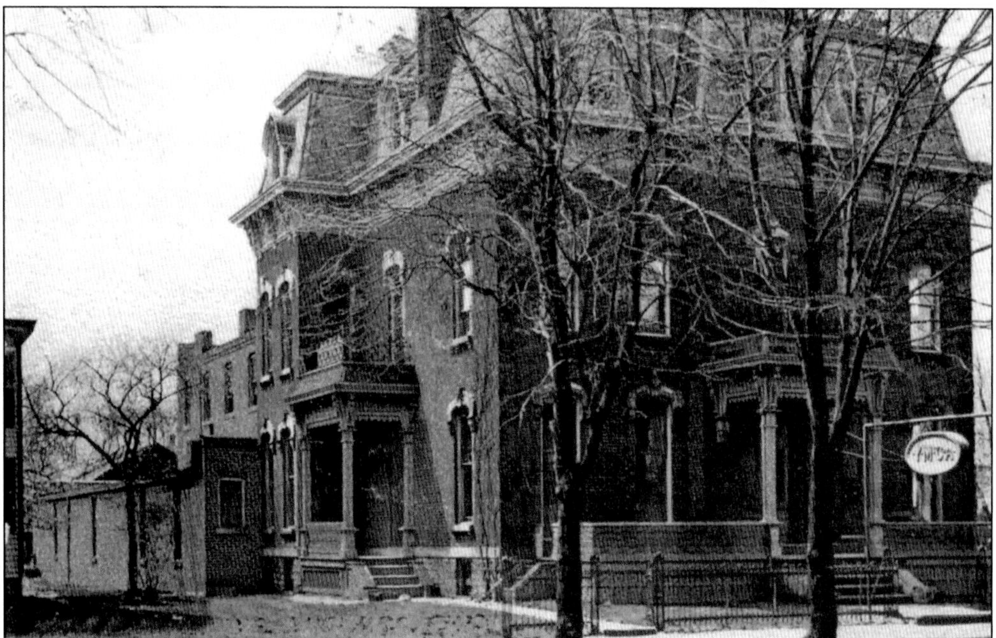

DEAL RESIDENCE. This Second Empire home still stands on East Mansfield Street but is camouflaged behind the facade of the former YMCA. The Deal family operated the Deal House hotel, formerly located on the southeast corner of Washington Square. (Courtesy of the Bucyrus Historical Society.)

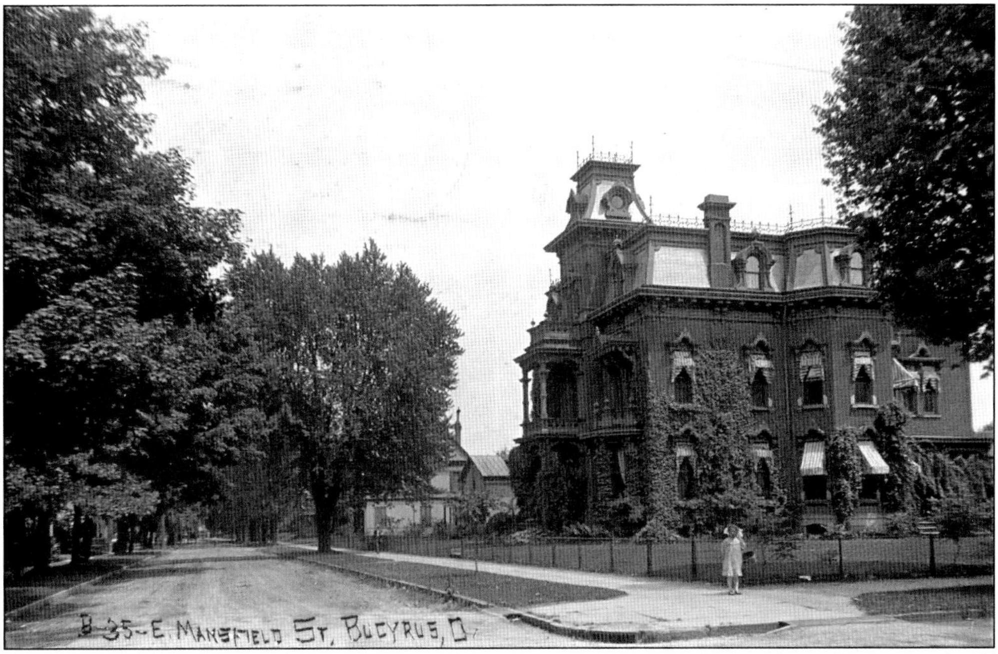

KEARSLEY MANSION. Bucyrus's most elaborate Second Empire-designed residence was built on East Mansfield Street by Edmund Kearsley. The brick house contained over 20 rooms, including the third-floor ballroom, bay windows, and numerous balconies. (Courtesy of the Bucyrus Historical Society.)

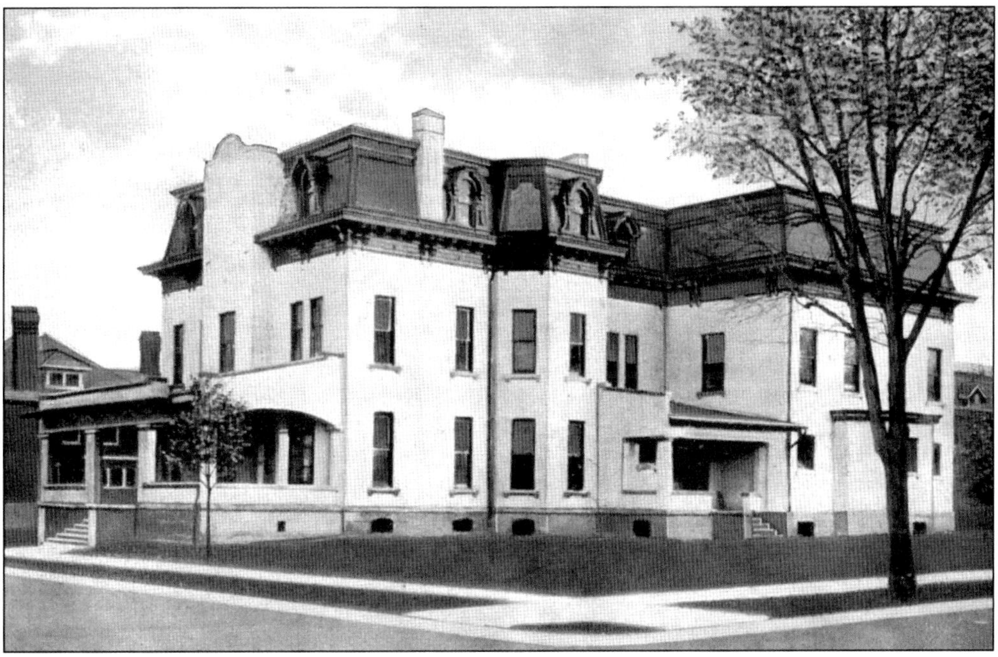

ELKS LODGE. In the early 20th century, the Kearsley mansion on East Mansfield Street was purchased by the Elks Lodge and modernized through the removal of much of its Victorian decorative trim and the covering of the brick with a stucco finish. (Courtesy of Stuart Koblentz.)

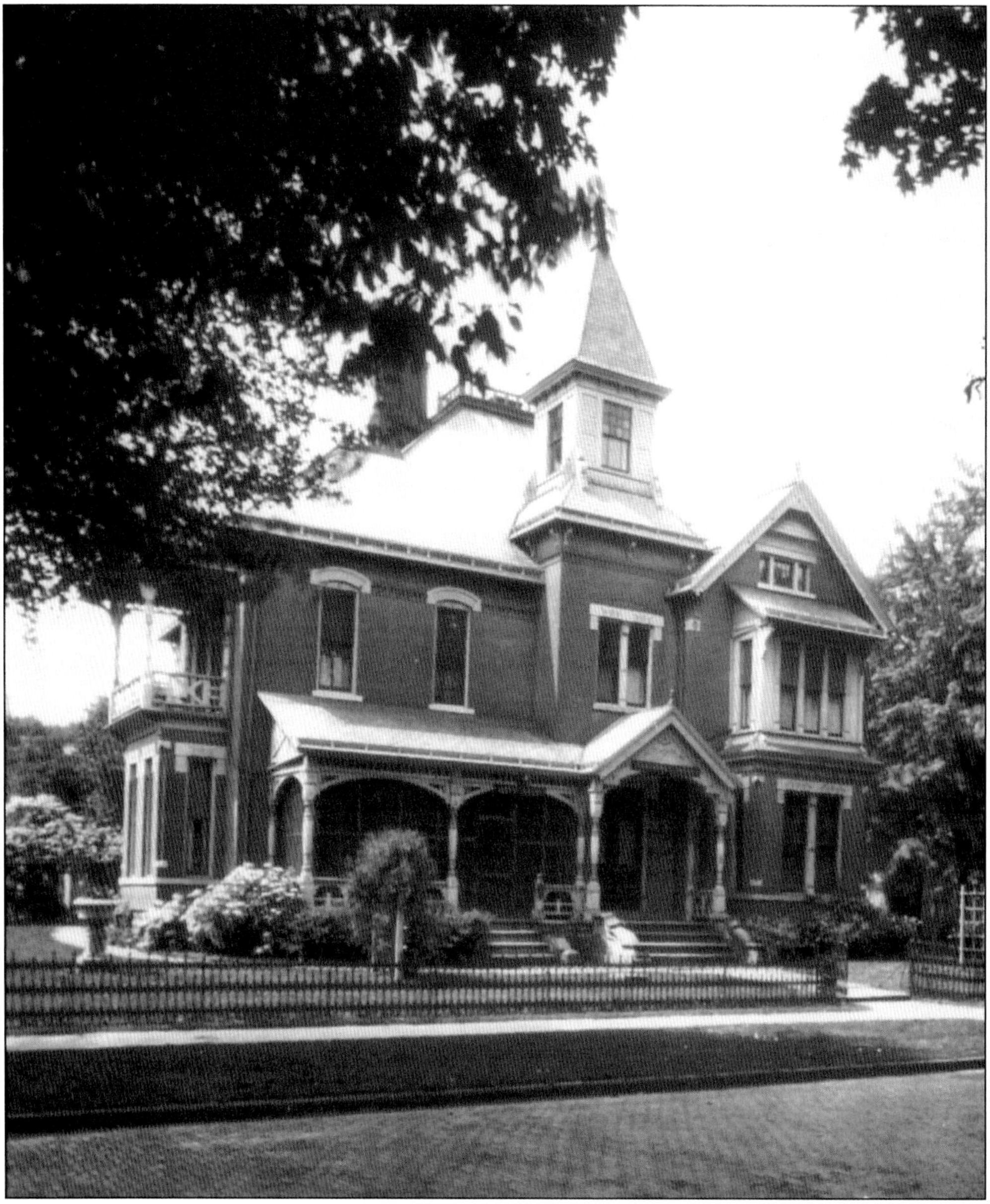

Mervin Monnette Mansion, 125 West Rensselaer Street. Mervin J. Monnette purposely chose the corner of Rensselaer and Poplar Streets for the construction of this imposing mansion in the 1880s. The house was designed in the Eastlake Victorian style and built to impress, as no expense was spared in its construction that included pressurized water and electric lights. (Courtesy of the Bucyrus Historical Society.)

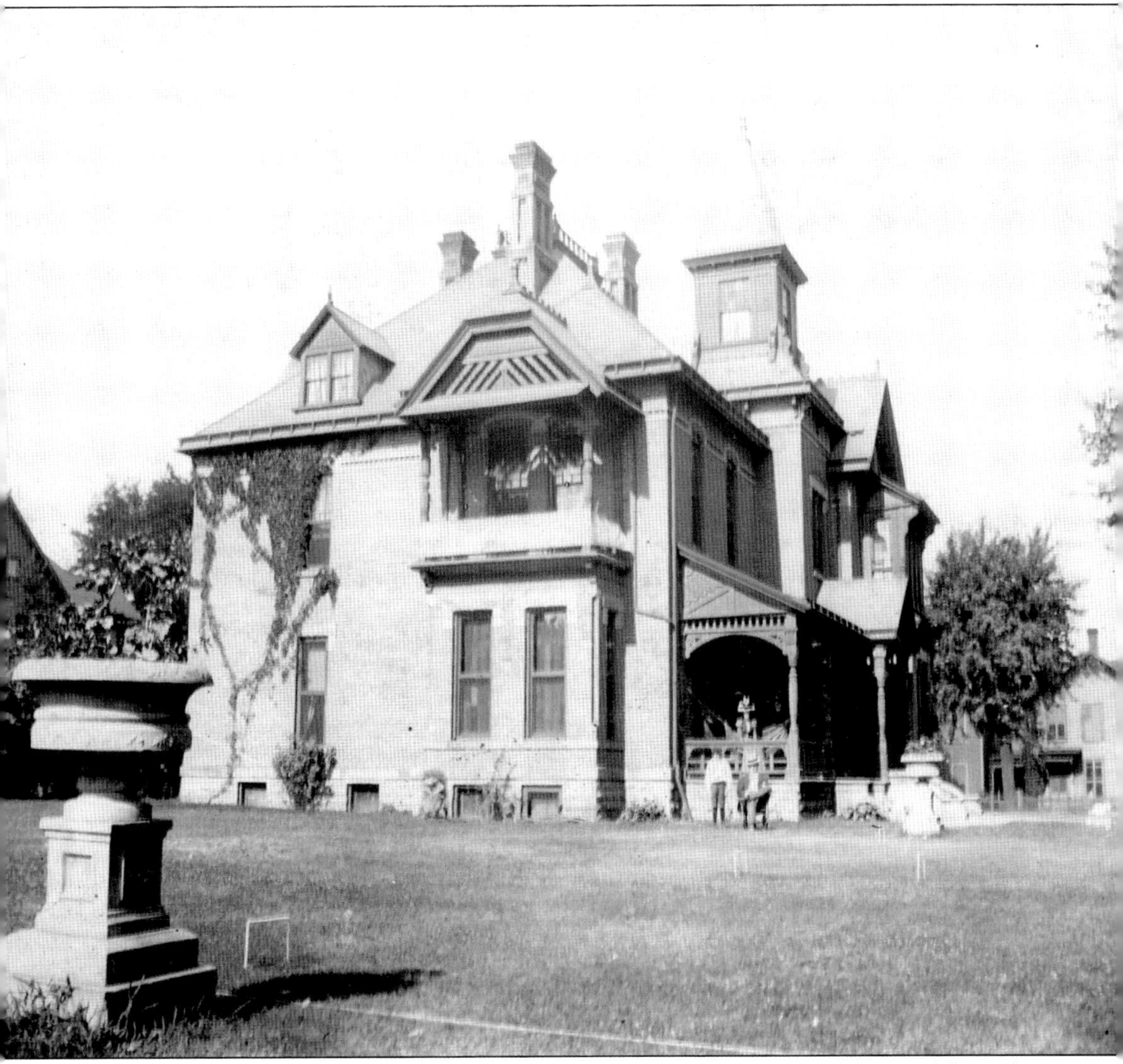

MONNETTE-FISHER RESIDENCE, EAST FACADE. Mervin J. Monnette chose the Eastlake style when building his mansion, which celebrated the then-novel idea that woodwork could be mass-produced by machine instead of handcrafted. Eastlake characteristics include repetition of pattern and upright lines, eschewing the rounded forms found in Queen Anne–style houses of the same era. (Courtesy of the Bucyrus Historical Society.)

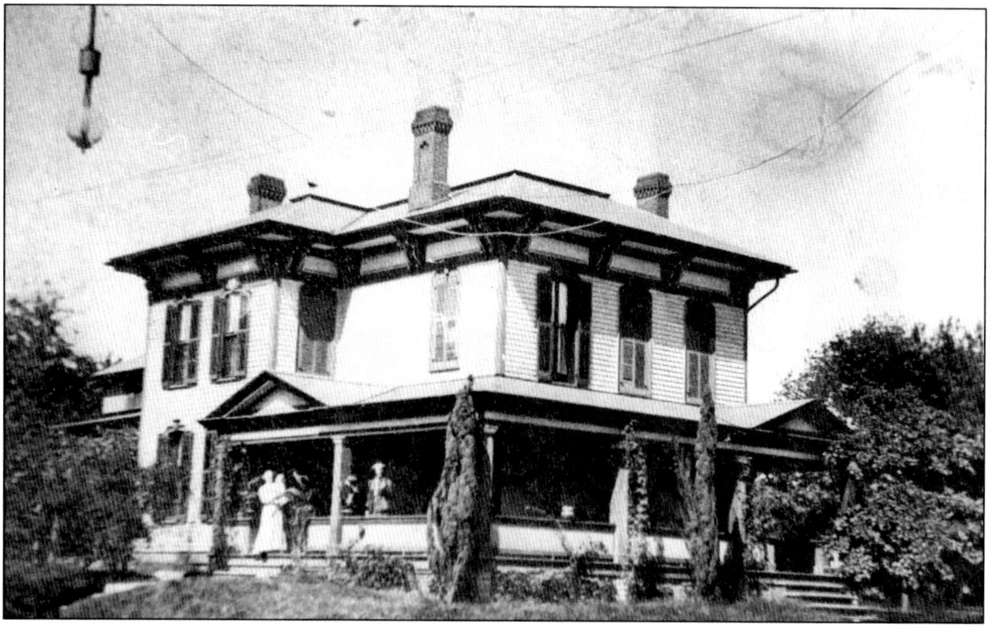

JAMES MALCOLM RESIDENCE. Located at 705 North Sandusky Street (at Gaius Street) is the former city home of James and Elsie Malcolm. Built in the Italianate style, the house was featured on one of the more popular postcards from the early 20th century of Bucyrus, which shows that the house was once painted yellow with green trim. It has since been converted to apartments. (Courtesy of Stuart Koblentz.)

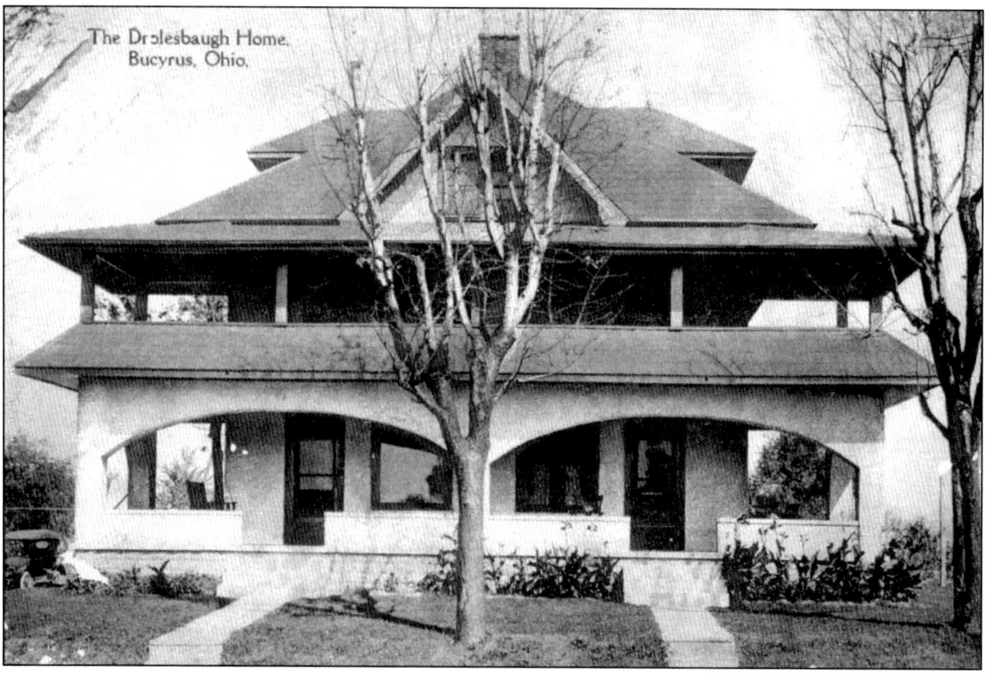

DROLESBAUGH HOME. One of the more eclectic residences in Bucyrus was the Drolesbaugh family home. The house was built in a plain fashion; however, the Drolesbaughs customized their home with large verandas and outside galleries. (Courtesy of the Bucyrus Historical Society.)

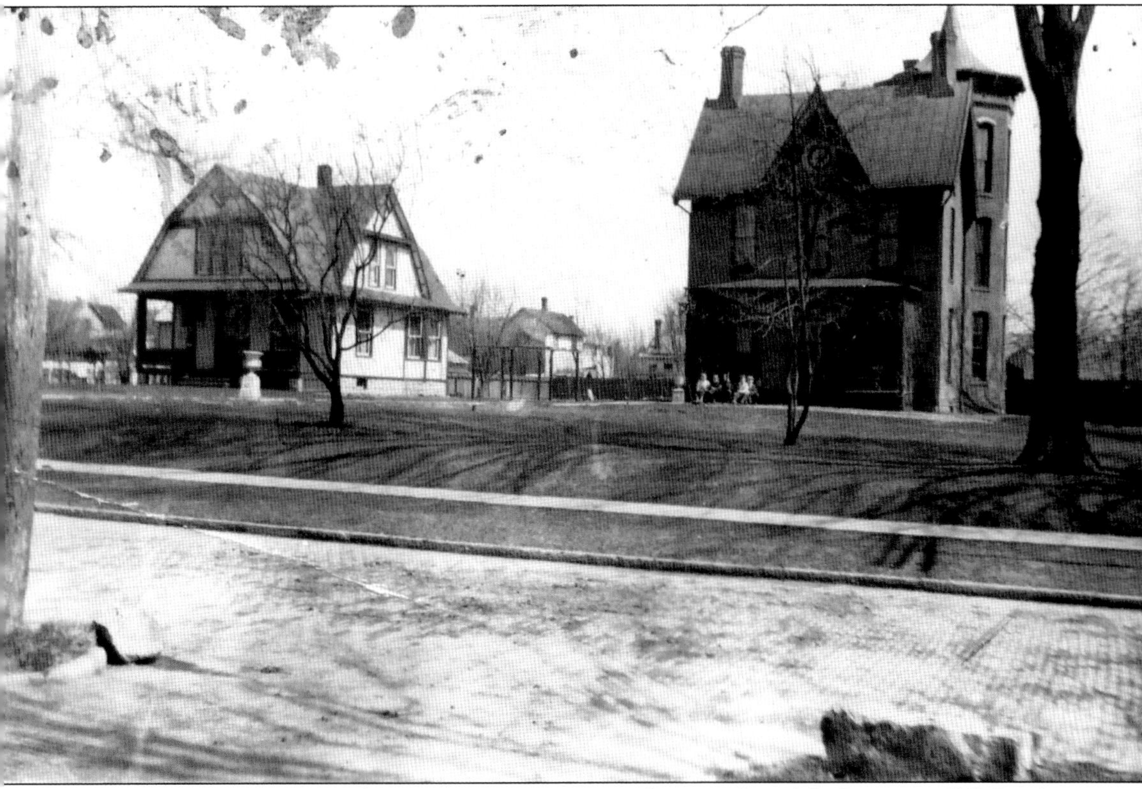

ROSEDALE COTTAGE. One of Bucyrus's most unique residences is Rosedale Cottage at 548 South East Street. Built by Stephan R. Harris in 1863, the house, with its side tower, was an exact copy of the Gothic-style cottage in which Harris was raised in England. Harris married Mary Jane Monnett; their daughter Sallie married Rufus Sears, and the house remained in the family until 1966. Harris's daughter Nellie bequeathed a substantial gift to the Bucyrus Public Library at her death. Rosedale Cottage was listed on the National Register of Historic Places in 1980. (Courtesy of the Bucyrus Historical Society.)

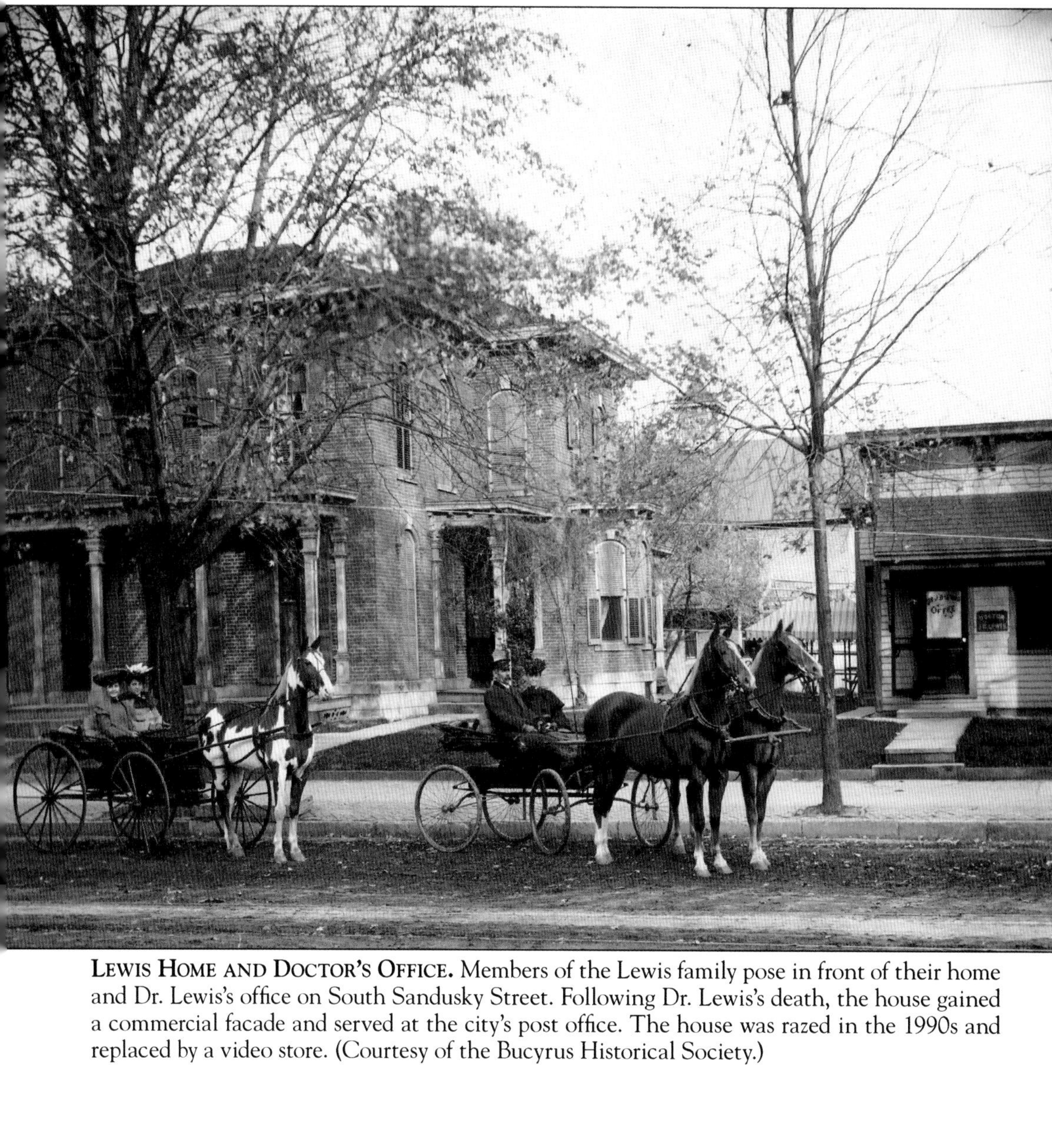

LEWIS HOME AND DOCTOR'S OFFICE. Members of the Lewis family pose in front of their home and Dr. Lewis's office on South Sandusky Street. Following Dr. Lewis's death, the house gained a commercial facade and served at the city's post office. The house was razed in the 1990s and replaced by a video store. (Courtesy of the Bucyrus Historical Society.)

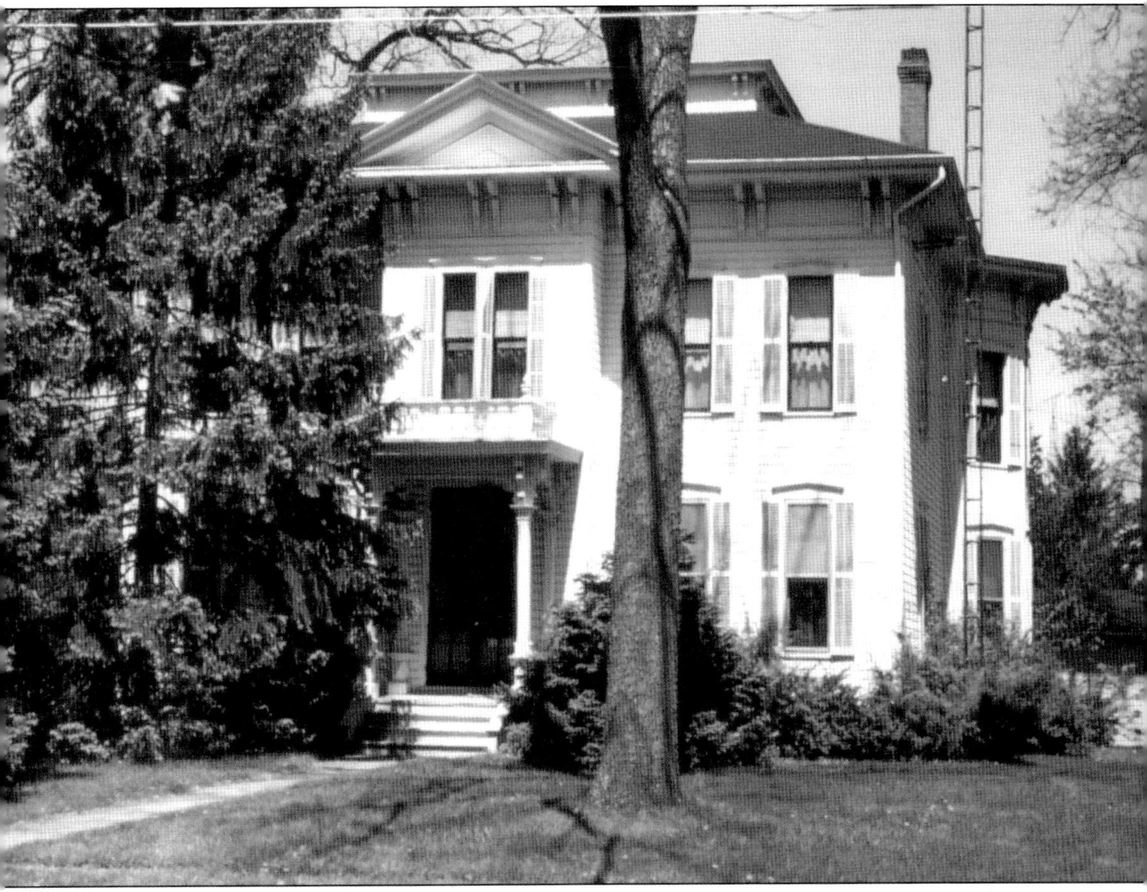

JUDGE THOMAS BEER RESIDENCE. Located at 306 West Southern Avenue is the Judge Thomas Beer residence. The Beer family lived in the home until 1977, when it was sold to the Zahn family. Both the Beer home and the Scroggs residence (now the Bucyrus Historical Society) were built by contractor George Ross. (Courtesy of the Bucyrus Historical Society.)

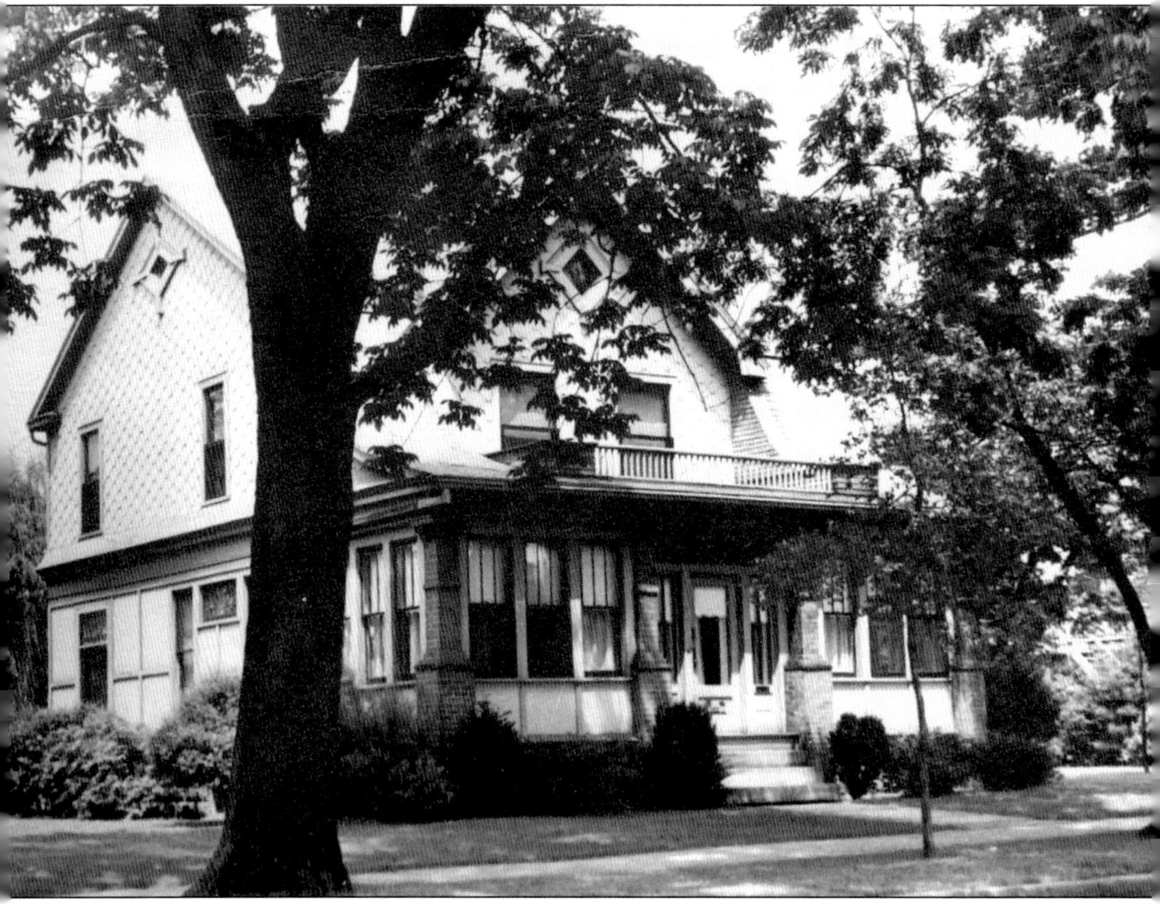

THE ROBERT PICKING HOUSE. Located on East Rensselaer Street is the Robert Picking residence, which now houses the Bucyrus Area Chamber of Commerce. The Picking residence is an example of a transitional style of architecture often referred to as the Picturesque style because of its storybook feel achieved through the combination of its neoclassical and Victorian elements. (Courtesy of Helen Picking Neff.)

Ten

SIX OF ONE

In compiling this book it became apparent that there were some photographs that could have fit in many chapters, and others that lacked a specific place in the arrangement of the book where they would have been at home. In discussing these particular images with various people who helped with this book, each one agreed that the inclusion of these images would preserve a special part of the past that helped to make Bucyrus the community it is today. Each photograph has a compelling story behind it. In some images it is possible to see people as they have never been seen. These visual odds and ends follow in this chapter.

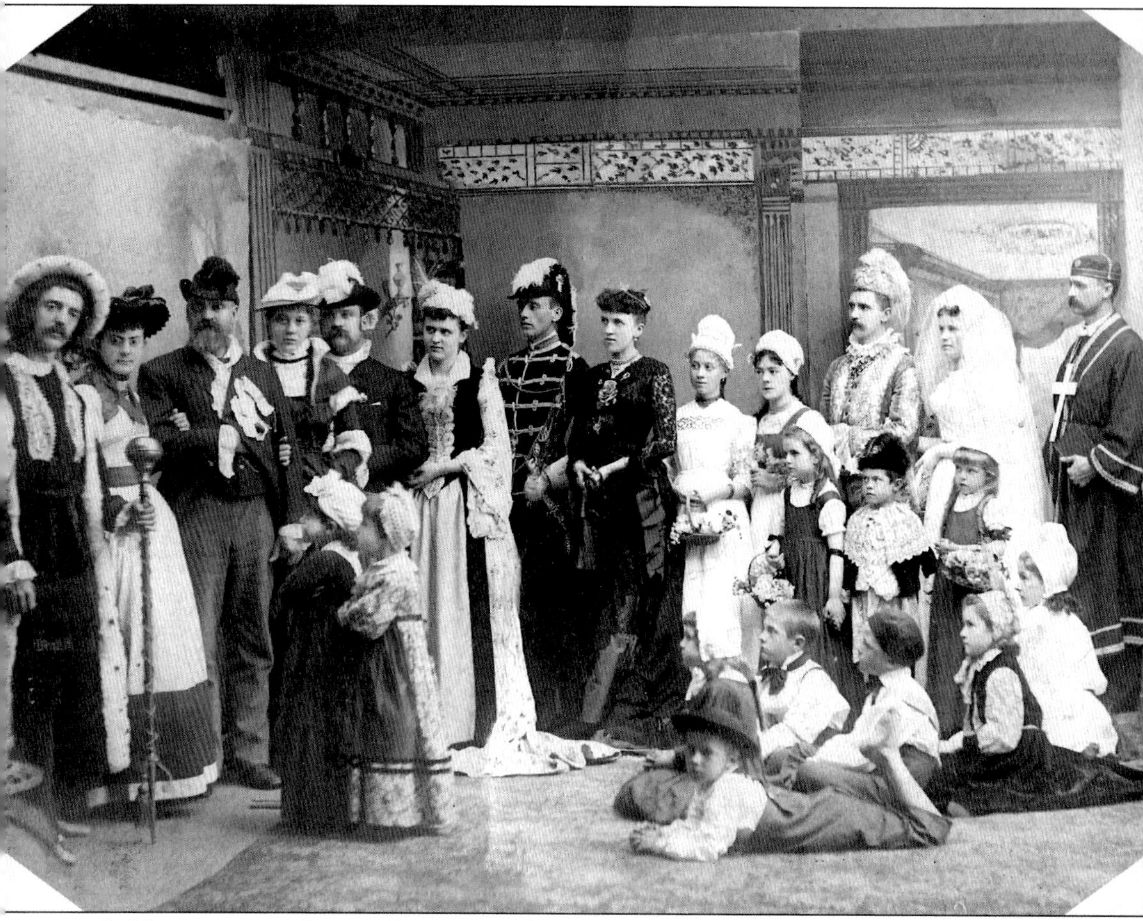

A Night at the Light Opera. Local residents pose in costume at the opera house that was once located in the Vollrath Building. Standing on the left is William Monnett, Annetta Monnett Gregory, and their father Ephraim Monnett, third from left. Melvin Monnett is fifth from left, Guy Monnett is seventh from left, and Sallie Harris is standing 10th from the left. Nella Ross is the third child standing from the right (with a flower basket), and her second cousin, Edna Gregory, is standing in front of the bride. (Courtesy of Nancy Clague.)

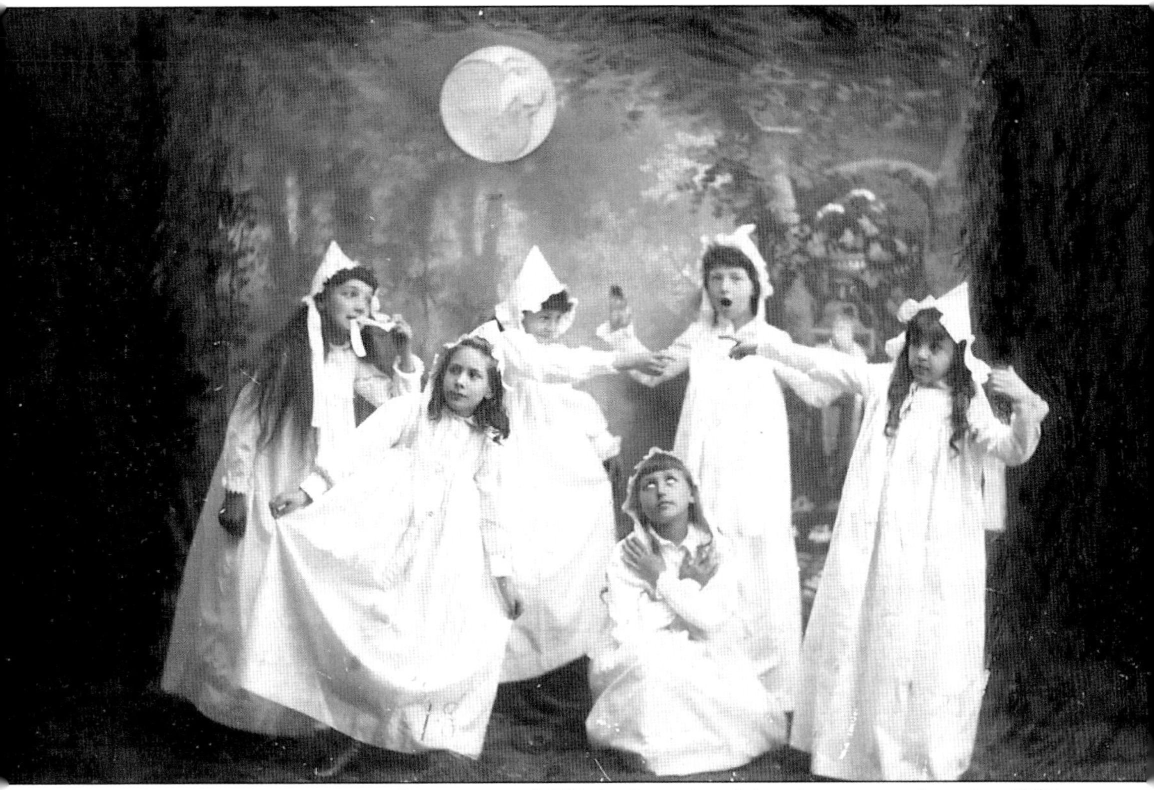

BEWITCHED, BOTHERED, AND BEWILDERED? While the title of the play captured in this 1888 photograph is unknown, what is recorded is that local children appeared in the production at the opera house. They are, from left to right, Mina Retter, Emma Workman, Lillie Ruther, Nita Keil, Iva Buger, and Nella Ross. (Courtesy of Nancy Clague.)

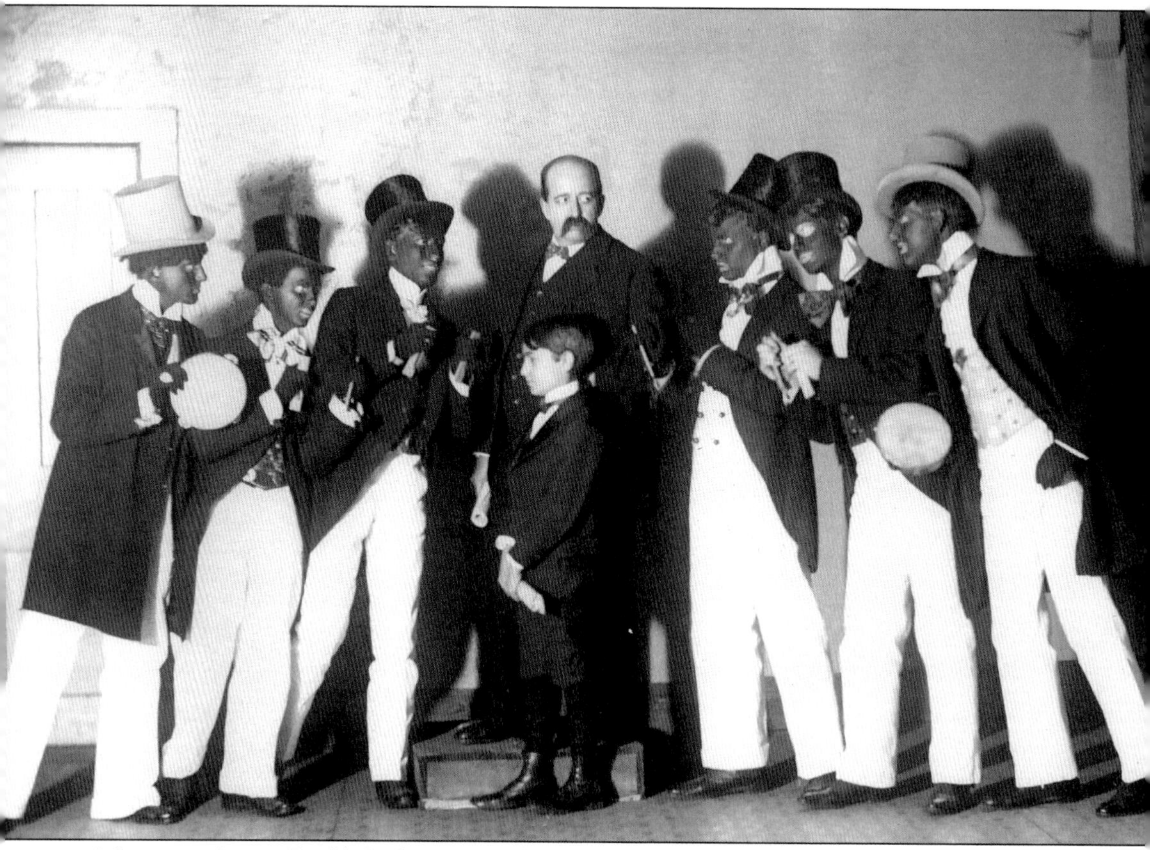

MINSTREL SHOW. Established at a time when minstrel shows were common and in great demand as entertainment, this troupe was organized by Charles Picking for his sons and their friends. This troupe performed in Bucyrus and in neighboring communities, often in churches on off days and nights. Robert Picking is third from left, and Wilfred Picking is third from right. Charles Picking stands in the center, in his role as the troupe's interlocutor. (Courtesy of Helen Picking Neff.)

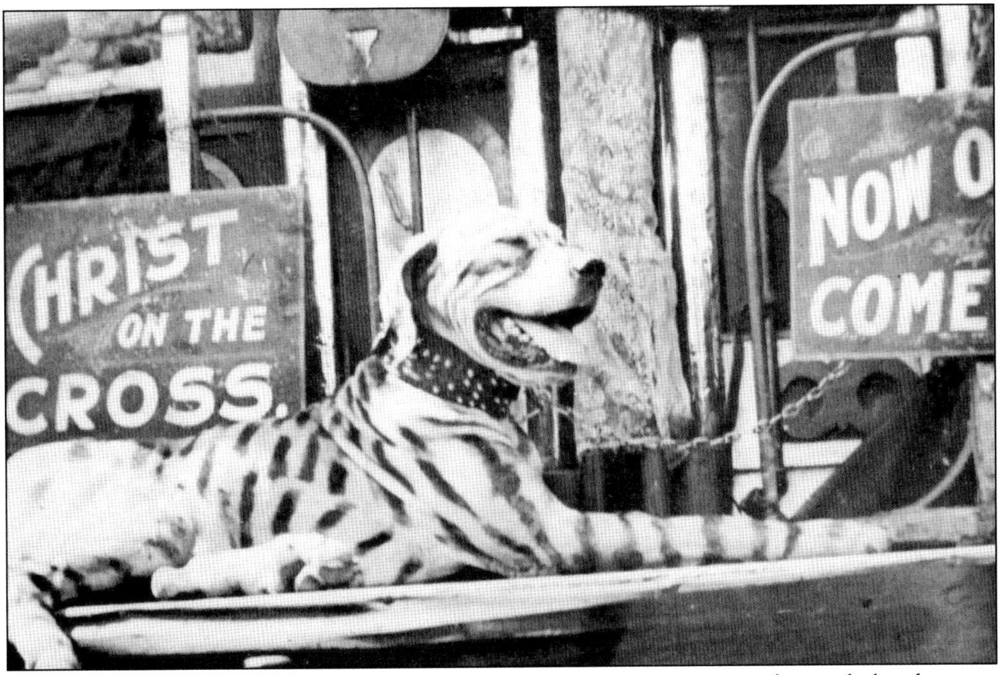

Dog-Tired Tiger. One of the sideshows at the 1910 Crawford County Fair featured a brief passion play of sorts. The troupe reenacted the crucifixion of Jesus Christ, but lacking a tiger, painted boot-black stripes on the producer's dog, and a star was born. (Courtesy of Stuart Koblentz.)

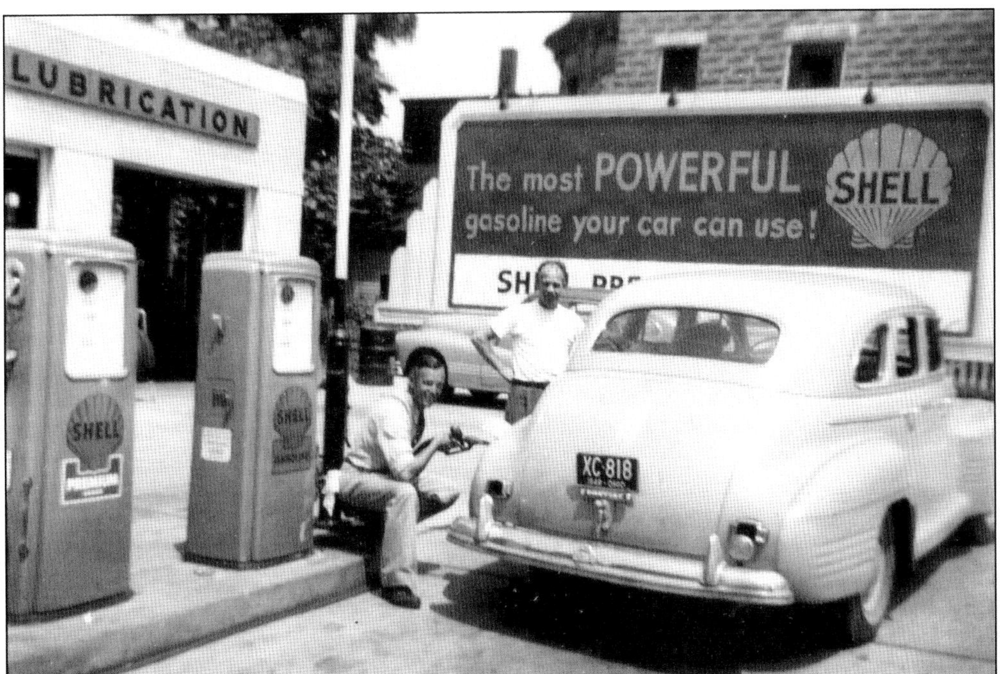

Service With a Smile. There once was a time when filling up the car with gasoline was both inexpensive and a duty that gas stations performed for their customers. Gas stations also changed oil, fixed breaks, and tuned cars up as well. (Courtesy of the Driscoll family.)

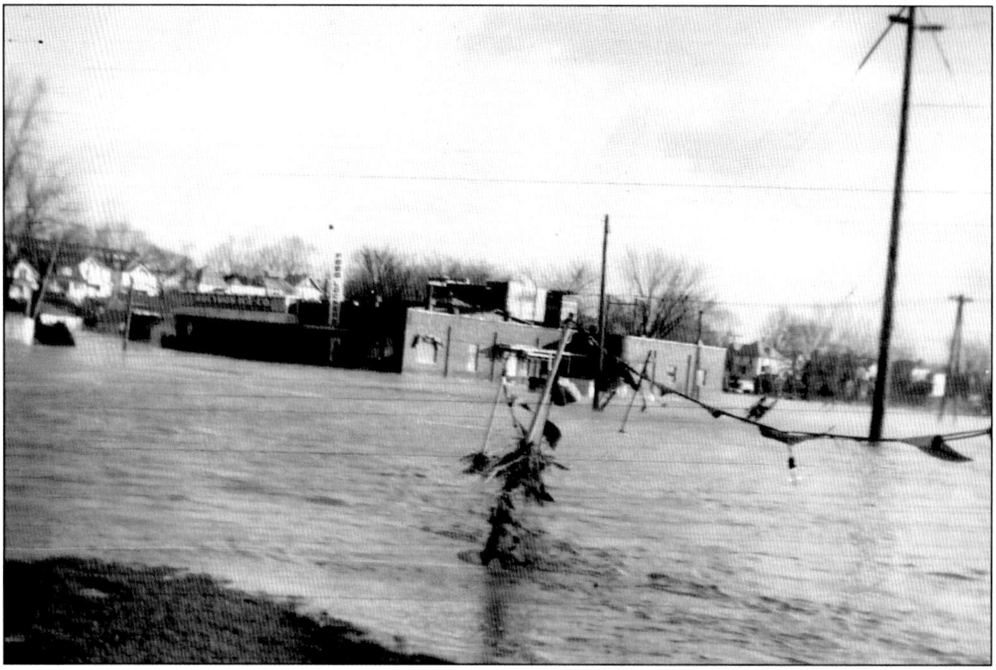

ICE WATER. The second major flood to hit Bucyrus occurred in 1957. While not the magnitude of the 1913 flood, the rising tide did surround the Bucyrus Ice Company plant, and thus, Bucyrus also had plenty of ice water. (Courtesy of the Rittenhour family.)

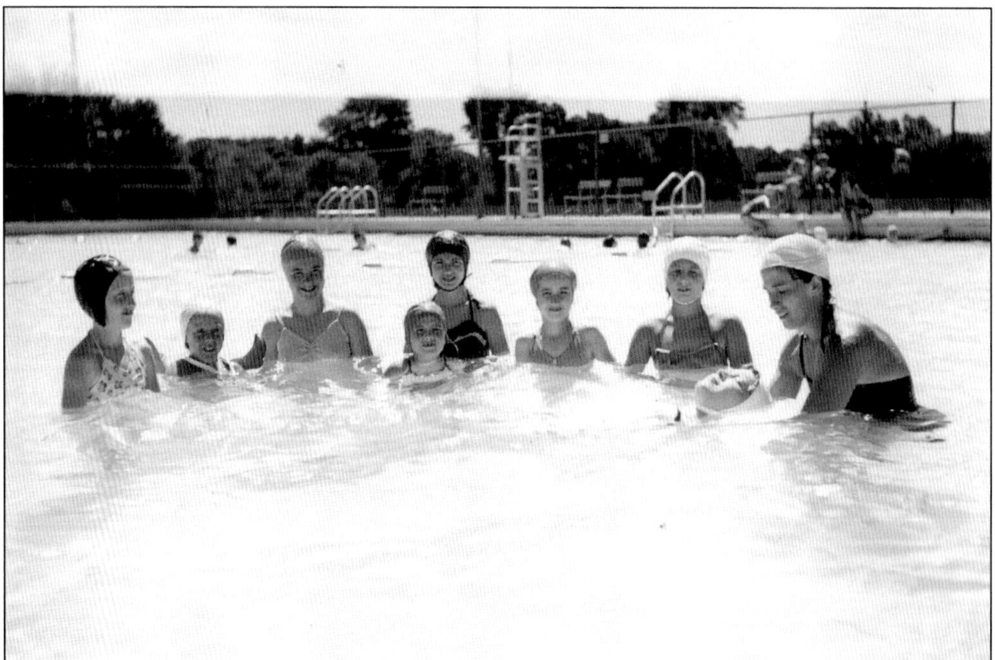

SWIMMING LESSONS. Something that almost every child in Bucyrus experienced were Red Cross swimming lessons at Aumiller Park Pool, on the west side of town. (Courtesy of the Rittenhour family.)

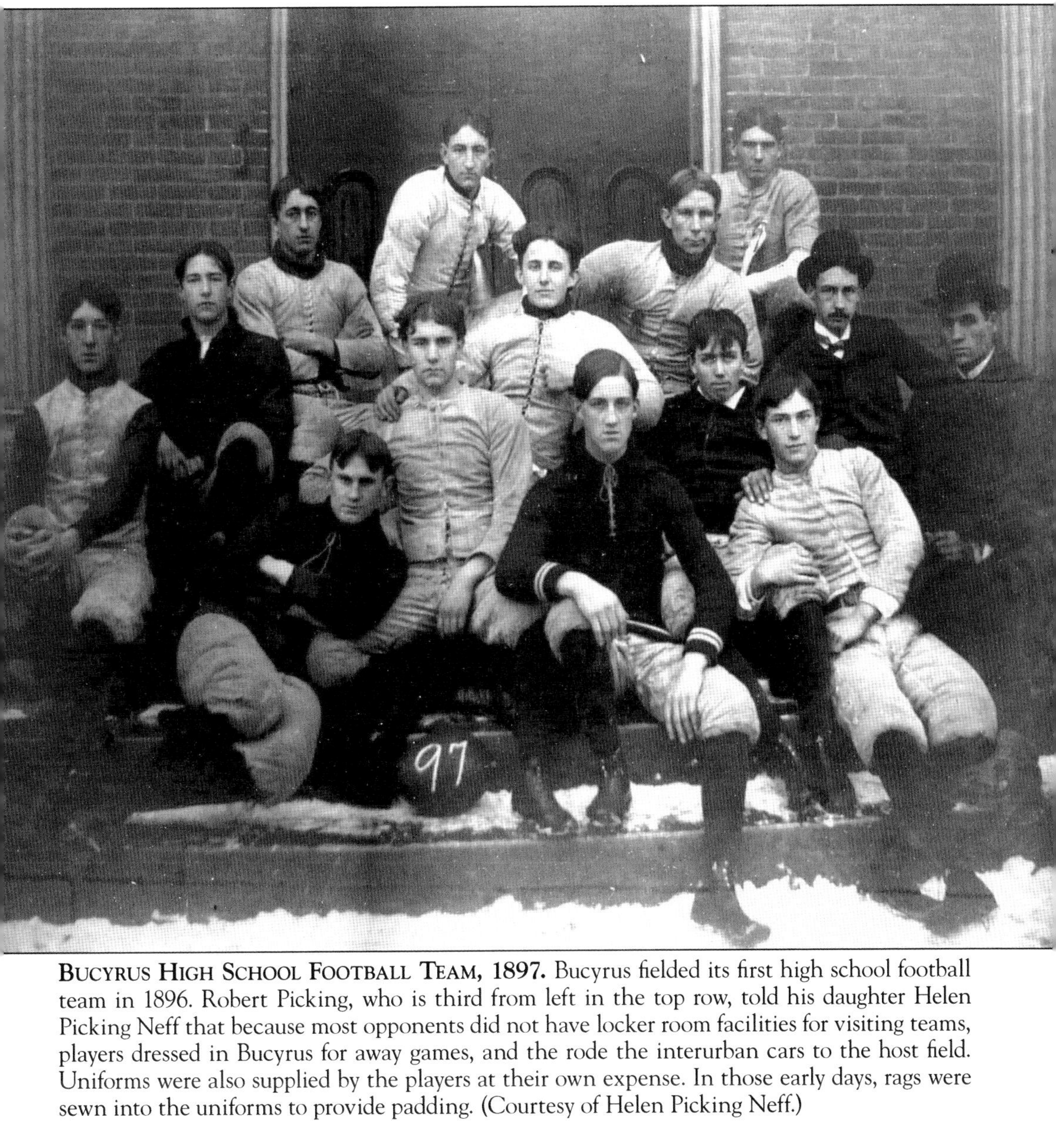

Bucyrus High School Football Team, 1897. Bucyrus fielded its first high school football team in 1896. Robert Picking, who is third from left in the top row, told his daughter Helen Picking Neff that because most opponents did not have locker room facilities for visiting teams, players dressed in Bucyrus for away games, and the rode the interurban cars to the host field. Uniforms were also supplied by the players at their own expense. In those early days, rags were sewn into the uniforms to provide padding. (Courtesy of Helen Picking Neff.)

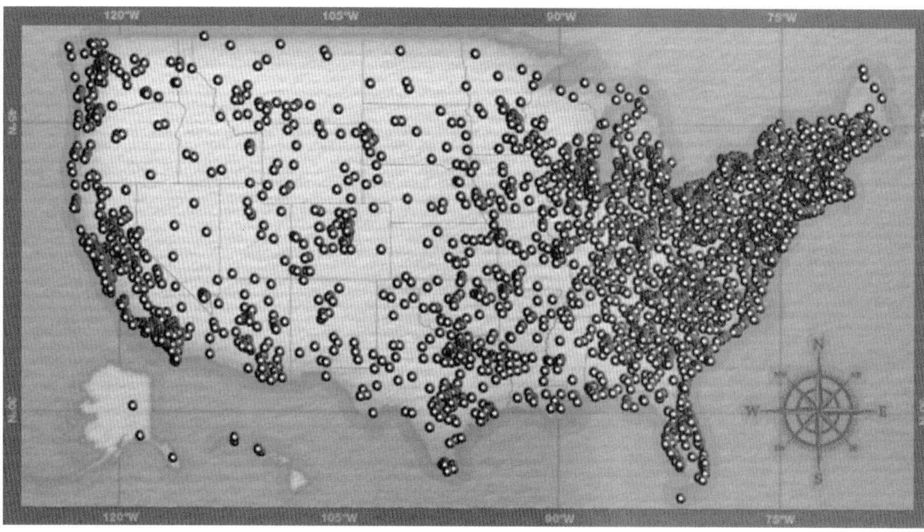